$ 8.00
FW
3/19

History of American Cooking

History of American Cooking

Merril D. Smith

ABC-CLIO

Santa Barbara, California • Denver, Colorado • Oxford, England

Library of Congress Cataloging-in-Publication Data

Smith, Merril D., 1956–
   History of American cooking / Merril D. Smith.
     p. cm
   Includes bibliographical references and index.
   ISBN 978-0-313-38711-1 (hardcopy : alk. paper) — ISBN 978-0-313-38712-8
(ebook) 1. Cooking, American—History. I. Title.
   TX715.S6655 2013
   641.5973—dc23   2012035382

ISBN: 978-0-313-38711-1
E-ISBN: 978-0-313-38712-8

17 16 15 14 13   1 2 3 4 5

This book is also available on the World Wide Web as an eBook.
Visit www.abc-clio.com for details.

ABC-CLIO, LLC
130 Cremona Drive, P.O. Box 1911
Santa Barbara, California 93116-1911

This book is printed on acid-free paper ∞

Manufactured in the United States of America

For my mother,
Sylvia L. Schreiber

Contents

Acknowledgments

Writing acknowledgments gives me an opportunity to thank all of the people who have helped me to write this book. In this case, some of them will never know the debt I owe them. As I have labored with the writing of this book, I have been inspired by the words of so many cooks of the past who have stirred me with their passion for food and cooking. Similarly, the ardent food bloggers of today whose recipes and photographs sometimes cause me to quite literally drool over my computer have also inspired me and sometimes have made me laugh as well as they shared their attempts to create or re-create various dishes.

The idea for this book came from Wendi Schnaufer, my former editor at ABC-CLIO. I hope this final product is something close to what she envisioned. Michael Millman stepped in as editor for this book when Wendi left. He has provided astute commentary and encouragement. Although he probably does not remember, Ken Albala gave me some early support and advice for this project (as well as scaring me and making me wonder, "Oh no. What did I get myself into?!") He suggested that I look into joining the Association for the Study of Food and Society. I have been a frequent lurker on that list, and have enjoyed the amazing knowledge and humor of these dedicated food scholars.

Else Hambleton, my dear friend and enthusiastic reader, has as usual given me support and advice. She has read many of the chapters of this book and helped to improve them.

My husband, Douglas Smith, has given me love and companionship. He eats whatever I cook, and if that's not true love, then I don't know what is. Plus, he does the dishes!

My mom, Sylvia Schreiber, taught me the *shit arein* method of cooking. For those unfamiliar with that term, it is a Yiddish expression that means "to throw in a little of this and that." I dedicate this book to her. I know she is thrilled that I have passed this great cooking tradition along to my daughters, Megan and Sheryl.

Introduction

Cooking is like love. It should be entered into with abandon or
not at all.
— Harriet Van Horne, "Not for Jiffy Cooks," *Vogue* (1956)

Archaeological evidence indicates that humans were cooking in North
America at least 12,000 years ago, perhaps earlier. Because they left
no written records, we do not know if they enjoyed cooking or if
there were any among them who were particularly skilled cooks. In
these hunter-gatherer societies, most likely women did the cooking.
We know that 11,500 years ago seminomadic people set up a tempo-
rary camp in Alaska, where they caught, cooked, and ate salmon and
squirrels. We do not know the fine points of their cooking methods
or what they thought as they cooked their meals. Undoubtedly they
were content and probably grateful to have food to feed their children, kinspeople, and friends.[1]

WHY COOK?

Although we do not know exactly when humans first cooked, or how
or where it happened, most people agree that cooked food tastes
good. Humans can taste sweet, sour, bitter, and umami (often described as a rich and satisfying mouthfeel), and over thousands of
years, we have learned to catch, grow, produce, and combine ingredients and textures in different ways to make a wide-ranging, perhaps
infinite variety of foods. When food is cooked, chemical reactions take

place that deepen flavors and change textures: sliced onions cooked slowly in a pan become golden and sweet, meat roasted over a flame or in an oven acquires a crisp brown exterior through the Maillard reaction (discussed in chapter 7), rice and grains boiled in water soften and swell, and vegetables combined with meat or fish and boiled in water become soup or stew, something new and different from its individual parts. Although there are some who believe raw food diets are the healthiest, and others who advocate a paleo-diet, consisting of single, uncombined meats, fish, fruit, and vegetables—or what they imagine our prehistoric ancestors ate—most people enjoy and have flourished on cooked food. Some scientists now believe that eating cooked food helped humans' large brains to evolve; moreover, they suspect that the activity of cooking itself helped humans to evolve as social creatures. By ingesting cooked food, our human ancestors did not have to spend as much time chewing and swallowing raw foods, and they could absorb more calories quickly. They then had more time to spend in social interaction, as well as in making tools and pursuing other activities. As a consequence of cooking, however, women probably had less time to become involved with other activities than men did, because they were the ones who did the cooking and food preparation, as well as foraging for plants and seeds.[2]

ORIGINS OF AMERICAN COOKING AND FOODWAYS

The food and food production techniques of mainland American Indians, Caribbean Indians, Europeans, and West Africans intersected in America hundreds of years ago. A partial list of the plants and animals brought to the Americans from Europe, Africa, and Asia includes pigs, cattle, chickens, horses, turnips, yams, onions, lettuce, carrots, celery, wheat, barley, chickpeas, oats, rice, rye, sugarcane, apples, grapes, lemons, peaches, plums, pears, and watermelon. European explorers and settlers also inadvertently brought weeds such as dandelions, rats, earthworms, and diseases, such as smallpox and measles, for which the native population had no immunity. English settlers brought European honeybees along with flowers and other plants they wanted to cultivate in the New World. Without these bees, Georgia peaches and apple orchards throughout the United States would not have been possible.[3] Historian Alfred W. Crosby Jr. coined the term Columbian Exchange in his 1972 book, *The Columbian Exchange: Biological and Cultural Consequences of 1492,* to describe the mixing and collision of plants, animals, and diseases that journey back and forth between the Old and New Worlds.[4]

Food items also traveled from the Americas to Europe, Asia, and Africa, and sometimes back again. Pumpkins, sweet potatoes, vanilla, sweet and hot peppers, beans, corn (maize), wild rice, cranberry, cacao, tomatoes, and tobacco are just a few of the crops that Europeans brought back to Europe, Asia, and Africa. Yet not all of the new items found universal appeal in Europe when they were first introduced. Corn, for example, found favor in Spain and Italy, where it replaced sorghum or millet to produce polenta, but northern Europeans believed corn was good only for feeding to their livestock.[5]

Corn (maize) was one of the most important staples of American Indians.[6] It most likely was cultivated in Mexico first—as early as 5000 BCE—and then spread south and north. By about 1000 CE, Northern Flint, a type of corn that was able to withstand colder temperatures, was being grown in the American Northeast. A number of different types of maize were cultivated throughout South, Central, and North America. There were more than 100 types of maize of many colors grown in North America when Europeans first began exploring the continent. Native Americans throughout the New World consumed corn, using every part of the plant, and eating it in a number of different ways—roasted, boiling, using the husks as wrappers for tamales, popping it (remains of popped corn that date from 3600 BCE have been found in Bat Cave, New Mexico), and making it into bread.[7] Francisco Vásquez de Coronado commented that the Zuni "eat the best cakes that ever I saw." These "cakes" were the bread made of cornmeal that the Spanish called tortillas (or cakes). Coronado explained, "They have the finest order and way to grind that we ever saw anyplace."[8]

The processing and grinding of maize is significant. The native inhabitants of the Americas used a process called *nixtamalization* to prepare maize. As one scholar of ancient cuisines explains, "[N]ixtamalization is the complex process that starts with soaking the ripe maize grains and then cooking them with lime or wood ashes." This process removes the outer later on the grain so it is easier to grind. "But the major contribution of nixtamalized maize to the unprocessed kind is that it much enhances the protein value of the maize for human beings." Nixtamalization is an ancient technique, and archaeologists have found that it was in use in Guatemala between 1500 and 1200 BCE. Women used special grinding stones called metates and monos to grind grain, beans, and nuts. When Europeans began growing, processing, and eating maize, they did not use

xiv INTRODUCTION

nixtamalization, thereby creating nutritional deficiencies among some people who began to rely on the grain.⁹

Sugarcane originated as a grass in New Guinea. In the eighth century, Arabs, who had learned how to process it to make sugar, were trading the valuable and exotic substance to Europeans. When he returned to Hispaniola on his second voyage, explorer Christopher Columbus brought sugarcane with him. The cane grows easily in tropical and subtropical areas, but harvesting it and processing it into sugar is extremely labor intensive. It required many steps between the hacking of the tough stems with machetes to the packaging of the sugar loaves in blue paper (to make the sugar appear whiter), and first the Spanish, and then the English, required a labor force to produce the valuable commodity. One historian asserts, "[S]ugar played the most significant role in forcing nearly 11 million Africans to the New World between 1500 and 1800."¹⁰

As a consequence of the enslavement of millions of Africans, West African foods and foodways traveled to the West Indies and then to the mainland. The style and flavors of traditional West African cooking with its emphasis on one-pot meals, peppers, and spices has influenced American cooking to the present day, and can be seen in dishes such as gumbo and Hoppin' John. Equally important is the influence that African and African American cooks had in disseminating foods, food preferences, and styles of cooking to the white population around them, since black cooks predominated in the antebellum plantations of the South, as well as in many white kitchens after the Civil War.

Most of the African cooks who labored in southern kitchens remain nameless. When 19-year-old Isabella Lenox Dunlop of Petersburg, Virginia, began writing down recipes, in what became a two-volume collection, she chose to credit both black and white cooks. For example, recipe titles read, "Cook Mary" and "Aunt Osborne's Cook Abby." On occasion, Dunlop even included directions of the black cook, as she did in the recipe for boiled ham: "Abby says changing the Ham from one pot to another would make it too fresh." Volumes like Dunlop's are rare.¹¹

As one historian observes, for black women cooking could take on "heightened emotional significance" and could even be considered an act of political rebellion. One man recalled that his mother, a slave, used to help slaves on their plantation who were hiding after being punished. "They would stay in the woods and come in at night, and mother would give them something to eat."¹²

After the Civil War, many black women continued to work in the homes and kitchens of white women in both the South and the North. According to one scholar, a servant notorious for her carelessness on the job might enjoy the praise of family and neighbors for her culinary skills and generosity. As former domestic worker May Anna Madison recalled, the Thursday "day-off get-togethers" in her Kentucky neighborhood that rotated between households were "hard work, but people didn't mind because they wanted to do that and they were working for themselves. They were working with people they liked and at the end they made this grand meal."[13]

In the post–Civil War period, thousands of African Americans moved to western territories to make better lives for themselves and their families. An even greater number of black Americans moved from rural southern areas to the urban North in the early years of the 20th century, in what is called the Great Migration. With them came barbecue, sweet potato pie, and other foods that were labeled soul food in the 1960s.

From the 16th century on, Europeans have been traveling to America, bringing their foods with them. A typical dinner in one of the northern cities of the United States in the 1850s would probably feature roast or boiled beef. Pies, including apple, were extremely popular and eaten at all times of day. Neither roast beef nor apple pie would have been possible without European immigrants bringing cows, wheat, and apple seeds. Subsequent immigrant groups from around the globe, among them Dutch, Germans, Scots Irish, Italians, Greeks, Polish, Russian, Chinese, Japanese, Mexican, Indian, and African, have all added their food knowledge and culture to American society. Dishes such as shoofly pie, spaghetti, bagels, and gumbo are popular in the United States because immigrants brought their culinary traditions with them. Other dishes such as chop suey and General Tso's chicken may owe their popularity more to Americans enjoying them, rather than authenticity.

Immigrants brought their own foods to America and found them to be a source of comfort and familiarity. Others have adopted the foods of the mainstream white culture around them, willingly or not. Sometimes they do it so that their children will feel more comfortable and accepted. Jhumpa Lahiri's poignant novel of Indian Americans, *The Namesake,* makes this point. The son, Gogol, writes of his parents, "They learn to roast turkeys, albeit rubbed with garlic and cumin and cayenne, at Thanksgiving." He notes that his parents continue to eat traditional Indian food, although they pack him bologna sandwiches, and "at his insistence" his mother "concedes and makes him an American dinner once a week as a treat, Shake 'n Bake chicken or Hamburger Helper prepared with ground lamb."[14] It is beyond the scope of this book to discuss recipes and traditions from every ethnic and religious group that has influenced American culinary culture, but I have tried to include a variety of styles within each chapter.

Transportation systems, first canals and roads, then the railroads, and finally highways and trucks, have made it easier for food and people to travel throughout the continent. In 1876, Frederick Henry Harvey opened his first railway depot restaurant in Topeka, Kansas. As one scholar notes, "'Meals by Fred Harvey' became a guarantee not only of delicious food in generous portions at a reasonable price but of outstanding service by welcoming, efficient, and impeccably groomed waitresses called Harvey Girls." The restaurants and Harvey Girls remained in existence until the late 1950s.[15]

Wars and events, such as the Great Depression, also had an effect on what people ate and cooked because food was often not available, was too expensive, or was rationed. During the Revolutionary War, women formed mobs and raided the warehouses of merchants suspected of hoarding coffee, sugar, and other staples. The prolific letter writer Abigail Adams, wife of the second president of the United States, John Adams, reported one such incident; a hundred or more women attacked "an eminent, wealthy, stingy merchant (also a bachelor)." The women forced him to give them the keys to his warehouse, hoisted the coffee "into trunks and drove off. . . . [A] large concourse of men stood amazed silent Spectators."[16]

The disruption caused by the war also meant that some women and their families were displaced from their homes—and food supplies. Inflation made the purchase of food difficult, even when supplies were available. In some areas of the country, a soldier's pay over a few months was still not enough to buy a barrel of wheat. The wife of one soldier wrote to her husband, "I am without bread . . . my children will starve, or if they do not, they must freeze, we have no wood, neither can we get any—Pray Come Home."[17]

Soldiers and civilians on both sides during the Civil War faced difficulties in obtaining food. Even the elite faced shortages. A German pastry chef on the private staff of a Confederate general was seldom able to make pastry because of a lack of supplies. According to one soldier, the pastry chef's "skill and ingenuity were often taxed to the utmost in providing dinners, from the scantiest materials."[18]

Although black troops in the Union army were often not treated well by white soldiers, the 54th Massachusetts regiment did receive a "mobile field kitchen mounted on a wagon." In May 1863, a sergeant in the regiment proclaimed, "We have a new style of cooking department here. It is a large wagon, covered similar to an omnibus, with a

stove and all the appurtenances of a well ordered kitchen." The sergeant believed it would be "a very handy affair" if adopted throughout the army, but it was not.[19]

Civil War nurse Kate Cumming noted, "Hunger is a good antidote
for even dirt," as she attempted to transform the hospital kitchen with
the help of women in Natchez. With their help, she obtained dishes
and supplies to feed wounded soldiers, and with "negroes for cooks,
[and] a good baker," they were able to "eat like civilized people."
When she was told that the men would not touch arrowroot, she
discovered a way to make it palatable, although she did not tell the
men what it was made of. "I make it quite thin, and sometimes beat
up a few eggs and stir in while hot; then season with preserves of any
kind—those that are a little acid are the best—and let it stand until it
becomes cold. This makes a pleasant and nourishing drink . . . especially beneficial in cases of pneumonia."[20]

The U.S. government published numerous documents during both
World War I and World War II that explained how to economize and
cook without the use of rationed ingredients. During both wars, the
government encouraged people to have meatless days and to grow
their own produce. The title page of one such pamphlet reads, "What
Shall We Eat on Wheatless and Meatless Days? The Soldiers Need
WHEAT[.] The Folks at Home Can Use CORN OATS RICE BAR-
LEY POTATOES." The booklet, written by the home economics
department of the University of Wisconsin, declares that unlike some
of the recipes in newspapers and magazines, the recipes "in this bul-
letin are planned to answer the housekeeper's need for reliable recipes
for wartime cookery. The menus are prepared to help the housewife
conform to the requests of the United States Food Administration for
one meatless and two wheatless days each week."[21]

Home economics became a fully professional field in 1899 with
degreed programs and professional organizations, although domestic science groups and advocates had existed since the late-19th century. The women who were part of this movement were passionate
about adapting scientific principles and technology to the kitchen. As
one scholar of the movement remarks, "[D]omestic scientists were
inspired by the nutritive properties of food," rather than the taste.
"Containing and controlling food, draining it of taste and texture,
packaging it . . . these were some of the major culinary themes of
the domestic-science movement." Some advocates of the scientific
way of cooking covered everything in white sauces to present food as
neat and clean. Home economists also partnered with food processing

companies and helped to advertise products, such as Crisco. Advertisements for Crisco promoted it as "a pure cream white, with a fresh pleasant aroma." It is "put up in immaculate packages, perfectly protected from dust and store odors."[22]

CHANGES IN COOKING TECHNOLOGY

Modern-day Americans still use skillets and Dutch ovens, but the technology of cooking has changed significantly over the centuries.

Undated book illustration of an 18th or early-19th-century farmer's kitchen. The kitchen was the main living space in most early American houses. This illustration depicts a range of activities taking place at the same time in this area, including cooking, laundry, and childcare. Notice the large cooking pot suspended over the fire, where a woman tends a smoking skillet or grill. The brick oven, which would have been used for baking bread, pies, and other dishes, is attached to the fireplace. Additional pots and cooking tools are hung nearby. Although perhaps still dangerously close to the fire and oven, the toddler is confined to a type of infant seat so that the women can attempt to work without interruption. (Corbis)

Cooks labored over hot fires, sometimes with the help of cranes and spits. Food was chopped with knives and stirred with sticks or wooden or metal tools. Now cooks have electric mixers, blenders, food processors, and of course electric ovens and microwaves. Ovens and stoves have probably changed the most over the centuries, although many ordinary kitchen devices, such as egg beaters, did not exist in the 17th century. Some kitchen equipment, tools, and techniques are discussed in the following chapters, but what follows is a brief discussion of changes in kitchen technology.

Although the Spanish brought wheat to America in the 16th century, they could not bake loaves of wheat bread without ovens. A Spanish explorer, Juan de Oñate, is credited with introducing adobe ovens, called *hornos* (pronounced OR-noes), to the Pueblo Indians of the American Southwest in 1598. *Hornos* are dome-shaped aboveground ovens that have an opening at the front and a vent at the top. They were commonly found in wheat-producing areas of Spain's New World territories, but not in areas such as central Mexico, where corn was the predominant grain. They were built on pueblo rooftops and within the courtyards of Spanish-style homes. Women built fires inside these ovens, and then allowed the fires to burn until the interior became very hot. When the fire burned out, the women swept the charcoal and ashes from the interior, placed the risen bread dough inside, and used a stone slab to close the opening of the *horno*. The clay interior held the heat inside and baked the bread.[23]

The enslavement of the Pueblo by the Spanish led to a successful rebellion by the Pueblo in 1680. In a backlash against their conquerors, the Pueblo destroyed their food, crops, churches, and slaughtered or set the livestock free. The Spanish returned and took over the Pueblo and their lands again 15 years later. Spanish and Pueblo culinary traditions melded over time. *Hornos* can still be found within Pueblo villages, and they are used for baking both wheat and maize breads. *Horno* styles differ somewhat from village to village and from family to family, and they are often passed down through generations. Modern-day *hornos* are sometimes used to bake dishes such as corn pudding in addition to various breads.

Native Americans also fashioned earth ovens to bake corn and other vegetables, fish, and bread. First a pit was dug in the ground, probably by men of the tribe, and then it was lined with stones. The stones were then covered with kindling, and a fire was started and allowed to burn down until only coal remained. Then a layer of dirt and leaves was placed on top to provide insulation against the direct heat, and the food was positioned on top of the leaves. The food was then covered with more greens and baked until done.[24]

Most European-style households outside of the Southwest used ovens that were built into or alongside of fireplaces. Baking kettles, sometimes called Dutch ovens, were also used to bake breads, cakes, and other items. These Dutch ovens usually had three legs, and they were placed within the fireplace on a bed of hot coals, rather than over an open flame, and then hot coals were placed on top of the lid. The tight-fitting lids kept the heat from escaping and allowed foods to bake within the kettle.[25]

Dutch ovens have been in use in America since the 17th century, and they have never completely disappeared from American kitchens. Modern-day Dutch ovens do not have legs or deep lids for holding coals. Instead, they are designed to go in the oven and used to make pot roasts, casseroles, and braised dishes. Over the years, however, Americans have made various improvements to the design of Dutch ovens. For example, in 1832, New York merchant John Pintard wrote to his daughter, Eliza Davidson, who lived in New Orleans, to tell her that her sister had recently purchased "a Dutch oven on an improved plan." Reporting that the appliance when placed before the fire "bakes Johnny Cakes, pies, &c., as well as roast small joints & cooks a beef stake on the gridiron," he told Eliza that he had ordered one for her. Two days later, the oven was ready, and the doting father noted that he was sending Eliza additional pans with the oven, "so that you can forthwith make an experiment whether the oven will bake a chicken pie & pudding, as quickly as your sisters, whose cook in one hour." Pintard declared that the oven "bakes cakes admirably, & serves to roast coffee to perfection, in short it is adapted for almost every culinary, except stews & fricasees, which are better prepared in casseroles."[26]

With or without ovens, kitchens dominated the homes of European colonists in the earliest settlements of 17th-century America. These 17th-century kitchens contained large fireplaces, which served to heat the house (often a one-room structure), as well as to provide a cooking site. The fireplaces of 17th-century New England kitchens were large enough to stand up in, and indeed, housewives did stand within them to manage the various cooking fires.[27] As homeowners became more established and prosperous, they expanded their houses by adding rooms to the original structure.

Homes built later in the 18th century began to locate the kitchen away from the more public areas of the house. Urban residents often put kitchens in the basement of the house, while 18th-century

southern plantation owners began placing their kitchens in outbuild-
ings away from the main house.[28] This was probably because of a
number of factors, including a desire to keep the heat and smells of
the kitchen away from the rest of the household, but it also indicated
an increasing separation between public and private life. For southern planters, the location of a kitchen away from the main house provided a conspicuous display of wealth and status, because a separate
kitchen indicated that there were slaves to do the kitchen tasks so that
the mistress of the house did not have to perform menial labor. Archaeological evidence suggests that workplaces on large plantations
were further divided into "clean" and "dirty" zones. The kitchen and
dairy were in the clean zone, but the smokehouse bridged the two
zones, and its door would open into the dirty zone.[29]

By the end of the 18th century, many northeastern kitchens of the
well-to-do featured new style Rumford fireplaces and stoves. These
fireplaces were shallower than the earlier kitchen fireplaces and had
smaller chimney throats, which permitted them to radiate more heat
while burning less wood. Ovens were built into the side of the wall
next to the fireplace.[30] By the 1820s stoves with baking ovens were
just beginning to become popular and replace open-hearth cookery and brick ovens. In the 1873 edition of her cookbook, Mary
Cornelius noted that "stoves and cooking-ranges have so generally
taken the place of brick ovens, that the following directions [for constructing a brick oven], which were appropriate when this book was
first published [in 1845] will seldom be of use now."[31]

Cookstoves began appearing in the 1820s, and by the 1870s, most
American kitchens, except for those of the poor and those living in remote areas, had cast iron stoves with ovens. By this time, they had developed into massive pieces that often mimicked the ornate furniture
of that time. A range called The Housekeeper, designed by Charles
Noble and Company of Philadelphia, won a medal at the 1876
Philadelphia Centennial Exhibition. This model was the top-of-the-
line model, and as one scholar writes, it "had six burners, two ovens,
and was embellished with cast-iron panels depicting standing stags,
bunnies, and lion's heads; Renaissance ornaments crowned the top.
In appearance, it would have been just as suitable in a bedroom or
parlor as in a kitchen."[32]

During the mid-19th century, reformer Catharine Beecher advocated the building of home kitchens that were models of efficiency
and convenience, with doors that closed it off from the rest of the
house yet kept everything necessary for cooking close at hand. She

expressed these views in her *Treatise on Domestic Economy,* which was first printed in 1841 and reprinted many time between 1841 and 1856. She expanded her views in *The American Woman's Home,* cowritten with her sister, the author Harriet Beecher Stowe, in 1869.[33]

Fancy baking and the modern kitchens of the mid-19th century were unavailable, of course, to those traveling west on overland trails. Because most of the women in the wagon trains were accustomed to cooking on stoves and baking in ovens, they were often unpleasantly surprised by the difficulty of cooking over a fire. Eighteen-year-old Esther Hanna, the wife of a minister, recorded her reactions to the difficulties of trail life: "Had to haul our water and wood for night. . . . I have also to bake tonight. It is very trying on the patience to cook and bake on a little green wood fire with the smoke blowing in your eyes so as to blind you, and shivering with cold so as to make the teeth chatter."[34]

Gas ranges became available in the United States by the 1850s, although they were not common because gas supplies from municipal sources varied and were unreliable. The stoves, too, needed constant maintenance, and many feared that gas stoves would leak gas into their houses, causing an explosion or asphyxiation of its residents. Gas companies, however, began to produce and market their own gas stoves, and gas delivery systems also improved. Gas companies advertised the advantages of cooking with gas by noting, as a Portland, Oregon, company did, "Its cleanliness, economy, and easy control make it decidedly superior to all other fuels." The American Stove Company introduced a gas stove with an oven thermostat in 1915, and by the 1920s most American homes had gas stoves.[35]

Electric stoves, although they existed earlier, did not begin to be popular until the 1920s, when manufacturers began to improve them. Most importantly, they introduced an electromechanical thermostat, which kept oven temperatures constant. They also placed ovens under the stove burners, permitting women to continue stovetop preparations at the same level as kitchen counters. These new electric stoves came in a variety of colors, as well. Still, electric stoves did not become widespread in American homes until the cost of electricity lessened and more homes were wired for electricity in the 1930s and 1940s. Electric stoves began to outsell gas stoves in the 1950s. Later, broilers were added to ovens, as well as timers, self-cleaning features, and storage drawers.[36]

With gas and electric ovens, housewives no longer had to clean out ashes, as they did with wood and coal stoves. Nevertheless, it was the self-regulating oven temperatures that made the most impact on American cooks. Baking times and temperatures could now be indicated in recipes. New cookbooks began to include standard oven temperatures, instead of stating something should be cooked in a "hot" oven.[37] An example of a cook's desire to have oven temperatures regulated precisely can be seen in Estelle Woods Wilcox's *Buckeye Cookery* (1877). After a detailed explanation of what type of wood should be used when heating an oven to bake cakes (she recommended ash), how the dampers should be adjusted, and how the oven should be tested, she writes, "All systematic housekeepers will hail the day when some enterprising Yankee or Buckeye girl shall invent a stove or range with a thermometer attached to the oven, so that the heat may be regulated accurately and intelligently."[38] Clearly, the fact that they were self-regulating with a turn of a dial was a major selling point for gas and electric ovens.

Twentieth-century technology brought new types of ovens and methods of cooking. The microwave oven came about as an accident. Percy L. Spencer, an engineer at the Raytheon Company, helped to perfect the design of magnetron tubes. These tubes were important for use in shortwave, or microwave, radar, which British scientists were developing during World War II in order to "see" German planes, even during nighttime raids. According to some sources, in 1945, Spencer discovered that a candy bar in his pocket had melted as he stood in front of a magnetron tube. He did additional experiments, and eventually the Raytheon Company produced a microwave oven. It was named the Radarange, and it was enormous, standing 62 inches tall and two feet deep, and weighing 670 pounds. The first countertop sized microwave became available in 1967, after Raytheon acquired Amana Refrigeration, Incorporated, which made it easier for the company to distribute the new appliances to consumers.[39]

Amana hired JoAnne Anderson to organize a team of women to demonstrate the new microwave ovens. She carefully monitored her team, and told them, "You must always dress, look, and act like a lady." She strongly suggested that the team refrain from demonstrating cakes in the microwave, since they were not foolproof, and highly advocated they prepare bacon because it had "a marvelous odor, and it traveled from one department to another." Anderson referred to the microwave as "a woman's appliance," and suggested that it was safe for children to use by themselves after school. The microwave has been so popular that other technologies and businesses have adapted to it. For example, frozen foods come in microwave-safe plastic bags and plastic or cardboard containers, rather than metal trays, and manufacturers now create products specifically to be heated in the microwave.[40]

Also available to consumers in the 1960s was the first Easy-Bake Oven, a toy oven that baked tiny cakes and other treats with the help of a light bulb. The toy was marketed with mixes and was aimed at girls between ages 8 and 12. It was turquoise and included a fake stovetop. Over the years, the toy has changed with the times, so that by the late 1970s, it looked more like a microwave oven. In 2011, the toy was totally redesigned and the light bulb eliminated. New compact fluorescent bulbs are too energy efficient to use for baking. The new oven has a heating element that heats the inside but allows the exterior to get only a little bit warm.[41]

Convection ovens use fans to circulate hot air. The ovens can run at lower temperatures, but food is cooked more quickly because the heat transfer is better than it is in conventional ovens. There are also microwave convection ovens that combine the speed of a microwave with the browning capability of a convection oven. Newer still are supersteam microwave ovens, which combine a steamer, microwave, and convection oven.

Other appliances have made cooking either easier, or at least entertaining. Some have remained popular with home cooks; others have disappeared. In the 1930s, electrical gadgets were very popular. Hostesses entertained their guests with supper parties featuring waffle irons, hot plates, and an electric roaster, which was a portable oven. Advertisements for the electric roaster suggested that the hostess could prepare the dinner and then relax or even go for a swim while the meal roasted in the electric roaster. There were also fancy toasters. The Toast-O-Lator had an art deco design. The bread entered at one end and traveled by a conveyor belt and out the other end.[42]

During the 1970s slow cookers became very popular, especially with women who wanted to come home from work to find a hearty meal simmering in the pot. Slow cookers do not brown food, and they cannot be used for all dishes. Soups, stews, beans, and other dishes that require long simmering still work well in slow cookers.[43]

Neither the hunting and foraging societies of early North America nor the colonial goodwives of the 17th century could have imagined the ease with which 21st-century Americans buy food in modern supermarkets, nor could they envision an electric or gas oven, much less a microwave oven. Canning, freezing, and food processing techniques have revolutionized American cooking. The following chapters provide a brief history of cooking in America. Each chapter focuses mainly on one technique, such as baking or boiling, although many dishes, of course, use more than one method to prepare. The final chapter looks at some of the most recent techniques and trends. Readers beware—this is not a cookbook; it is a history of cooking. Many of the recipes included here have not been tested or revised for modern kitchens. Rather, they serve as examples of how cooks in the past used particular techniques to prepare food.

Cooking in America has come full circle. While some indulge in high-tech kitchens, others are content to use simpler tools and equipment. In a 2012 article in *Slate* magazine, Brian Palmer explains "the fine art of guerilla cooking." In the article, he describes the meals he has prepared in his office using a frying pan, hot plate, or an electric fondue pot, and provides some tips on how to make it work. For example, he suggests cutting the vegetables and doing other preparation at home and keeping small quantities of "kitchen essentials" in a desk drawer at work. The inspiration for his guerilla cooking came from a third-grade vocabulary assignment. When a classmate forgot to do his homework, he quickly borrowed Palmer's dictionary and wrote, "Cook: to prepare with heat." To prepare food with heat is the subject of this book. Who knows what the future will bring?[44]

NOTES

1. Laura Schenone, *A Thousand Years over a Hot Stove: A History of American Women Told through Food, Recipes, and Remembrances* (New York: Norton, 2003), 4–5; Ben A. Potter et al., "A Terminal Pleistocene Child Cremated and Residential Structure from Eastern Beringia," *Science* 331, no. 6020 (February 2011), 1058–62.

2. For a detailed discussion of these ideas, see Richard Wrangham, *Catching Fire: How Cooking Made Us Human* (New York: Basic Books, 2009). Jared Diamond argues that that the adoption of an agricultural lifestyle was "the worst mistake in the history of the human race," leading to malnutrition, disease, and gender inequality. See Jared Diamond, "The Worst Mistake in the History of the Human Race," *Discover Magazine* (May 1987), 64–66.

3. Charles C. Mann, *Uncovering the New World Columbus Created* (New York: Knopf, 2011), 72.

4. Alfred W. Crosby Jr., *The Columbian Exchange: Biological and Cultural Consequences of 1492* (Westport, CT: Praeger, 2003). Also see Megan Gambino, "Alfred W. Crosby on the Columbian Exchange," October 5, 2011, Smithsonian.com, http://www.smithso

nianmag.com/history-archaeology/Alfred-W-Crosby-on-the-Columbian-Exchange.html.

5. Linda Civitello, *Cuisine and Culture: A History of Food and People,* 3rd ed. (Hoboken, NJ: John Wiley & Sons, 2011), 120–24, 136–37.

6. The English generally referred to any type of grain as corn. What Americans now call corn is maize. English and Anglo-Americans often referred to it as Indian corn.

7. For more on the origins and uses of maize, see Sophie D. Coe, *America's First Cuisines* (Austin: University of Texas Press, 1994), 9–16; Schenone, *A Thousand Years,* 9, 12.

8. Quoted in Schenone, *A Thousand Years,* 22.

9. Coe, *America's First Cuisines,* 14.

10. James E. McWilliams, *A Revolution in Eating: How the Quest for Food Shaped America* (New York: Columbia University Press, 2005), 29.

11. Nancy Carter Crump, *Hearthside Cooking: Early American Southern Cuisine Updated for Today's Hearth and Cookstove,* 2nd ed. (Chapel Hill: University of North Carolina Press, 2008), 30, 127.

12. Jacqueline Jones, *Labor of Love, Labor of Sorrow: Black Women, Work, and the Family, from Slavery to the Present* (New York: Vintage Books, 1986), 31.

13. Jones, *Labor of Love,* 5.

14. Jhumpa Lahiri, *The Namesake* (New York: Houghton Mifflin, Mariner Books ed., 2004), 64, 65.

15. Barbara Haber, *From Hardtack to Home Fries: An Uncommon History of American Cooks and Meals* (New York: Free Press, 2002), 87.

16. Quoted in Carol Berkin, *Revolutionary Mothers: Women in the Struggle for America's Independence* (New York: Knopf, 2005), 32.

17. Quoted in Berkin, *Revolutionary Mothers,* 33.

18. William C. Davis, *A Taste for War: The Culinary History of the Blue and the Gray* (Lincoln: University of Nebraska Press, 2011), 53.

19. Virginia Matzke Adams, ed., *On the Altar of Freedom: A Black Soldier's Civil War Letters from the Front* (Amherst, MA: University of Massachusetts Press, 1991), 17, quoted in Davis, *A Taste for War,* 58.

20. Quoted in Haber, *From Hardtack to Home Fries,* 40, 41.

21. "What Shall We Eat on Wheatless and Meatless Days?" Circular 106, May 1918, published by the Agricultural Extension Service of the University of Wisconsin, the United States Department of Agriculture Cooperating.

22. Laura Shapiro, *Perfection Salad: Women and Cooking at the Turn of the Century*, with a new afterword (Berkeley and Los Angeles: University of California Press, 2009), 5–8, 203–4.

23. Linda Murray Berzok, *American Indian Food* (Santa Barbara, CA: Greenwood, 2005), 26–27; Richard L. Nostrand, "The Highland-Hispano Homeland," in *Homelands: A Geography of Culture and Place across America*, ed. Richard L. Nostrand and Lawrence E. Estaville (Baltimore: Johns Hopkins University Press, 2001), 163.

24. Schenone, *A Thousand Years*, 7.

25. Jane C. Nylander, *Our Own Snug Fireside: Images of the New England Home, 1760–1860* (New Haven, CT: Yale University Press, 1994), 198; Sandra L. Oliver, *Food in Colonial and Federal America* (Santa Barbara, CA: Greenwood, 2005), 110.

26. John Pintard, "Letters to His Daughter, 1819–32," in *American Food Writing: An Anthology with Classic Recipes*, ed. Molly O'Neill (New York: Library of America, 2009), 20.

27. Laurel Thatcher Ulrich, *Good Wives: Image and Reality in the Lives of Women in Northern New England, 1650–1750* (New York: Oxford University Press, 1982), 20.

28. Oliver, *Food in Colonial*, 90–95.

29. Michael Olmert, "Smokehouses," *Colonial Williamsburg Journal* (Winter 2004–2005), http://www.history.org/foundation/journal/winter04-05/smoke.cfm.

30. Oliver, *Food in Colonial*, 99–101.

31. Mary Hooker Cornelius, *The Young Housekeeper's Friend*, rev. ed. (Boston: Thompson, Brown, & Co., 1873), 21.

32. Susan Williams, *Food in the United States, 1820s–1890* (Santa Barbara, CA: Greenwood, 2006), 56.

33. Kathryn Kish Sklar, *Catharine Beecher: A Study in American Domesticity* (New York: W.W. Norton, 1976), xi–xii, 151.

34. Esther Hanna's quote is from Eleanor Allen, *Canvas Caravans: Based on the Journal of Esther Belle McMillan Hanna, 1852* (Portland, OR: Binfords & Mort, 1946), no page number given, quoted in Lillian Schlissel, *Women's Diaries of the Westward Journey* (New York: Schocken Books, 1982), 80.

35. Andrew F. Smith, "Stoves and Ovens: Gas and Electric," in *The Oxford Companion to American Food and Drink*, ed. Andrew F. Smith (New York: Oxford University Press, 2007), 563–64; Advertisement of the Portland Gas & Coke Co., in *The Neighborhood Cook Book* (Portland, OR: Bushong & Co., 1914).

36. Smith, "Stoves and Ovens," 564–65.

37. Megan J. Elias, *Food in the United States, 1890–1945* (Santa Barbara, CA: Greenwood, 2009), 49.

38. Estelle Woods Wilcox, *Buckeye Cookery, and Practical Housekeeping: Compiled from Original Recipes* (Minneapolis, MN: Buckeye, 1877), 44.

39. Raytheon Company website, http://www.raytheon.com/our company/history/leadership/index.html.

40. William Hammack, "The Greatest Discovery since Fire," *Invention and Technology Magazine* 20, no. 4 (Spring 2005), http://todayin sci.com/Events/Technology/Microwave%20Oven%20History%20-%20The%20Greatest%20Discover%20Since%20Fire.htm.

41. Erika Niedowski, "Easy-Bake's Lightbulb Moment," *Philadelphia Inquirer*, September 15, 2011, http://articles.philly.com/2011-09-15/news/30160564_1_easy-bake-ultimate-oven-million-ovens-hasbro.

42. Sylvia Lovegren, *Fashionable Food: Seven Decades of Food Fads* (Chicago: University of Chicago Press, 2005), 46. The Toast-O-Lator still has a cult of enthusiasts who buy and sell old Toast-O-Lators and make You Tube videos of it working. There is also at least one Facebook page devoted to the Toast-O-Lator.

43. Lovegren, *Fashionable Food*, 345.

44. Brian Palmer, "You Don't Need a Kitchen to Become a Chef," *Slate*, posted February 17, 2012, http://www.slate.com/articles/life/food/2012/02/liberate_yourself_from_the_kitchen_become_a_guerilla_chef_.html.

Chronology

ca. 10000 BCE   Humans were cooking in North America.

During a 1938 dig, a member of an archaeological expedition cleans an ancient fire pit. The members of the expedition were excavating a Native American village located in what is now Colorado. The village was inhabited about 700 CE. It is uncertain how old the fire pit is. (AP/Wide World Photo)

ca. 3600 BCE	Humans were popping corn in Bat Cave, New Mexico.
1492	Christopher Columbus's voyage launches "the Columbian exchange" of plants, animals, and foods.
1567	Saint Augustine, Florida, established by Spanish. First permanent European settlement in America.
1607	Jamestown, Virginia, England's first permanent colony is established.
1620	Plymouth Colony is settled by the Pilgrims.
1625	Dutch establish New Amsterdam (now New York City).
1654	Twenty-three Sephardic Jews arrive in New Amsterdam after fleeing Brazil. They begin the practice of kashruth (or keeping kosher) in America.
1663	Court in Virginia rules that children born to slave mothers are slaves.
1680	Pueblo Revolt forces Spanish out of parts of New Mexico for about 15 years. Pueblo people attempt to reassert their traditional culture.
ca. 1685	Rice is brought to South Carolina.
1747	*The Art of Cookery* by Englishwoman Hannah Glasse is published. It is reprinted in Virginia, with a new American section in 1805.
1759–63	Seven Years' War fought in Europe and North America (also called the French and Indian War in the United States), killing, wounding, and displacing thousands.
1764	English Parliament passes Revenue (Sugar Act), placing taxes on sugar and other goods.
1773	English Parliament passed the Tea Act, which lowered the price of tea, but gave the East India Company control over who could sell tea in the colonies. Colonists in Boston and elsewhere protest.
1775–83	American colonies declare independence from England, fight a revolution, and win independence.
1781	British General Cornwallis surrenders at Yorktown, Virginia.

1782   Oliver Evans develops a grain mill in Newport, Delaware, using conveyor belts to move the grain through, requiring less human labor to produce flour.

1796   Publication of *American Cookery*, by Amelia Simmons, credited with being the first American cookbook.

1796   American Loyalist Benjamin Thompson (Count Rumford) publishes a work on fireplace design. The new Rumford fireplace becomes the standard fireplace.

1803   United States buys the Louisiana Territory, doubling size of the new nation and opening up more land for settlement.

1807   The importation of slaves into the United States is made illegal. Slavery remains legal.

1824   Cookbook *The Virginia Housewife*, by Mary Randolph, is published in Washington, DC.

1825   Erie Canal opens, allowing travelers and goods to travel more quickly and easily. The cost of wheat is greatly lowered in the East.

1825   First tin can is patented in the United States by Thomas Kensett.

1828   Eliza Leslie's *Seventy-Five Receipts for Pastry, Cakes and Sweetmeats* published in Boston.

1829   Publication of Lydia Maria Child's *American Frugal Housewife*.

1830   *Godey's Lady's Book* begins publication in Philadelphia.

1833   Sylvester Graham begins lecturing on vegetarianism.

1839   Publication of *The Good Housekeeper*, Sarah Josepha Hale's first cookbook.

1841   Publication of Catharine Beecher's *Treatise on Domestic Economy*.

1845   Irish Potato Famine begins. Over the next several years, nearly a million Irish migrants arrive in the United States, many settling in the Boston, Philadelphia, and New York City areas.

1848   End of U.S.-Mexican War; California and much of American Southwest become U.S. Territory.

1849	California Gold Rush begins.
1850	American Vegetarian Society founded in New York City.
1853	Gale Borden invents process for producing condensed milk.
1858	John Landis Mason patents glass canning jar with zinc screw cap.
1861–65	American Civil War.
1863	President Abraham Lincoln declares Thanksgiving a national holiday. Timothy Earle of Smithfield, Rhode Island, patents first rotary eggbeater.
1866	Cadwallader C. Washburn opens a flour mill in Minneapolis, Minnesota. It eventually becomes General Mills. Charles Pillsbury opens a mill there three years later.
1869	Transcontinental Railroad completed.
1876	Frederick Henry Harvey opens his first railroad restaurant in Topeka, Kansas.
1877	Publication of Estelle Woods Wilcox's *Buckeye Cookery*.
1879	Opening of Boston Cooking School.
1880	First matzoh factory opens in Cincinnati, Ohio.
1880	Publication in Boston of Maria Parloa's cookbook, *Miss Parloa's New Cook Book: A Guide to Marketing and Cooking*.
1896	Publication of *The Boston Cooking-School Cook Book* by Fannie Merritt Farmer.
1898	Spanish-American War; reports of U.S. soldiers becoming sick from eating canned rations. Hawaii becomes a U.S. Territory. Puerto Rico becomes a U.S. possession.
1900	Good Housekeeping Research Institute opens a test kitchen.
1901	Philippines become a U.S. territory.
1902	Horn and Hardart open first automat in New York City.
1903	James Dole first cans pineapple.

1910	Westinghouse introduced the first electric toaster. Ward Bakery, the largest bakery in the United States, opens in Brooklyn, NY.
1910–30	Great Migration of southern rural black Americans to urban North.
1911	Crisco is invented.
1915	Corning introduces Pyrex cookware. American Stove Company introduces a gas stove with an oven thermostat.
1917	United States enters World War I. There is voluntary rationing of wheat, meat, fat, and sugar. Girl Scouts begin selling home-baked cookies to raise money.
1918	Kelvinator refrigerator is introduced.
1920	Most Americans consume bread baked in commercial bakeries. The 18th Amendment goes into effect, banning the production, sale, and consumption of alcohol.
1923	Clarence Birdseye perfects a method of freezing food.
1927	Harry Baker invents a recipe for chiffon cake. He sells the recipe to General Mills in 1947.
1929	The stock market crashes, beginning the Great Depression.
1930	Sunbeam Mixmaster introduced.
1932	Campbells introduces its tomato soup.
1933	Prohibition repealed.
1937	The Hormel Company introduces Spam. The Waring blender (invented in 1922) is marketed as an aid to make cocktails.
1938	Teflon is discovered.
1939	Nestlé Company begins selling semisweet chocolate morsels.
1941	America enters World War II, following the Japanese attack on Pearl Harbor. Voluntary rationing of meat, wheat, fat, and sugar goes into effect.
1944	American troops are introduced to K rations.
1945	World War II ends. Earl W. Tupper invents a line of resealable food containers.

1946   The National School Lunch Act is passed. Frozen French fries introduced.

1947   Rise of suburban neighbor and growth of refrigeration lead to creation of large supermarkets. Cake mixes from Betty Crocker and Pillsbury start appearing.

1948   Dick and Mac McDonald open the first McDonald's in San Bernardino, California.

1949   Introduction of the electric dishwasher.

1952   Colonel Sanders sells first Kentucky Fried Chicken franchise. Lipton company markets dehydrated onion soup mix.

1954   Swanson company begins marketing the first TV dinner.

1955   Lender's Bagel Bakery begins selling bagels in a supermarket in New Haven, Connecticut. They begin selling frozen bagels in 1962.

1961   Publication of *Mastering the Art of French Cooking* by Julia Child.

1963   Easy-Bake Oven, a toy oven that really bakes, is marketed for girls. Premiere of Julia Child's first television series, *The French Chef*.

1965   Shake 'N Bake is introduced.

1967   First countertop microwave ovens become available.

1970   Hamburger Helper is introduced.

1971   The first Cuisinart Food Processor is introduced.

1986   Swanson replaces the metal tray in its TV dinners with a microwavable plastic tray.

1988   Molecular Gastronomy is created.

2001   Julia Child donates her kitchen to the National Museum of American History in Washington, DC.

2011   The multivolume *Modernist Cuisine* by Nathan Myhrvold, Chris Young, and Maxime Bilet is published. Easy-Bake Oven is redesigned to heat without a light bulb.

CHAPTER 1

Baking

There is nothing in any department of cooking that gives more satisfaction to a young housekeeper than to have accomplished what is called good baking.
—Elizabeth Ellicott Lea, *Domestic Cookery, Useful Receipts, and Hints to Young Housekeepers* (1853)

Baking is a method of food preparation that uses dry heat to cook food, usually in an oven or oven-type appliance. This technique is used most often for cooking bread, cake, cookies, pies (meat, fruit, and custard), and pastries, although apples, potatoes, casseroles, and pasta dishes, such as lasagna, are also baked. Over the centuries, the type of baking that has been done and the technology of baking have changed as ingredients have become available and ovens have evolved and developed.

Supermarkets in the United States now carry a wide variety of baked goods. At the local supermarket I frequent in suburban South Jersey, one can find packaged pita, rye, Indian naan, multigrain breads, bagels, and gluten-free bread, as well as white and whole-wheat sliced bread. The freezer section carries phyllo dough and puff pastry, along with piecrusts and tart shells. The in-store bakery bakes artisan-type breads, rye and pumpernickel, semolina bread, multigrain loaves, bagels, and a wide variety of rolls, cakes, and cookies. Moreover, the store shelves hold a great range of baking ingredients, supplies, and prepared mixes. Of course, this bounty and diversity was not always the case.

A display of ingredients and tools often used in baking. (AP Photo/Larry Crowe)

Before contact with Europeans and the introduction of wheat, Indian tribes living in North America made various types of bread from corn (maize), acorns, and other ingredients. European colonists used corn when wheat was not available and, when possible, adapted their traditional recipes for bread, cake, and pudding to use with the grain.

In the 18th century, wheat flour commonly was used to bake breads, cakes, and pies in many areas, but the availability of wheat and wheat flour in North America varied from place to place and over time. Wheat did not grow well everywhere, and in some locations it was more profitable to sell the wheat that was produced, rather than consuming it. A study of the 18th-century Chesapeake region indicates that corn remained the more commonly consumed grain there, particularly outside of the towns of Williamsburg and Annapolis, although as one historian notes, "the half of Williamsburg's and third of Annapolis's population who were enslaved likely ate little or no wheat." In contrast, Philadelphia laborers ate approximately one pound of wheat bread per day, as did Continental soldiers, along with their allotment of cornmeal.[1]

Even when wheat was available, corn in various forms continued to be a staple in the diets of early Americans, both Indian and European. Cornmeal (also known as Indian meal) was made into mush, baked as nonyeast breads, fried as fritters, or mixed with other flours to make bread. Whether baked in an oven, on a griddle, or in the fire embers, cornbreads and cakes have remained a popular feature of American cooking.

Cornmeal, however, does not react with yeast as wheat flour does, and early American settlers who did not have wheat flour could not produce the type of loaves they were accustomed to eating. The gluten—a type of protein—in wheat dough traps the carbon dioxide bubbles produced by yeast and makes the dough rise, but corn does not have the high gluten content that wheat has. Thus, American colonists adapted the Indian technique for producing *pot-ash* by leaching wood ashes in a pot. They then used this potash to make corn breads rise. A concentrated form of potash became known as pearl ash, and when it is mixed with molasses, sour milk, or some other acid, it becomes a quick leavening agent.[2]

The first cookbook to print recipes using pearl ash was Amelia Simmons's *American Cookery,* published in 1796. Although other cookbooks were available in the United States before this time, *American Cookery* was the first cookbook written by an American woman. The cookbook was also the first to emphasize American foods, such as corn, cranberries, potatoes, and turkey. One of her recipes using pearl ash as a leavening is Molasses Gingerbread. Molasses came from the sugar plantations of the Caribbean, and it was a popular sweetener, especially in New England, where it was also used to make rum. Gingerbread was very popular in early America.[3]

MOLASSES GINGERBREAD

One table spoon of cinnamon, some coriander or allspice, put to four tea spoons pearl ash, dissolved in half pint water, four pounds flour, one quart molasses, four ounces butter, (if in summer rub in the butter, if in winter, warm the butter and molasses and pour to the spiced flour,) knead well 'till stiff, the more the better, the lighter and whiter it will be; bake brisk fifteen minutes; don't scorch; before it is put in, wash it with whites and sugar beat together.

———
Source: Amelia Simmons, *American Cookery, or the art of dressing viands, fish, poultry, and vegetables, and the best modes of making pastes, puffs, pies, tarts, puddings, custards, and preserves, and all kinds of cakes, from the imperial plum to plain cake: Adapted to this country and all grades of life* (Hartford, CT: Printed for Simeon Butler, Northampton, 1798).

BREAD AND BREAD BAKING

"Only when the gods made people out of maize dough were true human beings created," according to the Mayans. Bread in a variety of forms, shapes, and textures has sustained human culture since ancient times, and it has been a feature of religious rituals for thousands of years. During Passover, matzoh, "the bread of affliction," is eaten. In Christian churches, communion is celebrated with sacramental bread, sometimes leavened and sometimes unleavened. In the recent young adult novel, *The Hunger Games,* set in a dystopian society that might be the United States, bread saves the young heroine from death more than once.[4]

When most Americans hear the word *bread* they probably picture loaves of yeast bread. Yet bread comes in a variety of forms, and quick breads are made with baking powder, baking soda, or potash, as described above. Quick breads, as the name indicates, are made quickly. They do not require time to rise or proof, they are not usually kneaded or shaped (some quick breads such as biscuits are briefly kneaded and shaped or rolled and cut), and they can usually be cooked in skillets, Dutch ovens, or regular ovens. Quick breads can be sweet or savory. They can include fruit, vegetables, or nuts, and they can be made of wheat, corn, or other flours. They can be baked as loaves or smaller cakes, or even as flatbreads. European colonists and American Indians both baked corn and pumpkin breads, and both types remain popular American favorites. Banana and other fruit breads are also popular. A website for the Solar Oven Society even includes a recipe for Mango Banana Bread to be baked in a solar oven.[5]

American Indians made a variety of flatbreads from maize (corn) that they baked on stones or in the embers of a fire. Maize had to be hulled, dried, and pounded into meal before it could be mixed with water to make bread. (For more on processing maize, see the introduction.) Sometimes Indian women added other ingredients such as fruit or animal fat to the mixture before baking it. Hopi women prepared piki bread, a flatbread made from very finely ground blue-maize meal and culinary ash that was baked on a special piki stone. Blue cornmeal comes from a special blue corn. Rather than soaking in wood ash or lime, the meal is mixed with the substances, providing additional nutrition and maintaining the color. A young Hopi woman would make piki bread and, escorted by her mother and maternal uncle, would leave it at the home of the young man she wanted to marry. If he and his family wished to accept the proposal, they brought the bread inside.

If not, they left it at the doorway. In the 16th century, when Spanish explorers and priests arrived in the American Southwest, the traditional method of baking piki bread was already several centuries old. Producing the thin, almost transparent sheets of this blue bread took great skill and gave a woman status in Hopi society. Pueblo and Hopi women also made tortillas from ground yellow corn and water. Women of many American Indian tribes baked bread by wrapping a cornmeal mixture in leaves before cooking it on a stone or in the ashes of a fire.[6]

White Americans continued to feel disdain for the bread and bread-baking techniques of American Indian women well into the 20th century. Domestic scientists who worked on reservations in the late-19th century attempted, as one put it, to teach them the "refinements of a cultured home." A teaching syllabus for educating Indian children suggested starting with a discussion on how bread was prepared in their homes. "The primitive manner of grinding grain between stones, mixing the flour with water and baking on hot stones or before the fire will form a practical beginning," observed the syllabus, "and will lead up to the flour of commerce which is purchased at the mills or stores and from which our bread is made."[7]

Seventeenth-century New England housewives who did not have access to wheat flour prepared Indian bread. After wheat became available, many, such as Beatrice Plummer of Newbury, Massachusetts, often used a mixture of wheat and other grains, usually rye. Plummer most likely baked a type of bread called *maslin* bread. This type of bread dates to the medieval period, when the poor, who could not afford white bread, most frequently ate it. Beatrice would have made a sponge by carefully sifting the flour to remove the coarsest bits of grain, then mixing a small amount of the flour with warm water and yeast to produce a wet, sticky dough. She probably obtained yeast from her home-brewed beer or from a saved bit of dough from a previous batch of bread. The sponge would be mixed at night and left to rise in a warm area. In the morning, Beatrice would mix more flour into the dough, knead it, shape it into loaves, let it rise again for a short time, and then bake it. While the bread was rising, she would be heating the oven.[8]

In early-17th-century American houses, ovens were usually built into the fireplace. Later in the century, ovens began to be built into the wall alongside of the kitchen fireplace. Because heating and baking in these ovens took time and experience, cooks continued to use Dutch ovens when they did not have a large amount of baking to do.

Elizabeth Ellicott Lea's 1853 *Domestic Cookery* provided instructions for baking bread both in a Dutch oven and in a brick oven. Although she took many of her recipes directly from other cookbooks, Lea tested them, and in some cases made improvements and suggestions. Thus, after she gave detailed instructions about how to make a loaf to be baked in a Dutch oven, she cautioned her readers to "set it near the fire, but not so near that it will scald." She continued with instructions on how to arrange the loaf, the lid, and the coals, and then advised cooks to "see that it does not bake too fast; it should have but little heat at the bottom, and the coals on the top should be renewed frequently; turn the oven round occasionally."[9]

Even in the late-18th and early-19th centuries, however, not all homes had baking ovens. For example, in Hallowell, Maine, midwife Martha Ballard's neighbors often used her oven to bake their bread. In this frontier town, neighbors exchanged, borrowed, and bartered goods and services. Martha Ballard was able to exchange the use of her oven for other products within the local female trade network.[10]

Heating a baking oven took a great quantity of wood, and this wood had to be cut and split—a difficult job usually done by men. Without firewood, there could be no bread. Martha Ballard discovered this when her husband was jailed for debt in 1804, and her sons neglected to cut wood for her. The 70-year-old Martha recorded her exertion and distress in her diary, as she struggled to cut up old logs and pulled stakes from the snow. On October 29, she reported that she had eaten "the Last bread I had for Breakfast and have sustained without the rest of the day."[11]

Because it took so much wood, time, and effort to heat and use an oven, many households baked only once a week. Large households or well-to-do families that entertained often needed to bake more frequently, or even daily. Elizabeth Lea declared, "If you have a large family, or board the laborers of a farm, it is necessary to have a brick oven, so as to bake but twice a week."[12] Late-18th- and early-19th-century New England ovens were about 40 inches deep and could hold about 10 or 12 pie plates. It could take two hours to heat an oven of this size. The fire was allowed to burn down, and then the cook shoveled out the coals and sometimes swept the oven with a damp broom.[13]

Items were baked in order, according to how long they needed to cook. Breads were normally baked first, then pies, cakes, and smaller cakes or cookies. Custard pies, which are made from milk and eggs and are more delicate, were baked last.[14] Lea suggested putting in the bread, then pies, and "if you have a plain rice pudding to bake, it should be put in the middle of the front, and have two or three shovels of coal put round it, if the oven is rather cool." She noted that bread took an hour to bake, rolls took about half an hour, and "pies made of green fruit will bake in three-quarters of an hour; but if the fruit has been stewed, half an hour will be long enough."[15]

Affluent people, as well as the poor and those in frontier areas, sometimes chose not to bake their own bread. In urban areas, bread and other baked goods could be purchased from commercial bakers. Philadelphia Quaker Elizabeth Drinker also purchased bread when she and her family stayed in their summer home a few miles outside of the city. In an August 13, 1794, diary notation, Drinker wrote that she and her family "have a good baker [who] supplies us with bread from Germantown."[16]

Then, as now, bread quality varied. Some 18th-century bread could get lethally hard, if a report in the 1733 *Pennsylvania Gazette* is correct. According to the account, a man was committed to prison and sentenced for manslaughter for killing his wife. " 'Tis said that upon some Differences he threw a Loaf of Bread at her Head, which occasion'd her Death in a short Time."[17]

In *The American Woman's Home* (1869), the reformer Catharine Beecher and her sister, the author Harriet Beecher Stowe, expounded over several pages the essentials of bread baking, noting, for example, "[T]he true housewife makes her bread the sovereign of her kitchen." They viewed true yeast bread made with brewer's or distiller's yeast as the only truly satisfactory type of bread. They also accepted that stoves and ranges were now a fixture in American kitchens, but lamented the loss of brick ovens. As they stated it, "We can not but regret, for the sake of bread, that our old steady brick ovens have been almost universally superseded by those of ranges and cooking-stoves, which are infinite in their caprices, and forbid all general rules." To produce a good loaf of bread that was cooked thoroughly, yet without heavy sections, cooks needed to know their own ovens and watch them carefully.[18]

Pancakes and other skillet breads were commonly prepared on the overland trails, but women also baked bread in Dutch ovens. They often did so under adverse conditions. For example, one man wrote of a woman who kneaded bread dough and then held an umbrella over the fire for two hours while the bread baked. Another traveler recorded seeing mosquitoes in the bread dough—so many that they turned the dough black.[19]

During the height of the forty-niner gold rush fever, Luzena Stanley Wilson, her husband, and two small sons made the difficult journey west to Sacramento, California, in search of gold. Wilson discovered that hungry men in frontier areas were willing to pay for a woman's cooking. After putting her tired children to bed in the wagon one night, Wilson noticed a miner who said to her, "I'll give you five dollars, ma'am, for them biscuit." She recalled,

> It sounded like a fortune to me, and I looked at him to see if he meant it. And as I hesitated at such, to me, a very remarkable proposition, he repeated his offer to purchase, and said he would give ten dollars for bread made by a woman, and laid the shining gold piece in my hand.[20]

According to one scholar, "[I]n 1890, 90 percent of American bread was baked at home by women." Small bakeries existed then and had existed before, but toward the end of the 19th century larger commercial bakeries began to appear. The Ward Bakery, the largest bakery the United States had ever seen, opened in Brooklyn, New York, in 1910. In 1929, it became the Wonder Bakeries, producers of Wonder Bread. By 1930, the same scholar notes, factories baked 90 percent of the bread in the United States—and this bread was the "standardized, homogenized product of food science and assembly-line manufacture."[21]

White bread has not always been the ideal for Americans. Bread fashions and ideals have changed throughout American history. In the 1820s, the health reformer Sylvester Graham began speaking to audiences about the dangers of ingesting stimulating foods, including meat, white bread, spices, caffeine, and alcohol. Graham believed anyone could achieve good health by choosing to avoid these substances. He found white flour particularly dangerous to humans—body and soul—because separating the bran from the white flour went against God's plan. According to a food scholar, "[W]hite flour was so denatured—so out of harmony with Creation—it took a particularly devastating toll on the bodies and souls of those who ate it." Graham also believed that women should be using locally grown and ground wheat to produce bread they baked in their own homes. During and after Graham's life, there were advocates for and those against Graham bread. A humor column in the *Chicago Daily Tribune* in 1875 joked, "Graham bread is said to be excellent for the children on account of its superior bone-giving qualities. You can feed a child on that bread until he is all bones."[22]

Early-20th-century manufacturers used science to turn consumers against the appeal of home-baked bread. Bakers, they contended, were knowledgeable and used up-to-date techniques to consistently produce superior bread. An article in the *New York Times* in 1904 quoted the manager of a large bread factory who demeaned "that wonderful bread that mother used to make." He commented on how often something went wrong with that bread, and declared, "It was because mother didn't know how to mix dough properly, or because there was something wrong with her ingredients, and she didn't know enough to remedy it."[23]

Many early-20th-century home economists, however, believed women could bake bread using efficient and up-to-date scientific methods. The home economics professors who compiled the 1920 *Manual of Home-Making,* aimed at rural women, included a recipe for Salt-Rising Bread, stating that it was an "old-fashioned bread, the making of which is almost a lost art to-day. . . . [G]as from a certain type of bacteria found in cornmeal is the leavening agent. . . . [T]he odor of salt-rising bread during fermentation and proofing is characteristic. No other dough is like it."

During World War I, the government and organizations called upon women to prepare meals, including baked goods made without or with only minimal amounts of wheat. "The time is at hand when

RECIPE FOR SALT-RISING BREAD (3 LOAVES)

(1) In the evening make a mush of 2 tablespoons of cornmeal and about 1/2 cup scalded milk. Keep it in a warm place overnight. (2) In the morning mix together 1 cup lukewarm water, 1/2 teaspoon salt, 1/2 teaspoon soda, 1 1/2 cups flour, cornmeal mush. (3) Cover the mixture, and place the dish in warm water until the mixture is light. (4) To 2 cups lukewarm water add 2 teaspoons of salt and 3 cups of flour. Add to this the cornmeal leavening mixture. Allow the mixture to rise until it is light. Then add sufficient flour to make a dough. Knead it until smooth, make it into loaves, place in tins, and allow to rise until it is double in bulk. Bake according to the general directions [Bake at 380° to 400°F for 50 to 60 minutes.].

Source: A Manual of Home-Making, compiled by Martha Van Rensselaer, Flora Rose, and Helen Canon (New York: Macmillan, 1920), 505.

the great question for each of us must be, 'How can I order my life today that I may be of service in shortening this conflict? How can I arrange my meals and manage my household so that I am using only such amounts of wheat, meat, sugar and animal fats as are a bare necessity?'" asked Mrs. Alexander J. Barrons, director of Food Conservation for Allegheny County [Pennsylvania] Woman's Committee, Council of National Defense in a 1918 publication, *The Twentieth Century Club War Time Cook Book*. The book was sold to raise money for war work. The recipes for bread include only small amounts, if any, of wheat flour. The volume includes many recipes for cornbread. Some include wheat; some do not. Some include milk and eggs, but others, much closer to the bread of Indian women and colonial settlers, use only cornmeal, water, and salt. There are also suggestions about economizing and saving resources by using stale bread, saving butter from people's plates to reuse in recipes, and rendering and substituting beef suet for butter.[24]

After the horrors of war, Americans looked forward to a world filled with new ideas in art, literature, and design. The sleek shape of commercially produced white loaves held an aesthetic appeal for Americans of the 1920s and 1930s. Trains, furniture, skyscrapers, and fashion favored sleek, smooth, and modern designs. The first commercially sliced loaves of white bread were a huge hit. Soft white bread was difficult to slice at home, but the uniform slices were also a visual delight to many Americans. Commercial white bread became even more popular in the 1940s and 1950s, when it became associated with American values. It also freed women from having to bake bread for their families—often so they could concentrate on other activities within the home. Whole-grain breads began to be popular again in the 1960s, and now in 2012, whole-grain, organic, artisan, and gluten-free breads are more popular in the United States than refined white bread.[25]

CAKES AND COOKIES

Wood- and coal-fired stoves, along with the other conveniences of the mid-19th century, made cooking and baking much easier for American women. Yet this greater ease in cooking increased the work of many women, because cultural norms and expectations changed, as well. Seventeenth- and 18th-century housewives often prepared one-pot meals, but mid-19th-century housewives were expected to produce multicourse meals. Cake styles and baking techniques changed as well.

In 17th- and 18th-century America, cakes were usually versions of plum (fruit) cakes, pound cakes, or sponge cakes. These cakes were made to rise by beating air into the butter and eggs. Without the use of electric mixers, this could take an hour or more of beating. Some cakes also used yeast, or *emptins,* the American terms for what the English called *ale yeast.* Emptins combined hops with the dregs left from beer or cider. Amelia Simmons's "Plain cake" called for "Nine pound of flour, 3 pound of sugar, 3 pound of butter, 1 quart emptins, 1 quart milk, 9 eggs, 1 ounce of spice, 1 gill of rose-water, 1 gill of wine."[26]

Colonial women baked cakes for special occasions. Sometimes these were female-only events, such as when a woman's relatives and friends came to support her physically and emotionally during labor and childbirth. One type of treat served during these occasions was called groaning cakes. The name marked the occasion rather than a particular recipe or type of cake. Women baked cakes for other types of female gatherings, too. Esther Burr, daughter of the famous minister Jonathan Edwards and wife of Aaron Burr, president of the newly created College of New Jersey (now Princeton), recorded in her journal on March 18, 1755, that she was "making Cake for spinning-frollick to day, which is to be attended tomorrow and several days after I suppose." Spinning frolicks were a type of work party, like quilting bees and harvest gatherings, where people got together to do work communally. Often there were dinners and sometimes dancing after the work was completed.[27]

Other common ceremonial events, such as birthdays and weddings, continue to be commemorated with special cakes. Bar and bat mitzvah and *quinceañera* celebrations may feature special elaborate cakes, as well. When Navajo girls reach puberty, a special ceremony is held called the Kinaalda. The ceremony is held after the girl has her first menstrual cycle, and it lasts for four days. It is based on the Navajo story of the Changing Woman. At the start of the ceremony, the girl prepares a special Kinaalda cake called an *alkon.* The cake is made of cornmeal and baked over cornhusks in a dirt pit. It is baked overnight, and slices are cut from east to west to honor the sun, with the most important people in the tribe served the largest, choicest pieces.[28]

In the 1830s, Americans developed new versions of the pound and sponge cakes to impress guests, but at less formal gatherings, women often used pearl ash in their cakes. This ingredient made their cakes rise but allowed the women to use fewer eggs and less butter, with the added benefit of requiring less beating. A type of cake called the *cup cake* was also invented at this time. In this type of cake, women measured the ingredients with a cup, instead of weighing them. A variation of the cup cake can be found in the 1904 *Blue Grass Cookbook*. Pound Cake (No. 2), An Old-Time Recipe is composed of the traditional 1 pound each of butter, sugar, and flour plus 12 eggs. The directions state, "The old-fashioned way was to bake this recipe in teacups and ice them with white icing, and they were called 'Snowballs.'"[29]

Throughout the 19th century cakes that alternated white (egg whites only) and yellow (egg yolks only) sections were popular. The 1877 *Buckeye Cookery* featured a version submitted by Miss Emma Fisher with the political name Hard-Money Cake. (Cookbooks during the 19th century often featured cakes with such names as election cake, Washington Cake, and Lincoln Cake, among others.) The gold part was flavored with lemon and vanilla, and the silver part was flavored with almond or peach. The two batters were to be placed alternately in the cake pan.[30]

By the 1880s, fancier cakes, such as jelly rolls and layer cakes, became popular. These cakes often featured caramel or fudge fillings. Mary Hooker Cornelius offered recipes for several jelly-roll cakes and layer cakes in her cookbook. Her cake recipes used cup measurements, but she advised readers that they should not use "the tea-table china cup, but the common large earthen teacup, except where a small

---

CHOCOLATE CAKE

One cup and a half of white sugar, half a cup of butter, half a teaspoonful of soda dissolved in half a cup of milk, three cups of flour, with one teaspoonful of cream-of-tartar stirred into it, and three eggs beaten thoroughly, yolks and whites together. Flavor with essence of lemon. Bake in three square pans. For the filling, use one cup of milk, half a cake of the sweet chocolate grated, and two eggs. Boil the milk, with the chocolate in it, for two or three minutes. Stir it often, and add the beaten eggs. Spread the chocolate between the sheets, like jelly-cake, or cut the sheets into square pieces of the right size for the table: split each one, and put the chocolate between the two parts. If the chocolate runs, add more to make it thicker.

Source: Mary Hooker Cornelius, *The Young Housekeeper's Friend*, rev. ed. (Boston: Thompson, Brown, & Co., 1873), 56.

one is specified." Her recipe for a chocolate cake is actually a lemon-flavored cake with a chocolate filling, and it uses baking soda and cream of tartar, the ingredients found in modern-day baking powder (cornstarch is often added, too, to help keep the mixture dry). By the late-19th century, these ingredients had replaced pearl ash.[31]

Recipes for these types of cakes, along with basic sponge and pound cakes, can also be found in Fannie Merritt Farmer's *Boston Cooking-School Cook Book*, first published in 1896. According to one historian, this cookbook "was to become the most influential cookbook in American history." It focused on standards of American cooking, provided clear instructions, and used level measurements. Fannie Farmer began her chapter on cakes with the statement, "The mixing and baking of cake requires more care and judgment than any other branch of cookery; notwithstanding, it seems the one most frequently attempted by the inexperienced."[32]

Cookie baking became more popular in the late-19th century, as new technology and the availability of ingredients made it easier to bake. Cookies, however, existed in colonial America. Most scholars believe the word *cookie* come from the Dutch for *little cake*. The colonial little cakes were usually sugar-type cookies that were rolled or shaped. Variations of spice or gingerbread cookies were also common. Cookies were usually baked around the Christmas season because they took so much work. Catharine Beecher's 1850 *Domestic Receipt Book* included a recipe for New Year's Cookies. Saleratus is baking soda, which reacts with acids, such as buttermilk.

NEW YEAR'S COOKIES

One pound of butter.
A pound and three quarters of sugar.
Two teaspoonfuls of saleratus, in a pint of milk (buttermilk is better).
Mix the butter and sugar to a cream, and add the milk and saleratus. Then beat three eggs, and add and grate one nutmeg. Rub in a heaping tablespoon of caraway seed. Add flour enough to roll. Make it one quarter of an inch in thickness, and bake immediately in a quick oven.

———

Source: Catharine Beecher, *Miss Beecher's Domestic Receipt Book: Designed as a supplement to her Treatise on Domestic Economy,* 3rd ed. (New York: Harper and Brothers, 1850), 142.

Many people today who do not bake often during the year bake cookies during the holiday season. There are thousands of cookie recipes available in cookbooks, magazines, and on the Internet.

One of the most popular cookie traditions in the United States is Girl Scout Cookies, which originated early in the 20th century. The tradition of selling cookies to help support the Girl Scout troops appears to have started in 1917. Throughout the 1920s and 1930s, girls and their mothers baked the cookies, usually sugar cookies, wrapped them, and sold them door-to-door for 25 to 30 cents per dozen. Today the cookies are produced at commercial bakeries, and they are certified kosher. There are eight varieties, although not all are available at all times. Recipes for Girl Scout Cookies can be found on many websites.[33]

By the 1930s, many women were cooking from the recipes manufacturers of food products printed on their cartons, as well as recipes printed in newspapers and magazines. Manufacturers of such products as baking powder also printed booklets of recipes using their creations. The Nestle Company, however, began manufacturing semisweet chocolate morsels in 1939 after Ruth Wakefield, the owner of the Toll House Inn in Whitman, Massachusetts, publicized her Toll House Chocolate Crunch Cookie. With the soaring popularity of this cookie, Nestle signed an agreement with Ruth Wakefield allowing the company to print her recipe on their new semisweet morsels packages. This cookie, now generally known as the chocolate chip cookie, is still extremely popular throughout the United States.[34]

During the Great Depression and World War II, food shortages and rationing led to creative baking recipes. Cookbooks written during the 1930s and 1940s, such as Alice Bradley's *Wartime Cook Book* (1943), provided advice on how to substitute molasses, corn syrup, honey, or maple syrup for sugar. Recipes for War Cake were often spiced or fruit cakes that also required little or no butter. Some also substituted margarine for butter. Maple syrup was not rationed, and it was also used for sweetening.[35]

California salesman Harry Baker invented chiffon cake in 1927. In 1947, he sold the recipe to General Mills, and *Better Homes and Gardens* magazine published it in 1948 with the exclamation, "The first really new cake in 100 years!" The cake is made by thoroughly beating salad oil and eggs rather than creaming butter. The cake is then baked in an ungreased tube pan. The most common flavors are lemon or orange, but almost any flavoring can be used.[36]

In the late-20th century, flourless chocolate cake became very popular in restaurants in the United States. Sweet, dense, and superchocolaty, it appealed to those looking for something different. Before long, cooks were making and developing new forms of this treat to bake at home. The cakes use eggs for leavening, sugar, and usually bittersweet chocolate for flavor. They are often are cooked in a water bath. These cakes have become very popular with those on gluten-free diets, but increasingly they are also making appearances on Passover Seder tables. Because observant Jews do not use wheat flour or most forms of leavening during Passover, flourless cakes and cookies have a long tradition in Jewish homes around the world. Often they use finely ground nuts and sometimes matzoh meal to replace the flour, and most use eggs or egg whites for leavening.

PIE

"Tell me where your grandmother came from and I can tell you how many kinds of pie you serve for Thanksgiving," food writer Clementine Paddleford wrote in her 1960 collection, *How America Eats.*[37] Although many people eat pie only on Thanksgiving and Christmas, it has a long history in both American history and pop culture. For example, in an episode of the television show *Twin Peaks,* the pie-loving FBI agent Dale Cooper (played by Kyle MacLachlan) exclaimed, "This must be where pies go when they die," as he tasted a slice of cherry pie at the local diner. Pies seem to be both homey and somehow elegant, as in Julia Child's famous chocolate mousse pie. While away at school, Pennsylvania Quaker Margaret Morris, Jr., wrote longingly to her grandmother, "I often wish for a piece of your good pye, and then dieting would not go so hard with me."[38]

Pie has been popular in America since the colonial period. English settlers brought apple seeds to North America in the 17th century, and apple orchards soon spread throughout the colonies, because apples could be dried for use during the winter or for long journeys. Apple pies have been popular throughout American history, but Americans have created pies from whatever ingredients were available: pumpkin, sweet potatoes, berries, rabbit, oysters, and more. Pennsylvania Germans were noted for shoofly pie, made with molasses; pie makers in Florida created Key lime pies from the limes that grow there; and New England bakers sometimes used maple syrup as a sweetener. The famous Harvey House

A BUTTERED APPLE PIE

Pare, quarter and core tart apples, lay in paste No. 3, cover with the same; bake half an hour; when drawn, gently raise the top crust, add sugar, butter, orange peel and a sufficient quantity of rose water.

No. 3

To any quantity of flour, rub in three fourths of its weight of butter, whites of eggs; if a large quantity of flour, rub in one third or half of butter, and roll in the rest.

———

Source: Anonymous, *The Cook Not Mad or Rational Cookery Being a Collection of Original and Selected Receipts* (Watertown, CT: Knowlton and Rice, 1831), 24, 33.

railway restaurants always offered dessert pies on their menus, and each pie was cut into four slices, instead of the more typical six.[39]

The anonymous author of *The Cook Not Mad,* first published in 1831, included recipes for many different types of pie in the cookbook. There were meat, fish, and something called Save-all Pie, which was made with meat left over from previous meals. The recipe stated, "All meats can be used in this way and with good paste and seasoning make a clever dinner." Despite the author's claim of original recipes, the above recipe for A Buttered Apple Pie is the same as the recipe published in Amelia Simmons's 1798 *American Cookery.* The recipe, which includes rose water and orange peel, is similar in style to earlier, 17th-century English recipes.[40]

Some pies have crumb crusts rather than pastry crusts. Crumb crusts can be made from Graham crackers, cookies, or cakes. One of the first published references to a crumb crust pie appeared in the *1938 Watkins Cook Book.* Some common crumb crust pies include cheesecakes, Key lime pies, chocolate pies, and almost any type of fruit pie.[41]

The availability of traditional ingredients, or the lack thereof, has also led to unusual recipes for baked goods, such as mock apple pie. Included in a book of recipes from the Civil War era is a recipe for Confederate Apple Pie without the Apples. It uses crumbled soda crackers "or even hardtack" mixed with a sugar syrup, placed in a pie crust, dusted with cinnamon, and dotted with butter. Modern versions use Ritz crackers.[42] Ingredients commonly used in a particular region may also change a traditional food. For example, noodle kugel, a common Eastern European Jewish baked noodle pudding, might include pecans in a southern version. Or instead of a traditional potato kugel, southern Jewish cooks might produce a sweet potato kugel.[43]

Yet factories were also producing products aimed at ethnic and religious subgroups of the populations. For example, the first matzoh factory opened in Cincinnati, Ohio, in the 1880s. Before this time, matzoh was made by hand and often wrapped in newspaper. Dov Behr Manischewitz, who was a rabbi and businessman, assured the success of his factory by gaining the endorsement of rabbis in Jerusalem. As one historian notes, "[H]e would subsequently display their endorsement—'There is none more faithful to be found'—in both English and Hebrew on the exterior of his mass-produced boxes." Just as the large bread manufacturers did, he and other matzoh factory owners also emphasized the cleanliness and sanitary conditions of their factories to a public that had become concerned about germs and dangerously adulterated food products.[44]

Ethnic foods that immigrants prepared for the American general public were, and often still are, foods that are not found in their native countries. Sometimes they are adaptations prepared in a blander fashion and with ingredients more palatable to most Americans. An Asian baked good, fortune cookies, has a curious history. Scholars have recently determined that fortune cookies were created in Japan and sold there in 19th-century bakeries. Japanese confectioners then sold them in San Francisco. During World War II, the Chinese and Chinese Americans living there took over the baking and selling of fortune cookies when Japanese Americans were interned and no one wanted to buy Japanese products. Servicemembers and travelers enjoyed the fortune cookies and asked for them when they went to Chinese restaurants in their hometowns. By the late 1950s, Chinese restaurants throughout the United States served fortune cookies.[45]

Italian immigrants who came to the United States in the latter part of the 19th century built bakeries with ovens that would produce the type of bread they ate in Italy. They also used these ovens to produce flatbreads, such as the focaccia of northern Italy and the pizza of southern Italy. Only Italians and Italian Americans ate pizza at first, but Americans began to eat it in Italian restaurants and pizzerias in the late 1930s. Pizza first appeared in an American cookbook in the 1936 *Specialita culinary italiane: 137 Tested Recipes of Famous Italian Foods,* which was a fund-raising cookbook published in Boston. It was called Neapolitan Pie or Pizza alla Napolitana. The recipe called for "raised dough," which "can be purchased in any Italian bake shop." The dough was to be flattened by hand, not rolled with a rolling pin. It was sprinkled with salt and pepper, then covered with a layer of scamorza cheese, a cow's milk cheese somewhat similar to mozzarella, tomatoes, sprinkled with Parmesan cheese, and moistened with olive oil. Readers were instructed to bake the pizza in a hot oven "until the edges are deep brown."[46]

Pizza has changed and developed with American tastes. New York–style pizza generally has a thin crust, similar to Neapolitan pizza. Thicker pizza crust is used as a base for many different toppings. Americans also make pizza at home with homemade or prepared dough, and sometimes the use of a pizza stone, which is preheated at a high temperature to produce an effect similar to a brick oven (although not as hot). More recently, gourmet pizzerias have installed wood-burning ovens that reach extremely high temperatures and allow pizzas to cook very quickly, producing a thin, crispy crust.

American cooks have sought to reproduce other European breads. Julia Child, the American cook who became a household name and beloved icon, began her culinary training when she was in her 30s and living in Paris with her husband, Paul. As she started working on her second cookbook, a complication arose when her editor asked her to include a recipe for French bread. She and Paul spent much of 1967 trying to create bread that was French. They tried different flours, yeasts, and steaming techniques for the oven. Finally, to create the effect of a French baker's oven, they used a hot brick or stone dropped into a pan of water and put in the hot oven. Paul also lined the oven with quarry tiles. *Mastering the Art of French Cooking II*, published in 1970, included a 19-page recipe (including 34 drawings) for French bread. The book declared that this was "the first authentic successful recipe ever devised for making real French bread—the long, crunchy, yeasty, golden loaf that is like no other bread in texture and flavor—with American all-purpose flour, in an American home oven." With that achievement, American bread-baking history came full circle from the crusty loaves baked in the brick ovens of colonial America through the idealization of soft white bread produced in modern electric ovens, and back to European-style breads baked in a hot (simulated brick) oven.[47]

NOTES

1. Lorena S. Walsh, "Feeding the Eighteenth-Century Town Folk, or, Whence the Beef?" *Colonial Williamsburg Interpreter* 21, no. 2 (2000),

http://research.history.org/Historical_Research/Research_Themes/Theme Respect/Feeding.cfm; Billy G. Smith, *The "Lower Sort": Philadelphia's Laboring People, 1750–1800* (Ithaca, NY: Cornell University Press, 1990), 97–98.

2. Betty Fussell, *The Story of Corn* (Albuquerque: University of New Mexico Press, 2004), 225–26.

3. Amelia Simmons, *American Cookery, or the art of dressing viands, fish, poultry, and vegetables, and the best modes of making pastes, puffs, pies, tarts, puddings, custards, and preserves, and all kinds of cakes, from the imperial plum to plain cake: Adapted to this country and all grades of life* (Hartford, CT: Printed for Simeon Butler, Northampton, 1798). Another version of 18th-century gingerbread can be found in Walter Staib with Beth D'Addono, *City Tavern Cookbook: 200 Years of Classic Recipes from America's First Gourmet Restaurant* (Philadelphia: Running Press, 1999), 131. Staib's recipe uses brown sugar instead of molasses. He notes that the exotic spices arrived in Philadelphia from the West Indies.

4. Sophie D. Coe, *America's First Cuisines* (Austin: University of Texas Press, 2005), 8; Suzanne Collins, *The Hunger Games* (New York: Scholastic Press, 2008).

5. "Mango Banana Bread," Solar Oven Society, http://www.solarovens.org/recipes/mango-banana-bread.html.

6. Linda Murray Berzok, *American Indian Food* (Santa Barbara, CA: Greenwood, 2005), 99–100, 114; Linda Civitello, *Cuisine and Culture: A History of Food and People,* 3rd. ed. (Hoboken, NJ: John Wiley and Sons, 2011), 114; Laura Schenone, *A Thousand Years over a Hot Stove: A History of American Women Told through Food, Recipes, and Remembrances* (New York: Norton, 2003), 27–28.

7. Alice C. Hewitt, "The Work of the 'Field Matron' among Indian Women," *New England Kitchen Magazine* (March 28, 1898), 216; *Teaching the Rudiments of Cooking in the Class Room* (Washington, DC: Government Printing Office, 1906), 45, both quoted in Laura Shapiro, *Perfection Salad: Women and Cooking at the Turn of the Century,* with a new afterword (Berkeley and Los Angeles: University of California Press, 2009), 139.

8. Laurel Thatcher Ulrich, *Good Wives: Image and Reality in the Lives of Women in Northern New England, 1650–1750* (New York: Oxford University Press, 1982), 20–21.

9. William Woys Weaver, *A Quaker Woman's Cookbook: The Domestic Cookery of Elizabeth Ellicott Lea,* rev. ed. (Mechanicsburg, PA: Stackpole Books, 2004), xl, 58–59.

10. Laurel Thatcher Ulrich, *A Midwife's Tale: The Life of Martha Ballard, Based on Her Diary, 1785–1812* (New York: Knopf, 1990), 85.

11. Ulrich, *A Midwife's Tale,* 276–77.

12. Weaver, *A Quaker Woman's Cookbook,* 59.

13. Jane C. Nylander, *Our Own Snug Fireside: Images of the New England Home, 1760–1860* (New Haven, CT: Yale University Press, 1994), 197–98.

14. Nylander, *Our Own Snug Fireside*, 198.

15. Weaver, *A Quaker Woman's Cookbook*, 60–61.

16. Elaine Forman Crane, ed., *The Diary of Elizabeth Drinker* (Boston: Northeastern University Press, 1991), 582.

17. *Pennsylvania Gazette*, June 21–28, September 21–28, 1733.

18. Catharine Beecher and Harriet Beecher Stowe, *The American Woman's Home; or, Principles of Domestic Science* (New York: J. B. Ford and Co., 1869), 173–75.

19. Lillian Schlissel, *Women's Diaries of the Westward Journey* (New York: Schocken Books, 1982), 80, 81.

20. Fern L. Henry and Luzena Stanley Wilson, *My Checkered Life: Luzena Stanley Wilson in Early California* (Nevada City, CA: Carl Mautz Publishing, 2003), 29.

21. Aaron Bobrow-Strain, *White Bread: A Social History of the Store-Bought Loaf* (Boston: Beacon Press, 2012), 23, 24, 25–29.

22. "Humor," *Chicago Daily Tribune*, January 20, 1875, 3; Bobrow-Strain, *White Bread*, 83, 86.

23. "As Mother Used to Make It," *New York Times*, July 24, 1904.

24. *Twentieth Century Club War Time Cook Book* (Pittsburgh: Pierpont, Siviter, 1918).

25. Bobrow-Strain, *White Bread*, 56–58, 14.

26. Simmons, *American Cookery*, 33.

27. Carol F. Karlsen and Laurie Crumpacker, eds., *The Journal of Esther Edwards Burr* (New Haven, CT: Yale University Press, 1984), 101.

28. Tess Kenner, "Kinaalda: The Hidden World of Girls," *The Kitchen Sisters*, (September 20, 2010), NPR Radio Series, http://www.kitchensisters.org/girlstories/kinaalda/; for a recipe gathered by anthropologist Floral L. Bailey and published in 1940, see her "Navaho Foods and Cooking Methods," *American Anthropologist* 42, no. 2 (April–June 1940), 281.

29. In October and November 2009, the American Antiquarian Society had bake-off contests first for pound cake, comparing an 1834 recipe and a modern recipe, and then comparing four apple pie recipes from the 18th century to the present. The tasters preferred the old pound cake recipe, but it required an hour of hand beating. They chose the modern-day version apple pie. See http://pastispresent.org/tag/dessert. Minnie C. Fox, *The Blue Grass Cook Book* (New York: Fox, Duffield, 1904), 264.

30. Estelle Woods Wilcox, *Buckeye Cookery, and Practical Housekeeping: Compiled from Original Recipes* (Minneapolis, MN: Buckeye Publishing Co., 1877), 54.

31. Mary Hooker Cornelius, *The Young Housekeeper's Friend*, rev. ed. (Boston: Thompson, Brown, and Co., 1873), 50, 56.

32. Megan J. Elias, *Food in the United States, 1890–1945* (Santa Barbara, CA: Greenwood, 2009), 11; Fannie Merritt Farmer, *Boston Cooking-School*

Cook Book (Boston: Little, Brown, 1896), 412. On my bookshelf sits the 13th edition of this classic cookbook, now called *The Fannie Farmer Cookbook*.

33. Girl Scout Cookies History, Girl Scouts, http://www.girlscouts.org/program/gs_cookies/cookie_history/today.asp.

34. Becky Mercuri, "Cookies," in Andrew F. Smith, ed., *The Oxford Companion to American Food and Drink* (New York: Oxford University Press, 2007), 156.

35. Elias, *Food in the United States, 1890–1945,* 32–33; Barbara Haber, *From Hardtack to Home Fries: An Uncommon History of Cooks and Meals* (New York: Free Press, 2002), 156–57.

36. Sylvia Lovegren, *Fashionable Food: Seven Decades of Food Fads* (Chicago: University of Chicago Press, 2005), 154.

37. Quoted in Janet Clarkson, *Pie: A Global History* (London: Reaktion Books, 2009), 77.

38. Margaret Morris, Jr., to Margaret Hill Morris, August 18, 1807, Howland Collection, Box 9, Quaker Collection, Haverford College, Haverford, PA.

39. Haber, *From Hardtack to Home Fries,* 97.

40. Anonymous, *The Cook Not Mad or Rational Cookery Being a Collection of Original and Selected Receipts* (Watertown, CT: Knowlton and Rice, 1831), 22, 24, 33.

41. Lovegren, *Fashionable Food,* 152.

42. William C. Williams, *A Taste for War: The Culinary History of the Blue and the Gray* (Lincoln: University of Nebraska Press, 2011), 168.

43. Marcie Cohen Ferris, *Matzoh Ball Gumbo: Culinary Tales of the Jewish South* (Chapel Hill: University of North Carolina Press, 2005), 16, 264–65.

44. Jenna Weissman Joselit, "The 4,452 Year Old Food," Reform Judaism Online (2010), http://reformjudaismmag.org/Articles/index.cfm?id=1009&pge_prg_id=5096&pge_id=1137.

45. Jennifer 8. Lee, "Solving a Riddle Wrapped in a Mystery Inside a Cookie," *New York Times,* January 16, 2008, http://www.nytimes.com/2008/01/16/dining/16fort.html; Jennifer 8. Lee, *The Fortune Cookie Chronicles: Adventures in the World of Chinese Food* (New York: Twelve, 2008.)

46. Robert W. Brower, "Pizza," in Smith, *Oxford Companion,* 462–63; *Specialita culinarie italiane: 137 Tested Recipes of Famous Italian Foods* (Boston: North Bennet Street Industrial School, 1936), 48.

47. Noël Riley Fitch, *Appetite for Life: The Biography of Julia Child* (New York: Doubleday, 1997), 325–26, 359–60. Julia Child's kitchen is re-created at the Smithsonian Institution. The website discusses her French bread baking, along with other stories and pictures. http://americanhistory.si.edu/juliachild/. . .

CHAPTER 2
Barbecuing

Maybe all of us who do not have the good fortune to meet or
meet again, in this world, will meet at a barbecue.
    —Zora Neale Hurston, *Dust Tracks on the Road* (1942)

Barbecuing is very popular in the United States. According to a survey
conducted by the Hearth, Patio and Barbecue Association in 2009,
"82 percent of all U.S. households own a grill or smoker . . . and
97 percent of grill owners actually used their grill in the past year."[1]
When most people talk about barbecuing, however, they actually
mean grilling. Although the terms *barbecuing, grilling,* and *broiling*
are often used interchangeably, they are actually three distinct methods of cooking. Broiling and grilling are techniques that cook food
quickly. In broiling, the food is placed directly *under* a high temperature heat source; in grilling, the food is placed directly *over* a high
temperature heat source. Barbecue, however, is a method of slowly
cooking food (usually meat) over low heat. Most scholars agree that
the word *barbecue* derives from the Taino or Carib word *barbricot,* a
wooden frame on which the native inhabitants of Hispaniola grilled
and smoked meat over a bed of coals. The Spanish pronounced the
word *barbacoa,* and eventually it became *barbecue* in English. Barbecue
was used first to describe the cooking frame, then the method of
cooking. It is also used to describe an event, as in attending a barbecue, or the food itself, as in eating barbecue.
    By the mid-18th century, barbecues had become ritualized events in
the American South. For example, in May 1769 George Washington

Barbecued ribs are a favorite in Kansas City and in many other areas of the United States. (PR News Foto/Kansas City Barbeque Society)

noted in his diary that he "went to Alexandria to a Barbecue and stayed all Night."[2] These rustic celebrations often included music and dancing as well as food. The Scottish publisher John M. Duncan described a barbecue he attended in Virginia in 1818. Duncan was visiting Mt. Vernon, the home of Bushrod Washington, an associate justice of the Supreme Court. Washington had inherited Mt. Vernon from his uncle, the former president George Washington. Washington invited Duncan to a barbecue, which was to be held nearby. Duncan was unfamiliar with the word *barbecue*, but Washington explained that it was a type of "rural fête." In his travel memoir, Duncan reported that he saw slaves occupied

> with various processes of sylvan cookery. One was preparing a fowl for the spit, another feeding a crackling fire . . . others were broiling pigs, lamb, venison, over little square pits filled with the red embers of hickory wood. From this last process the entertainment takes its name. The meat to be *barbecued* is split open and pierced with two long slender rods, upon with it is suspended across the mouth of the pits, and turned from side to side till it is thoroughly broiled.

Duncan then observed that the little glen had been transformed into "a rural banqueting-hall and ball room." To his dismay, he discovered he should not have sat down at the first seating. The men who really wanted to eat, rather than dance or flirt, waited for the second seating so that they would not have to attend to "the ladies," who ate at the first seating.[3]

Because barbecuing meat takes time and requires the cook to be available to oversee the process, it is most often done for special gatherings, rather than for everyday meals. In the pre–Civil War South, barbecues were often events hosted by plantation owners whose slaves prepared, cooked, and served the food. Martha McCulloch-Williams's romanticized account of food and foodways in the Old South, *Dishes and Beverages of the Old South* (1913), looks back upon how food was prepared and served in the antebellum South and the types of celebrations that took place when she was a young girl living on a plantation in Tennessee.

McCulloch-Williams noted that a barbecue was often held as part of a political event. In a time and place when newspapers were scarce, these political gatherings gave people a chance to hear the candidates speak, but it also gave them an opportunity to socialize and hear the local gossip. As McCulloch-Williams explained, "[A] real big barbecue was a sort of social exchange, drawing together half of three counties, and letting you hear and tell, things new, strange, and startling." As a child, she attended a barbecue held during the presidential campaign of 1856. There were speakers and supporters for both the Whigs and the Democrats, and the event was reported to have drawn a crowd of one thousand people. Even so, there was more than enough food, and those attending the barbecue, particularly the slaves, took leftovers home.[4]

In one passage, McCulloch-Williams described how meat was barbecued:

> Lambs, pigs, and kids, when barbecued, are split in half along the backbone. The animals, butchered at sundown, and cooled of animal heat, after washing down well, are laid upon clean, split sticks of green wood over a trench two feet deep, and a little wider, and as long as need be, in which green wood has previously been burned to coals. There the meat stays twelve hours—from midnight to noon next day, usually. It is basted steadily with salt water, applied with a clean mop, and turned over as needed from the log fire kept burning a little way off.

This whole process was more difficult than it seems, and McCulloch-Williams noted, "[T]he plantation barbecuer was a person of consequence." Because he was a slave, however, he could be "lent" as "an act of special friendship." McCulloch-Williams then described the importance of the secret *dipney*, the sauce brushed onto the meat just before it was taken from the heat. Her father's recipe included

> [t]wo pounds sweet lard, melted in a brass kettle, with one pound beaten, not ground, black pepper, a pint of small fiery red peppers, nubbed and stewed soft in water to barely cover, a spoonful of herbs in powder—he would never tell what they were,—and a quart and pint of the strongest apple vinegar, with a little salt. These were simmered together for half an hour, as the barbecue was getting done.

The mixture was lightly smeared on top of the cooking meat, and the cook was careful to make sure that no sauce dripped onto the coals because it would send smoke and ash up onto the meat.[5]

Politicians and barbecue seem to go together. When Jack C. Walton ran for governor of Oklahoma in 1922, he declared, "When I am elected governor there will be not be an inaugural ball. I am going to give an old fashioned square dance and barbeque. It will be a party for all the people, and I want you all to come." When Walton was elected, he kept his promise. More than 100,000 people were served on January 9, 1923. It took 19 railroad cars to ship the wood for the fire, and the barbecue that day consisted of meat from "289 head of cattle, 70 hogs, 36 sheep, 2,500 rabbits, 134 possums," and more. Newspapers reported it as the "biggest barbeque" ever held. The barbecue was Walton's most noteworthy action, because he was impeached later that year and did not complete his term of office.[6]

More recent political events have also included barbecues. Lyndon B. Johnson's first presidential state dinner was a barbecue for the West German chancellor Ludwig Erhard and his staff on December 29, 1963. This barbecue for 300 people was held at the LBJ Ranch in Texas. Lady Bird Johnson, the president's wife, recorded the menu in her diary: "beans (pinto beans, always), delicious barbecued spare ribs, cole slaw, followed by fried apricot pies with lots of hot coffee. And plenty of beer." Because it was too cold to sit outside, the actual meal was held indoors at a nearby high school that was decorated with bales of hay to create an outdoor barbecue appearance.[7] Since that time, both presidents and presidential candidates have hosted and attended barbecues to attract voters and reward supporters. In 1986, while he was a senator, Al Gore even participated in a Memphis barbecue competition.

TYPES OF BARBECUE BY REGION

In most of the American South, barbecue means pork. Hernando de Soto, the Spanish explorer, brought pigs to Florida in the 16th century, and English settlers brought them to Virginia and Massachusetts in the 17th century. These pigs were small and stringy because the colonists expected their livestock to forage for food. In fact, English observers noted and commented on the small size of colonial livestock, and one historian has reported "full-grown Chesapeake hogs may have weighed as little as 100 pounds, steers perhaps 500 pounds."[8] By the 19th century, pigs were larger because they were bred for meat. (Today, pigs are bred to be lean, since many people do not want to eat too much fat.) In Texas, however, cattle raising became important, and Hispanic and Anglo groups, and the German immigrants who arrived in the state later, barbecued beef instead of pork. In Kentucky, sheep raising led to barbecued sheep.

Although barbecue styles can vary from town to town, there are four main barbecue styles named for their geographical region: Memphis, Tennessee; North Carolina; Kansas City; and Texas. Memphis style features pulled pork shoulder in a sweet, tomato-based sauce. North Carolina style is typified by a whole hog barbecued with a vinegar-based sauce. Kansas City is noted for its barbecued ribs cooked with a dry rub. The barbecue choice of Texans is beef brisket.

Some people maintain that true barbecue must be pork. To them, Texas barbecued beef brisket or the barbecued mutton of Owensboro, Kentucky, is not true barbecue. Owensboro, however, calls itself "the world capital of barbecue," and the town has held an annual barbecue festival since 1834. Owensboro is located along the Ohio River, and it has been a sheep-raising area since the early 19th century. Mutton, which is the meat of older sheep, requires long, slow cooking.

A barbecued sheep recipe was included in the 1877 edition of *Buckeye Cookery*. This cookbook began as a charity cookbook for the First Congregational Church in Marysville, Ohio, in 1876.

For most of the South, however, pork is *the* meat for barbecuing. Although all agree that it must be cooked slowly, there are differences in the way the meat is served. In eastern North Carolina, chopped or sliced pork is served in a peppery vinegar sauce; in the western part of the state, the sauce often includes tomatoes. People in South Carolina and Georgia served chopped or sliced pork in a yellow-mustard-based sauce. Around Memphis, pork is "pulled," that is, it is hand shredded into threads and then covered in sauce. This sauce is generally a

BARBECUED SHEEP

Dig a hole in ground, in it build a wood fire, and drive four stakes or posts just far enough away so they will not burn; on these build a rack of poles to support the carcass. These should be of a kind of wood that will not flavor the meat. When the wood in the pit has burned to coals, lay sheep on rack, have a bent stick with a large sponge tied on one end, and the other fastened on one corner of the rack, and turn so that it will hang over the mutton; make a mixture of ground mustard and vinegar, salt and pepper, add sufficient water to fill the sponge the necessary number of times, and let it drip over the meat until done; have another fire burning near from which to add coals as they are needed.

—Mrs. Ella Turner

Source: Estelle Woods Wilcox, *Buckeye Cookery, and Practical Housekeeping: Compiled from Original Recipes* (Minneapolis, MN: Buckeye Publishing Co., 1877), 176.

tomato-based sauce with pepper and molasses. Sauces in Alabama are similar, but they are usually spicier.[9]

Of course, other types of meat, poultry, and fish *can* be barbecued. Some barbecue experts recommend brining poultry before it is cooked. A brine is a type of salt solution with added seasonings into which one places meat and soaks it for 1 to 12 hours (approximately 1 hour per pound). As a result, the weight of the meat will increase because water, salt, and sugar will enter its cells. This helps the meat to stay moist when it cooks, because the first moisture lost will be from the brine. Some barbecue chefs believe all poultry should be brined, but other meats and fish, such as smoked salmon and pork chops, can also be brined. Traditional barbecue meats, such as brisket and ribs, should not be brined because they will taste like ham.[10]

BRISKET AND PORK CUTS

Brisket, the usual choice for Texas barbecue, is a cut of beef that comes from the area on top of the legs and just under the shoulders. It is a large rectangle that has no bones, and it is very tough, unless it is cooked for a long time at a low temperature. In addition to its popularity in Texas barbecue, it is also used for pot roasts. Brisket is often divided into two sections. The "first cut" is flat with fat layered on the top. The "second cut" is smaller, thicker, and has fat interlayered throughout it. Despite the extra fat, many consider this second cut to have more flavor. Some people ask the butcher to cut the meat so that the second cut also contains a portion of the first cut.[11]

For pulled pork, barbecuers usually use a fatty pork roast or a whole hog. The pork shoulder is a popular choice. It is divided into two parts, the Boston butt and the picnic roast. Either can be used in barbecue. Spareribs come from the bottom section of the ribs; baby back ribs are from the smaller back ribs (not from baby pigs). Baby back ribs have less meat. They are traditionally used for the barbecued ribs served in Chinese restaurants.

BARBECUE RESTAURANTS

Although traditional barbecue began as a southern food, over time, it spread north and west as people migrated and brought this cooking technique with them. In the first few decades of the 20th century, many African Americans in search of employment moved from the rural South to urban areas in the North. This Great Migration also introduced many southern foods, including barbecue, to people in the North. Barbecue restaurants that were established to bring familiar foods to migrants also became popular with those who had no previous knowledge of it. Often these restaurants became family businesses. For example, James Lemons, the owner of a popular barbecue restaurant, came to Chicago from Indianola, Mississippi, in 1942, with his brothers when he was teenager. His brother opened a barbecue restaurant in Chicago in 1951, and James began working there a few years later. In an oral interview, he recalled that his father barbecued in Mississippi:

> [W]e used to barbecue pigs—pork, you know. They'd always kill hogs around Thanksgiving time, you know what I mean. My daddy had a little—made a little brick pit outside the house and we used to barbecue smoke—smoke meat; we had a smokehouse, you know, and things—. We always fooled around with it, you know—smoking meat and—and cooking meat on the grill; that's what we called it back then. We didn't call it a pit; we called it a grill. So that's how we got to working doing that, and when we came to Chicago we started working in restaurants. And mostly that was—most jobs back then and then the war [World War II] came, you know—came along so a lot of people went to the factories and we went to—my brother and I stayed in the cooking business. And years later, my younger brother came along, and that's when

we opened up the barbecue place. They opened up the barbecue place; I came in on there later on.[12]

Lemons barbecues pork ribs, never beef, at his restaurant. The meat is first seasoned with "sprinkling mix," which sometimes sits on the meat for a few days before the meat is cooked over the wood fire. A barbecue sauce is brushed on later, and it adds a bit of sweetness to the meat. Like most owners of barbecue restaurants, Lemons would not reveal the ingredients of the seasoning or the sauce. Chicago barbecue is a mixture of southern styles—dry rub with a sweet and slightly hot sauce. Unique to Chicago, however, is the aquarium smoker, which features a metal base topped by tempered-glass sliding doors, making it look something like a fish tank. Aquarium smokers burn wood or a combination of wood and coal. Lemons's restaurant uses an aquarium smoker, as do many other Chicago barbecue places.[13]

Barbecue restaurants can be found throughout the United States. They are often takeout-only places; those that do have seating tend to keep it simple and utilitarian, although there are some upscale places. One barbecue restaurant in Texas is actually run from a church. In fact, people often refer to it as "that church that sells barbecue." Members of the mostly elderly congregation prepare barbecued brisket and pork ribs in indirect-heat barrel smokers, using a secret recipe for the rubs and sauce. Some people drive hours to eat this barbecue in the small parish hall.[14]

BARBECUE TECHNIQUES

Pit barbecue is the oldest form of barbecue. The barbecued sheep recipe discussed above uses this technique. This method was used in the southeastern United States, most commonly to barbecue whole pigs or hogs. It is also used for pig roasts at Hawaiian-style luaus. Nineteenth-century California ranchers held barbecues in which hundreds of pounds of wood burned overnight in the pit. Wrapped and marinated beef then was lowered into the pit to cook for about 10 hours.[15] Clambakes use a similar technique in that a pit is dug into the ground—usually on a beach—but the addition of seaweed and water actually steams the ingredients rather than smoking them.

Many people, however, prefer to leave barbecuing to the experts. Because barbecuing is time-consuming and labor intensive, they prefer to get their fill of smoked and charbroiled meat by going to restaurants, competitions, and other events. Barbecuing requires the cook to maintain low temperatures with the cooking done away from the heat source. Charcoal and/or wood (hickory, oak, and fruitwoods are the most popular) are allowed to burn and then smolder before the meat is added. The cooking temperature should be between 200°F and 300°F, which produces smoke and helps to cook and flavor the meat. A pan of water should be placed near the coals at the bottom of the barbecue grill. The food is placed over the water, rather than over the heat, and the lid should be left on while the meat is cooking. If large pieces of meat are going to be cooking over several hours the fuel has to be replenished. For that reason, a supply of hot coals or wood should be kept nearby. The water also has to be replaced as necessary. Barbecuing is particularly well suited for very large pieces of meat and/ or for tough cuts, such as brisket, that benefit from long, slow cooking.

The use of gas grills is frowned upon in the world of true barbecue. As the authors of one barbecue cookbook write, only slightly tongue-in-cheek, the use of a gas grill is "so heretical that it is not even open for discussion among 'Q' fans. Polite grill society won't broach the subject. Even the most vehement arguments between Texans and Carolinians will never veer in this direction. It is off limits." These same authors then proceed to explain the advantages of "smokin' with gas."[16]

A gas grill is much easier to use, and the cooking process is much faster than with wood or charcoal because the cook does not have to wait for coals to burn down to ash. Gas grills do cook at higher temperatures than the ideal for barbecue, but by keeping the meat as far from the heat source as possible and using smoke to help cook the meat, barbecuing can be done on a gas grill. To provide a smoky, barbecue taste, use wood chips or chunks in the grill.[17]

Barbecue experts often use rubs, which are dry ingredients sprinkled or rubbed onto the meat before it is cooked. Common ingredients for rubs include salt and sugar, as well as various herbs and spices, such as garlic powder, chili powder, lemon pepper, dry mustard, cinnamon, nutmeg, ginger, thyme, cumin, and sage. Various combinations can be made, depending on the type of meat being cooked. Sugar can burn, however, so it should be used sparingly. Rubs should be applied thoroughly to the meat, and then the meat should be placed in the refrigerator for one hour to overnight.

While cooking, barbecue cooks often use *mops* or *sops.* These are terms that describe a type of thin liquid that is used to baste the meat while it cooks. It is not barbecue sauce. Often cooks boil a marinade and then use it as a mop. A mop should always be cooked, and then it is applied warm to the meat. Mops should not be applied at the start of cooking. If a rub has been used on the meat, it should have time to form a crust before the mop is applied. Then the mop should be applied every 30 to 45 minutes.[18]

Marinades and mops usually combine acidic ingredients and oil with spices. Sometimes fruit juices or alcoholic beverages are used. Sometimes both are used. For example, one barbecue cookbook contains a recipe for a marinade that can also be used as a mop. It combines apple juice, apple cider, Jack Daniel's sippin' whiskey, as well as a minced Golden Delicious apple, onion, and some other spices. The ingredients are mixed and heated, and the cook is advised to "Pour the shot glass of JD into a glass and sip while you cook."[19]

Because barbecuing takes so much time and effort, cooks have developed shortcuts to try to achieve barbecue flavor with less fuss. One method is to begin by cooking the meat on a grill. The meat is then removed from the grill and finished in the oven or in a slow cooker. This can still be a time-consuming process. A recipe for Memphis-Style Dry-Rub Ribs advises the cook to start the ribs on the grill over indirect heat for six hours. During this time, the fuel, temperature, and water levels have to be maintained. After the time on the grill, an additional one and one-half hours in the oven at 200°F then finishes the ribs. Carolina Pulled Pork Shoulder Barbecue is a bit easier and faster. After cooking the meat for just 15 minutes outside on the grill, it is then brought inside to cook in a slow cooker for 8 hours.[20] These methods give the cook time to attend to guests while still providing a meal of smoky barbecued meat.

Barbecue aficionados do not consider quickly grilled meat slathered with barbecue sauce to be true barbecue. Nevertheless, barbecue sauce is often used on or served on the side with slow-cooked barbecued pork, beef, or chicken. Barbecue sauces can be sweet tomato, peppery vinegar-based, or mustard-based sauces. Other ingredients, such as salsa or cola, might also be incorporated in the sauce. Unique to northern Alabama is a white barbecue sauce that is made with mayonnaise, vinegar, lemon, salt, and pepper. It is used on turkey and chicken.[21] Sometimes sauces are thinned and used as mops.

BARBECUE COMPETITIONS

Competitive barbecuing has grown extremely popular in the last two decades. There are many barbecue associations that sponsor competitions throughout the United States and Canada.[22] The authors of one barbecue cookbook stated that in 1998, "more than 6 million people attended more than 500 barbecue contests." Television shows, such as *BBQ Pitmasters* (TLC), *Barbecue University* (PBS), and *BBQ with Bobby Flay* (Food Network), have brought barbecue and barbecuing techniques to an ever-increasing audience, and they have pushed more people to enter barbecue contests.

The Memphis in May World Championship Barbecue Cooking Contest is the largest barbecue contest in the world, according to one source. One barbecue cookbook describes it as "Super Bowl week, the Mardi Gras and King Hell redneck picnic all rolled into one."[23] Although the main event is the barbecue competition—and hundreds of teams compete for more than $100,000 in prize money—the festival also includes a Miss Piggy Idol competition, a T-shirt competition, and a best barbecue booth competition.[24] The Kansas City Annual American Royal Barbecue and the Jack Daniels Invitational are the other major barbecue competitions, but there are barbecue competitions throughout the United States and Canada, and they are held all year long.

In the late 1980s, some members of Memphis's large Jewish community decided to hold a kosher barbecue competition. The event began in 1988. Since that time it has expanded, attracting corporate sponsors and celebrity judges. Now in its 21st year and known as the ASBEE (Anshei Sphard–Beth El Emeth) Kosher BBQ Contest and Festival, the competition offers a kosher alternative to the Memphis in May competition. According to its website, last year the festival "hosted 40 teams and more than 3000 attendees." Its Facebook page proudly declares it to be "the world's largest and possibly only Kosher BBQ Contest and Festival."[25]

Unlike traditional barbecue competitions, the kosher barbecue competition supplies contestants with kosher grills, kosher beef briskets, and beef ribs (there is no pork at this competition), and the approved ingredients for marinades, rubs, and sauces. Contestants choose their meat at a meeting in the synagogue on the Thursday evening before the competition on Sunday. They may begin preparations that night and continue them on Saturday night after sundown, when the Sabbath is over. The synagogue supplies all of the utensils and cooking supplies, and contestants must even have their snacks approved by the rabbi to ensure that they are kosher. As with other barbecue competitions, the teams at this kosher festival often sport interesting names, such as Three Brisketeers, Shofar Shogood, Grillin n' Tefillin, and The Holy Smokers. Rabbi Joel Finkelstein of Anshei Sphard–Beth El Emeth believes this festival is "the ultimate in the integration of the great traditions of Jews and Southerners."[26]

NOTES

1. "Grilling Facts and Figures," Hearth, Patio and Barbecue Association, http://www.hpba.org/consumers/barbecue/consumers/barbecue/grilling-facts-and-figures.

2. May 27, 1769, Donald Jackson and Dorothy Twohig, eds., *The Diaries of George Washington* (Charlottesville: University Press of Virginia, 1976–90), online at The George Washington Papers, 1741–1700, The Library of Congress, Manuscript Division, http://memory.loc.gov/ammem/gwhtml/gwseries1.html#D.

3. John M. Duncan, "A Virginia Barbecue," in *American Food Writing: An Anthology with Classic Recipes,* ed. Molly O'Neill (New York: Penguin, 2009), 21–23.

4. Martha McCulloch-Williams, *Dishes & Beverages of the Old South* (New York: McBride, Nast & Co., 1913), 275–78.

5. McCulloch-Williams, *Dishes & Beverages,* 273–74.

6. "World's Biggest Barbeque," Oklahoma Journeys, Week of January 9, 2010, Oklahoma History Center, http://www.okhistory.org/okjourneys/barbeque.html.

7. Craig "Meathead" Goldwyn, "In 1963, a First State Dinner for the Record Books," *Huffington Post,* posted November 24, 2009, http://www.huffingtonpost.com/craig-goldwyn/in-1963-a-first-state-din_b_369539.html.

8. Virginia DeJohn Anderson, *Creatures of Empire: How Domestic Animals Transformed Early America* (New York: Oxford University Press, 2004), 98–99, 118–19.

9. "All About Barbecue," The 3 Men Website, http://www.3men.com/allabout1.htm#TheHistoryofBarbecue.

10. The 3 Men Website, http://www.3men.com/allabout1.htm#TheHistoryofBarbecue.

11. David Rosengarten, *It's All American Food: The Best Recipes for More Than 400 New American Classics* (Boston: Little, Brown, 2003), 441.

12. James Lemons (Lem's Bar-B-Q), oral interview by Amy Evans, Chicago, IL, March 26, 2008, at Lem's Bar-B-Q, Length: 1 hour, 2 minutes, Project: Chicago Eats/TABASCO Guardians of the Tradition, Southern Foodways Alliance, http://www.southernfoodways.com.

13. Lemons interview.

14. Patricia Sharp, "New Zion Barbecue," *Saveur,* May 26, 2009, http://www.saveur.com/article/Travels/New-Zion-Barbecue.

15. The Culinary Association of Southern California re-created a 19th-century pit barbecue in 2007. See http://www.culinaryhistorian sofsoutherncalifornia.org/2007BBQ.htm, and more pictures on Professor Salt's blog, http://professorsalt.com/2007/07/24/how-i-know-my-bbq-from-a-hole-in-the-ground/.

16. Rick Brown and Jack Bettridge, *Barbecue America: A Pilgrimage in Search of America's Best Barbecue* (Alexandria, VA: Time-Life Books, 1999), 184–85.

17. Brown and Bettridge provide detailed instructions on using a gas grill for barbecuing in *Barbecue America*, 184–91.

18. "All About Barbecue," The 3 Men Website, http://www.3men. com/allabout1.htm#TheHistoryofBarbecue.

19. Brown and Bettridge, "Drunken Appul Whiski Marry-nade," in *Barbecue America*, 20.

20. Rosengarten, *It's All American Food*, 313–16.

21. Jennifer Ludden, "Dad, Daughter Write the Book on BBQ," *All Things Considered*, NPR, July 3, 2005, http://www.npr.org/templates/story/story.php?storyId=4728146.

22. For a list of the major associations and teams, see *The Smokin' Blue BBQ Rag*, http://www.smokinbluesbbq.com/Teams.html. This site also has detailed instructions on what to do and not do at barbecue competitions, helpful tips, recipes, and links to many other sites.

23. Brown and Bettridge, *Barbecue America*, 53.

24. World Championship Barbecue Cooking Contest—Hosted by Memphis in May, http://www.memphisinmay.org/bbq.

25. ASBEE 22nd Kosher BBQ Contest and Festival, http://www. asbeekosherbbq.com/.

26. Marcie Cohen Ferris, *Matzoh Ball Gumbo: Culinary Tales of the Jewish South* (Chapel Hill: University of North Carolina Press, 2005), 240–43; ASBEE 22nd Kosher BBQ Contest and Festival, http://www.asbeekosherbbq. com/.

CHAPTER 3
Boiling and Poaching

> I had an excellent repast—the best repast possible—which consisted simply of boiled eggs and bread and butter. It was the quality of these simple ingredients that made the occasion memorable. The eggs were so good that I am ashamed to say how many of them I consumed.
> —Henry James, *A Little Tour in France* (1884)

Boiling is a method of cooking in which foods are heated in a liquid that has reached the boiling point (212°F at sea level). It is used to prepare simple dishes, such as Henry James's boiled eggs, and for more complex dishes, such as boiled beef dinners and soup. Boiling can be done in two ways: food can either be placed in a boiling liquid, or it can be put into a cold liquid and then the food and liquid are brought to a boil together. A full boil is characterized by rapidly rolling bubbles, but generally food is not boiled for very long, since the intense motion can damage it. According to an old adage, "a stew boiled is a stew spoiled." If a stew is boiled too long, the meat and vegetables will fall apart, and the meat can become stringy and tough. Boiling too long also damages other foods. For example, custards should not be boiled because the high heat will cause the eggs to curdle. When preparing boiled eggs, the temperature of the water should be lowered after it comes to a boil to prevent the eggshells from cracking. Consequently, boiling food generally means bringing the liquid to a boil, then lowering the heat to a simmer, or just below the boiling point. In simmering, tiny bubbles appear on the surface of the liquid, but there is not a violent rolling boil.

Fresh pasta with arugula and chorizo is an example of a quickly prepared boiled meal. (AP Photo/Larry Crowe)

Lobsters and crabs are put into boiling water to cook them. The shellfish are supposed to be alive when placed in the boiling water of a huge lobster pot. In a memorable scene from Woody Allen's 1977 movie, *Annie Hall,* Alvy Singer, played by Allen, and his girl-friend, Annie Hall, played by Diane Keaton, chase lobsters around the kitchen as they attempt to get them in the lobster pot. Singer jokes about luring one out from behind the refrigerator by putting down melted butter and a nutcracker so he will run out the other side.

Poaching is used to cook delicate items, such as eggs and fish. The temperature of the liquid is kept between 140°F to 180°F, which is below a simmer. The poaching liquid, whether water, broth, wine, or syrup, should not appear to be boiling, although there may be tiny bubbles at the bottom of the pot.

In blanching, however, the water is kept to a rapid boil. Vegetables are often blanched to preserve their color and crispness before freezing them, adding them to another dish, or serving them as crudités. To blanch vegetables, add them to rapidly boiling water for a few minutes only. The exact length of time depends upon the type of vegetable and its size—finely chopped vegetables take less time to blanch, perhaps less than a minute. Remove the vegetables from the boiling water and plunge them into ice water to stop them from cooking.

Boiling water is used to make coffee and tea and to dissolve gelatin and is added to instant, dried foods. Many kinds of foods can be boiled, and the technique of boiling is sometimes used as one step in the creation of many dishes. This chapter will give examples of some foods and dishes that use boiling as a cooking method.

HISTORY

As a cooking technique, boiling probably came later than grilling or baking in ashes because some type of container is needed to hold the liquid. Before humans learned to create pottery and in cultures where pottery making is uncommon or unknown, baskets or containers made from animal skin were used for boiling food. In these instances, the cook boiled the food by heating a stone in a fire and then dropping it into the container.

The Nuu-chah-nulth (commonly referred to as Nootka) of the Pacific Northwest used wooden boxes to cook and serve food. Captain James Cook described this method in 1778.

> Boiling is performed in a wooden trough like an oblong box by putting red hot stones into the liquor, a heape of which always compose the fire hearth, they put them in and out of the pot with a kind of wooden tongs. In this manner, they boil all kinds of meat and make soups.[1]

Native American tribes of the Northwest and California mainly used the stone-boiling method. For example, Native Americans of the Northwest stone-boiled sea lion blubber in watertight baskets. After boiling, they skimmed the oil from the surface and stored it in containers made from the sea lion's stomach. The oil was used to season boiled plants and vegetables.[2]

American Indian women wove the baskets used for food gathering and preparation. It was a skill that was passed down through generations of American Indian women. The American Indians of western North America wove intricate baskets of all sizes and that were used for many purposes, including gathering berries, holding fish, cooking foods, and serving prepared food. One scholar states, "[W]atertight baskets were used to cook acorn mush, soups, and stews by heating smooth rocks in a fire, dipping them briefly in water to rinse off ashes, and dropping them into the basket, where they are stirred constantly until cool." The cooks used two sticks, "like chopsticks," to pick up the hot rocks.[3]

The Iroquois, who lived in what is now the northeastern United States, boiled cornmeal and pumpkin and mixed it with maple sugar to make a type of pudding. Many tribes made corn dumplings by mixing cornmeal and water and then dropping the mixture into boiling water or into a pot of boiling meat. Succotash was another dish made by many Indian tribes and later adopted by European settlers. The word *succotash* comes from the Narragansett *sukquttahash*. In the winter, the dish could be made from dried maize (corn), beans, and winter vegetables, all boiled and combined, but in the summer, it was made from fresh beans and green maize. Sometimes, meat was added to the dish, and some type of grease or oil might also be added for flavor.[4] Succotash was a very popular dish in New England. The 19th-century Rhode Island author and reformer Thomas Robinson Hazard recalled that his grandmother "used to always caution me about eating too much [succotash], as she had once known a naughty boy who burst asunder in the middle from having eaten too heartily of the tempting dish."[5] Twenty-first-century succotash recipes often use canned or frozen vegetables, and cooks are more likely to sauté the vegetables or cook them in a microwave oven than to boil them.

Boiled food was frequently prepared in colonial kitchens because meat and vegetables can easily be combined in one pot to make a meal, and making such a meal does not require much attention, at least compared to other open-hearth cooking techniques. In the 17th and early-18th centuries, kitchen fireplaces had lug poles from which pots and kettles could be suspended over a fire by way of pothooks. In the mid-18th century, cranes with hinges replaced the lug poles. A cook could swing the crane out of the fireplace in order to reach pots hanging on it, thereby eliminating the need to step into the fireplace. Pots and kettles came in a wide range of sizes, and some pots were footed. To move from a hard boil to a simmer, the cook moved the pot away from the flames.[6]

Boiling was more complicated for those who had to cook outdoors in remote areas. Travelers on the Overland Trail, for example, did not always have fuel or water, and when they found water, it was not always clean. They sometimes used cornmeal to filter the mud and silt from river water. At times, they had to camp without any water. Overland travelers called this a "dry camp." The diaries of men and women on the overland trails often record nights they "[c]amped without water."[7]

"Camped without wood" was another frequent complaint. When there was wood, it was often green willow branches. A minister's wife, Esther Hanna, grumbled, "It is very trying on the patience to cook and bake on a little green wood fire with the smoke blowing in your eyes so as to blind you, and shivering with cold so as to make the teeth chatter."[8] In the barren plains, overland travelers learned to collect buffalo dung or chips, which burned quite well. In the Rocky Mountains, they burned sagebrush.

Indoor fireplaces and ovens also required fuel. Early in the 19th century, the Maine midwife Martha Ballard complained in her diary about not having wood. Although she was used to chopping kindling and bringing in smaller pieces of wood, she could not haul and split large logs. At this point, she was in her 70s; her husband had been imprisoned for debt, and her sons were either ignoring her, or they were unaware of her plight. In one entry on April 19, 1804, she reported, "I have gathered Chips South side of my gardin. Broke the old logg fence to pieces and kept fire to do my work."[9]

In addition to fuel and water, cooks needed pots in which to boil the ingredients for a meal. In her popular 19th-century cookbook, N.K.M. Lee advised cooks to use the correct size pot when boiling food. "The size of the boiling-pots should be adapted to what they contain: the larger the saucepan the more room it takes upon the fire, and a larger quantity of water requires a proportionate increase of fire to boil it." She also cautioned cooks to "let the covers of your boiling-pots fit close, not only to prevent unnecessary evaporation of the water, but to prevent the escape of the nutritive matter."[10]

Of boiling, Mrs. Lee stated, "This most simple of culinary processes is not often performed in perfection." To boil meat, she noted, did not "require so much nicety and attendance as roasting." The key points were "to skim your pot well, and keep it really boiling (the slower the better) all the while, to know how long is required for doing the joint & c., and to take it up at the critical moment when it is done enough." These simple steps were "almost the whole art and mystery" of boiling.[11]

The advice Mrs. Lee gave about boiled foods holds true today. Although the taste of contemporary boiled dishes might be similar to those prepared in the 17th, 18th, and 19th centuries, their preparation does not require shifting pots away from flames or hot coals. The heat under a boiling pot can be adjusted quickly on modern stovetops. Nevertheless, if forgotten, the liquid in a pot can still boil away, leaving the pot to burn. Such inventions as electric rice cookers, slow cookers, coffee makers, and electric kettles, however, regulate the heat, and some models can be programmed to turn on and off, thereby eliminating scorched pots.

BOILED MEAT AND ONE-POT MEALS

Boiling was a popular method of preparing meat in the 18th and 19th centuries. Americans ate a great deal of meat, which was widely available to most people, and they boiled beef, mutton, lamb, pork, veal, poultry, and game. They also boiled seafood. They boiled roasts, chops, and other animal parts, such as tongues. Often these meats were combined with vegetables to make a one-pot meal. Animal parts were also used to make sausage, and animal fat was rendered to make tallow for candles and soap. The 18th-century Long Island farmwife Mary Cooper seemed to spend endless hours cooking and cleaning. On December 1, 1769, a few days after she reported they were "buesy killing hogs," she wrote in her diary, "Oh, I am distressed with harde worke making sassages and boile souse, bakeing and cooking." Souse, also called headcheese, is a gelled meat or sausage made by boiling pig heads and sometimes the feet, ears, and other parts.[12]

To boil meat for a meal, Mrs. Lee advised cooks to "put your meat into *cold* water" and then bring the water to a boil very slowly. The meat, she cautioned, should be of equal thickness throughout to keep one section from cooking faster than another, and the water in the pot should just cover the meat. Mrs. Lee provided another useful cooking tip. She recommended placing a "trivet or fish-drainer . . . on the bottom of the boiling-pot, raising the contents about an inch and a half from the bottom" to allow the meat to cook evenly all over.[13]

Seventeenth-century and early-18th-century American meals were very often one-pot meals, but later in the 18th century, meat and vegetables were more frequently cooked separately. One scholar attributes this change in food preparation—at least partly—to differences in the way colonists butchered their animals. He bases his views on the analyses of animal bones found at 17th- and 18th-century sites, noting,

[T]he earlier method, which is contemporary with the period of mixed cooking, was marked by chopping of the bone, probably with an ax. Such a quartering method did not permit the closest control over the size of the resulting portions, nor did it permit the production of small cuts, such as chops, steaks, or short ribs. Hacking a carcass into rather large chunks produced large pieces of meat that could be roasted and then corporately consumed, or cooked in a stew in which the meat would cook from the bone and blend with the other ingredients. This quartering technique was replaced by the use of saws to divide up the animal. . . . A saw can produce servings controlled to size.[14]

Nevertheless, one-pot meals remained popular because they were easy to prepare and did not require constant attention. In the antebellum Chesapeake region, one-pot meals were popular with both slaves and white settlers. For slaves, there were some advantages to preparing a one-pot meal, since less desirable types of meats, along with all kinds of plants, could simmer in a pot while the slaves worked. A historian of African American foodways notes, "The key difference between English and African meals of this type was that the latter added more spices to their one-pot meals while the English preferred their meals to be simpler with less spice. The pot was often used to both cook and serve the food."[15]

The traditional New England boiled dinner, consisting of boiled beef and vegetables, evolved over time. The necessity of making old or low-quality beef palatable, as well as transformations in kitchen design and technology, contributed to the evolution of this traditional dish. The earliest versions of the boiled dinner may have been a form of succotash that included meat. Later-18th- and early-19th-century versions attempted to make the boiled beef more elegant by adding stuffing, more elaborate seasonings, and wine, then allowing the meat to simmer for several hours. This dish was often called Beef Alamode or Alamode Beef. As ovens and kitchen technology developed, however, the fancier boiled-beef dishes disappeared, and another version of the boiled-beef dinner appeared. This is what is now called pot roast, a version of boiled beef cooked with root vegetables and water in a large roasting pot instead of in a kettle. Sometimes it is called Yankee Pot Roast. Yet traditional New England boiled beef can still be found. Most often, present-day recipes use corned beef, which is boiled with turnips, potatoes, carrots, and cabbage. It is also referred to as corned beef and cabbage, even when other vegetables are added.[16]

Some one-pot meals, such as chowders, were made with fish. Scholars argue over the origins of chowder, but most agree that the word *chowder* is derived from the French word *chaudiére,* a type of caul-dron. In addition, many centuries ago, fishermen in Brittany ate a stew called *la chaudrée,* which traveled with them to the coasts of France, England, Ireland, and Wales. Chowder may have come to Newfound-land with Breton fishermen and then traveled down the coast to New England. The ingredients for early chowders, consisting of fresh fish, salt pork, and hard biscuits or dry bread, would have been available to most early settlers who lived along the coast, as well as to those at sea. Moreover, it is likely that American Indians also made chowder-like fish stews or soups. One cookbook maintains, "Eastern Coastal tribes made a soup combining clams and potatoes long before the ar-rival of Europeans."[17]

Nineteenth-century chowder recipes usually include potatoes and sometimes clams. Milk was not considered a necessity, but some mid-19th-century recipes began to include it. Early recipes used crack-ers, hard bread, or ship's biscuits to thicken the soup. Later, crackers began to be served on the side with the chowder. New England chow-ders do not include tomatoes.[18]

In New England, chowder evolved from a subsistence food to one eaten during special occasions. One culinary historian writes, "[C]howder was probably eaten more often by people who could af-ford little meat and occasionally by other people because they liked it or desired variety in their menus." Chowder parties and picnics became very popular in mid-19th-century New England. Sometimes participants made chowder on the beach during these get-togethers. Chowder feasts were also sometimes used as fund-raisers, and chow-der was also served at gatherings for social or political groups.[19]

The 1896 edition of the popular *Boston Cooking-School Cook Book* includes five recipes for chowder. There are recipes for Fish Chow-der, Clam Chowder, and Lobster Chowder, all with milk and crackers added toward the end of the cooking time. Connecticut Chowder, however, uses stewed tomatoes in place of the milk. There is also a recipe for Corn Chowder made with canned corn, potatoes, salt pork, onion, milk, and crackers.[20]

In much of the South, particularly in Louisiana, gumbo served the same purpose as chowder did in New England. It was often served at parties and social gatherings, and one pot could be stretched with added ingredients to serve many people. *Gumbo* (or *gombo*) is derived from an Angolan word for okra, an important ingredient in most gumbos. When boiled, okra helps to thicken the soup. The word *okra*

OCHRA SOUP

Get two double handsful of young ochra, wash and slice it thin, add two onions chopped fine, put it into a gallon of water at a very early hour in an earthen pipkin, or very nice iron pot; it must be kept steadily simmering, but not boiling: put in pepper and salt. At 12 o'clock, put in a handful of Lima beans; at half-past one o'clock, add three young cimlins [squash] cleaned and cut into small pieces, a fowl, or knuckle of veal, a bit of bacon or pork that has been boiled, and six tomatos, with the skin taken off; when nearly done, thicken with a spoonful of butter, mixed with one of flour. Have rice boiled to eat with it.

Source: Mary Randolph, *The Virginia Housewife: Or, Methodical Cook*, stereotype ed. (Baltimore: Plaskitt & Cugle, 1838), 17–18.

comes from the West African word *nkru ma.* Okra was brought to the Americas through the slave trade.

Mary Randolph's 1838 cookbook, *The Virginia Housewife,* includes a recipe for Ochra Soup, which is similar to today's gumbo recipes. One culinary historian remarks, "What is certain is that various African okra stews characterize the cuisines of South Carolina and New Orleans, *with rice the obligatory accompaniment,* although not always explicitly so directed." (The successful cultivation of rice in South Carolina, discussed later in the chapter, was primarily because of its large African-born slave population.) Gumbos are sometimes thickened with filé (powdered dried sassafras leaves).[21]

Gumbo derived from a combination of various people and cuisines. Over time, it has evolved even more. As one historian puts it,

The creole world that German and French Jews encountered in midnineteenth-century New Orleans and rural Louisiana was as complex as the gumbo they ate—a rich seafood stew inspired by African, Indian, and Franco-Spanish cultures. Like the gumbo their society was heavily influenced by the Caribbean, by the French and Spanish, by Choctaw and Natchez Indians, by enslaved Africans and free "people of color," by French Canadian exiles, and later in the century by Irish, Italians, and Greeks. . . . Sephardic, German, and French Jewish immigrants added their own heritage to this rich stew as they mixed with the larger culture.[22]

In New Orleans's cultural fusion of cuisines, Creole and Jewish culinary traditions combined to make Matzoh Ball Gumbo, in which Creole matzoh balls are served with chicken and beef sausage gumbo.[23] Matzoh balls (*knaidlach* in Yiddish) are a type of dumpling prepared with matzoh meal, eggs, and sometimes oil or chicken fat. Most commonly, they are dropped into boiling water or broth (usually chicken or vegetable) to cook. Jews around the world eat matzoh, unleavened bread, during Passover.

Dumplings were created from the ingredients a particular group had at hand, as were the soups and stews with which they were served. Often they were used to make a soup or stew more filling. Every culture, ethnic group, and region had—and has—its own soups and dumplings. The dumplings made by American Indians and 17th-century British settlers were little more than cornmeal and water. Later, European settlers used wheat flour to make dumplings to add to soups and stews. Dumplings can also be steamed, fried, or baked, and some dumplings are filled. Italian ravioli and tortellini, Chinese wontons, and Jewish kreplach are all made from thin squares of dough filled with meat or cheese and boiled in soup (or water).

In contrast, fruit dumplings were not cooked in soup or stew. They were usually made of apples or peaches and were particularly popular in the mid-Atlantic region of the country. They appear to be part of both the Pennsylvania German and English culinary traditions. To prepare apple dumplings, the cook pared and cored apples, enclosed them in pie dough, and boiled them in water. Peach dumplings were made the same way. They were then served warm with cream, sugar, and butter and thus could serve as a simple meal.[24]

While traveling on the Overland Trail to California, Mary Rockwell Powers used the last of her dried strawberries to make dumplings. After stewing them and making some dough, she "rolled it out with a bottle and spread the strawberries over it, and then rolled it up in a cloth and boiled it, and then with the juice of the strawberries and a little sugar, and the last bit of nutmeg I had made quite a cup full of sauce to eat upon the dumplings. . . . The dumplings were light as a cork and made quite a dessert."[25]

Like dumplings, noodles and other forms of pasta can be added to soups. Noodles come in many different shapes and sizes. In addition to being added to soups, noodles can be combined with other foods and/or served with sauces. Most wheat-flour noodles are boiled in water before they are added to soups or other food to prevent them from absorbing too much of the liquid in the soup. However, they can be cooked directly in the soup. For example, orzo, a small rice-shaped pasta, is often boiled in soup. For macaroni and cheese, the macaroni is boiled in water and drained before it is combined with a cheese sauce. To prevent pasta from getting gummy or sticking together, it should be added to rapidly boiling water, and there should be enough water in the pot to allow individual pieces to float freely. Asian starch or rice noodles (also called glass or cellophane noodles) require only soaking in a hot liquid; they do not need to be boiled.

A web search for one-pot meals will generate thousands of results, including many types of chowders, gumbos, and noodle dishes. (Stews are one-pot meals, too, but they are discussed in chapter 9.) There are recipes for traditional fish and seafood chowders and for more unusual types of chowders, such as Cheeseburger Chowder. Like 17th- and 18th-century cooks, Americans today want the ease of preparing a meal that does not require too many steps or pots or much cleanup. Unlike the boiled meals prepared by 17th-century cooks, however, one-pot meals today might be cooked in an oven, slow cooker, or microwave oven, as well as in a large stockpot. Some dishes—those using pasta, for instance—might require boiling and mixing as a first step. After that, the dish can be baked in the oven. The initial preparation can be prepared in advance, refrigerated or frozen, and then baked at a later date.

BOILED PUDDINGS

Boiled puddings were another staple dish of 17th-century British colonists. Puddings were traditional in England. At first, they were cooked in bags made from the guts of animals, but by the 17th century, pudding cloths were being used. A pudding cloth or bag was an old piece of cloth. After the pudding was poured onto it, the ends were gathered together and tied with string. The cloths were washed and reused. English settlers in New England used pudding cloths to make puddings but substituted maize (corn) as the main ingredient. A history of New England foods declares, "[B]oiled bag corn puddings were one of the most successful adaptations of a New World food to English tastes." American Indians boiled cornmeal and water; New England colonists added berries or other ingredients to sweeten the pudding, then put the mixture in a pudding bag and boiled it for several hours in a pot. In this way, it could be added to a pot that was already being used to cook other foods.[26]

Although puddings were sometimes sweetened with maple syrup or molasses and enhanced with spices, butter, and even eggs, they were served during the meal and not at the end, as a dessert. Puddings started to appear at the end of the meal in the late-18th century. In Salem, Massachusetts, eating pudding at the end of the meal apparently signaled support of Jeffersonians. Federalists there continued to eat puddings at the beginning of the meal. Whether served at the beginning or the end, puddings were popular. Scholars note, "Boiled bag puddings remained a staple of New England cooking for almost three hundred years, continuing to be called for in standard cookbooks into the twentieth century."[27]

English-style boiled puddings were found throughout the English colonies. Martha Washington's *Booke of Cookery* contains several pudding recipes. This manuscript was a family heirloom created in England early in the 17th century and passed down to her. Martha Washington presented it to her granddaughter, Nelly Custis, in 1799. Amelia Simmons, author of the first American cookbook, *American Cookery,* initially published in 1796, included several pudding recipes in the cookbook. There are three Indian pudding recipes. The word *Indian* indicates the recipes use corn or Indian meal. Two of the Indian puddings are baked, but the third one is boiled.

In the 19th century, Esther Allen Howland, whose popular cookbook and household advice manual, *The American Economical Housekeeper and Family Receipt Book,* underwent several printings and included detailed instructions on making puddings. Her wording is very similar to those used by English author Hannah Glasse in her 1755 cookbook, *The Art of Cookery.*[28]

A NICE INDIAN PUDDING NO. 3

Salt a pint of meal, wet with one quart milk, sweeten and put into a strong cloth, brass or bell metal vessel, stone or earthen pot, secure from wet and boil 12 hours.

Source: Amelia Simmons, *American Cookery* (Hartford, CT: Printed for Simeon Butler, Northampton, 1798), 26.

109. OBSERVATIONS ON MAKING PUDDINGS

The outside of a boiled pudding often tastes disagreeably, which arises by the cloth not being nicely washed, and kept in a dry place. It should be dipped in boiling water, squeezed dry, and floured, when to be used. If bread, it should be tied loose; if batter, tight over. The water should boil quick when the pudding is put in; and it should be moved about for a minute, lest the ingredients should not mix. Batter puddings should be strained through a coarse sieve, when all is mixed; in others, the eggs separately. The pans and basins must be always buttered. A pan of cold water should be ready, and the pudding dipped in as soon as it comes out of the pot. And then it will not adhere to the cloth.

Source: E. A. Howland, *The American Economical Housekeeper and Family Receipt Book* (Cincinnati: H. W. Derby & Co., 1845), 109.

Mrs. Howland's cookbook contains several pudding recipes as well as sauces to serve with them. Some of the puddings were supposed to be baked, but many were boiled. There are recipes for bread puddings, both baked and boiled, various fruit and vegetable puddings, and rice puddings. Some of the recipes do not indicate how the pudding should be cooked. For one custard pudding, the recipe instructs the cook to pour the custard into a pan that is then tied into a cloth and boiled.

JAMS, PRESERVES, AND FRUIT SAUCES

Boiling is also used to preserve fruit, vegetables, and meat. Fruit can be preserved in boiled sugar syrup. Fruit preserves, as well as jelly and jam, use large amounts of sugar. Fruit preserves are whole fruits or large pieces of fruit that are boiled in a sugar syrup. For jam, the fruit is crushed before it is combined with sugar and boiled. To make jellies, the cook strains the cooked fruit, adds sugar to the juice, and boils it. When heated together, fruit and sugar gel by releasing pectin, a sugarlike substance found in plant cells. According to a food chemist, boiling the fruit and sugar together makes some of the water evaporate and brings "the pectin chains even closer together." Increasing the acidity of the mixture "neutralizes the electrical charge [of the pectin molecules] and allows the aloof pectin chains to bond to each other into a gel."[29]

Canned foods are boiled again, after being poured into sterilized jars and sealed. Many Americans were first exposed to canned foods during the Civil War. In 1858, John L. Mason patented the glass jar with the screw-on lid that sealed the jars. This invention made home canning safer and easier. Cane sugar had been expensive during the colonial period, but the price decreased in the 19th century, helping to make canning more affordable. After the Civil War, home canning became very popular, and the kitchens of many homes included large canning pots and kettles in which fruit could be boiled and jars could then be immersed in a boiling-water bath. In this way, the produce of summer and early fall could be preserved and enjoyed in the winter.

Apples, quince, and citrus fruits are particularly high in pectin, and they are sometimes added to berries or other fruit to help them gel. Pectin powder or liquids derived from apples or citrus can also be added to crushed fruit to make it gel, even without cooking. Scientists developed a special concentrated form of pectin that does not need additional sugar to create a gel. This has permitted manufacturers to produce low-calorie jams and preserves.[30]

Fruits are also boiled to make sauces. Applesauce is one common example. Cranberries can be boiled with sugar and water until the mixture gels, making it more of a jam or jelly (if all of the cranberry pieces are strained out) than a sauce.[31] Fruits can also be cooked until they form a butter, or thick paste, that is often spread on bread. Apple butter is prepared by boiling apples in cider for many hours. The Pennsylvania Germans introduced this spread to Anglo-Americans. It was also called *cider cheese*.[32]

RICE

Maize (corn) and wheat were staples in much of America, but rice became the major grain in early South Carolina, as it is in much of the world. According to one culinary historian, "[R]ice was established as a major crop in South Carolina by 1700." This was possible only because of the knowledge of its large slave population, many of whom were taken from rice-growing areas of West Africa. The English and French plantation owners had little knowledge of rice cultivation, and rice was not native to the Americas.[33]

The strain of rice grown in South Carolina became known as Carolina Gold. It is no longer grown commercially, but in the 18th and

19th centuries, it was prized. A field of Carolina Gold was a vision of glowing gold—hence its name—but when cooked, it produced an amazingly white, long-grained rice.[34]

The preferred method of cooking long-grained Carolina rice was to wash the rice, soak it, and then boil it briefly in a large amount of water. The water was then poured off, and the rice was covered and allowed to cook over a very low fire for up to an hour. It is very important not to overcook rice. The goal—then and now—is to produce rice that is just tender, or al dente, not rice that has become mushy. Each grain should remain separate. Today, rice can be prepared in electric rice cookers. Often these cookers can be programmed to turn on and off at a particular time.

There are probably more than 100,000 varieties of rice. Rice varieties include long-grain, medium-grain (like that used to make risotto), short-grain (preferred in China, Japan, and Korea), and sticky rice (used in Laos and Thailand). Some varieties of rice are aromatic. Examples of these are long-grain rice such as basmati and jasmine. Brown rice is unmilled rice that has its outer layers intact.[35]

Rice is often boiled and combined with beans in popular dishes. Rice and beans dishes are inexpensive, nutritious, and comforting. Hoppin' John is an African American dish that was also popular with white southerners. It consists of black-eyed peas and rice flavored with a boiled piece of bacon or ham. Other versions of beans and rice are popular throughout the United States, the Caribbean, and Latin America. Black beans are favored in Brazil, while red beans and rice, often served with a smoked sausage, are popular in Louisiana.

Rice, of course, can be used as a base for stir-fries and other foods. It is added to soups and made into puddings. It is almost always boiled before being added to a dish, or it is boiled with other ingredients. Fried rice, for instance, is prepared with rice that has already been boiled.

Wild rice is a North American water grass. American Indians gathered, boiled, and ate it long before Europeans came to North America. In 1672, François de Crepieul, a Jesuit missionary from France, recorded his observation of the native people he encountered in the Green Bay area on Lake Michigan and their use of wild rice. Wild rice is now grown commercially, but many Chippewa in Minnesota continue to gather true wild rice from their canoes, following the traditional way. After gathering the grass, they then beat the rice from the stems with wooden sticks. The Chippewa call wild rice *mahnomin*. A Mahnomin Festival is held every fall in Minnesota.

According to one cookbook, the traditional method used by the Chippewa to prepare wild rice was by boiling it "over slow fires in birchbark containers called *makuks*." The wild rice could them be mixed with various ingredients, such as "venison, fish, bear meat, wildfowl, berries, maple sugar, and animal fat for seasoning." Wild rice was also "ground into a kind of meal and used for baking bread. And, like corn, it could be popped."[36]

VEGETABLES

When green vegetables are boiled for only a few minutes, they become a bright green. In their uncooked state, the chloroplasts that make vegetables green are obscured by microscopic air pockets. When the vegetables are cooked, the gas that is ordinarily trapped in the cells of the plant expands and escapes. Additional cooking, however, produces chemical changes that dull the color as well as soften the vegetables. To maintain the color, vegetables should be cooked for only a brief time. In addition, acidic coatings, such as lemon juice, should be added only at the last minute, since acids also damage the chloroplasts.[37]

Vegetables of all kinds were added to soups and boiled meats to provide additional nutrients and flavor, as well as to increase the number of portions. Overland travelers gathered mustard greens (a significant source of vitamin C), wild onions, garlic, and prairie peas to supplement their provisions and to make their meals tastier. American Indians also gathered greens to add to their dishes.[38]

In their domestic manual *The American Woman's Home*, the 19th-century reformers Catharine Beecher and Harriet Beecher Stowe, wrote, "As regards the department of *Vegetables*, their number and variety in America are so great that a table might almost be furnished by these alone." The passage continued, noting that vegetables are easy to cook and little more had to be said about them. Of potatoes, however, the sisters declared, "The soggy, waxy, indigestible viand that often appears in the potato-dish is a down right sacrifice of the better nature of this vegetable." To produce "snowy balls of powdery whiteness," they explained, the potatoes must first be peeled, then "boiled as quickly as possible in salted water," drained as soon as they are done, then "gently shaken for a moment or two over the fire to dry them still more."[39]

There are many varieties of potatoes. New potatoes have thin skins that do not require peeling. They can be boiled and served or mashed, made into salads, and added to other foods. Sweet potatoes can also be boiled and mashed.

Although technically tomatoes are fruits, they are usually treated as vegetables. According to one authority, "[I]n the United States tomatoes are second only to potatoes in annual vegetable consumption." The first tomato recipe known to have been written by an American is that of South Carolinian Harriott Horry, daughter of Eliza Lucas and Charles Pinckney. The recipe To Keep Tomatoes for Winter Use is dated 1770. Horry advised cooks to peel the tomatoes and cut them in quarters, and then to cover them with salt and pepper, and let them sit for an hour. After that, the tomatoes should be cooked until "the liquor is boild away." Then they should be put into pots and cooled. When they are cooled, Horry said, a layer of melted butter should be poured on top of them. Presumably this was to seal the pots. She further noted, "Each pott will make two soups."[40] Tomatoes can be prepared many different ways, as well as eaten raw, but they are often boiled to make sauces and added to soups and stews.

EGGS

Because this chapter began with Henry James's remarks on boiled eggs, it seems fitting to close with eggs, as well. Eggs contain many important amino acids and other valuable nutrients. When cooked, an egg is an extremely nutritious food. Even its high cholesterol count in not a problem for most people because most of an egg yolk's fat is unsaturated, and recent studies indicate human blood cholesterol is affected more by saturated fat than by the actual intake of cholesterol. Egg yolks also contain phospholipids, fatty substances that help to prevent absorption of cholesterol in the yolk.[41]

Eggs can be prepared in many ways, among them, scrambled, fried, baked, poached, and boiled. They are made into omelets and custards. Poached eggs are the basis of elegant dishes, such as Eggs Benedict. Boiling eggs is one of the easiest methods for preparing eggs, because the egg is contained within its own shell. On the Overland Trail, at least one enterprising woman used the water taken from hot springs to boil an egg. Mary Bailey put the egg in "fresh water & in a tin bucket in the hot water," making a type of double boiler. Within a few minutes, her egg was cooked.[42]

In the mid-19th century, Eliza Leslie provided detailed instructions for boiling eggs in her popular cookbook.

TO BOIL EGGS FOR BREAKFAST

The fresher they are the longer time they will require for boiling. If you wish them quite soft, put them into a saucepan of water that is boiling hard at the moment, and let them remain in it five minutes. The longer they boil the harder they will be. In ten minutes' fast boiling they will be hard enough for salad.

If you use one of the tin egg-boilers that are placed on the table, see that the water is boiling hard at the time you put in the eggs. When they have been in about four or five minutes, take them out, pour off the water, and replace it by some more that is boiling hard; as, from the coldness of the eggs having chilled the first water, they will not otherwise be done enough. The boiler may then be placed on the table (keeping the lid closed,) and in a few minutes more they will be sufficiently cooked to be wholesome.—

Source: Miss [Eliza] Leslie, *Directions for Cookery In Its Various Branches* (Philadelphia: E.L. Carey & Hart, 1849), 207.

NOTES

1. Quoted in Beverly Cox and Martin Jacobs, *Spirit of the Harvest: North American Indian Cooking* (New York: Stewart, Tabori, & Chang, 1991), 206.

2. Linda Murray Berzok, *American Indian Food* (Santa Barbara, CA: Greenwood, 2005), 111.

3. Ken Hedges, *Fibers and Forms: Native American Basketry of the West* (San Diego: San Diego Museum of Man, 1997), 17.

4. Berzok, *American Indian Food,* 111–13.

5. Thomas Robinson Hazard, *The Jonny-Cake Papers of "Shepherd Tom,"* introduction by Rowland Gibson Hazard (Boston: Merrymount Press, 1915), 51, quoted in Keith Stavely and Kathleen Fitzgerald, *America's Founding Food: The Story of New England Cooking* (Chapel Hill: University of North Carolina Press, 2004), 41.

6. Sandra L. Oliver, *Food in Colonial and Federal America* (Santa Barbara, CA: Greenwood, 2005), 101, 107.

7. Jacqueline Williams, *Wagon Wheel Kitchens: Food on the Oregon Trail* (Lawrence: University Press of Kansas, 1993), 89–92.

8. Lillian Schlissel, *Women's Diaries of the Westward Journey* (New York: Schocken Books, 1982), 80.

9. Laurel Thatcher Ulrich, *A Midwife's Tale: The Life of Martha Ballard, Based on Her Diary, 1785–1812* (New York: Knopf, 1990), 275–77.

10. N.K.M. Lee, *The Cook's Own Book* (Boston: Munroe & Francis, 1832), xvi.

11. Lee, *The Cook's Own Book*, xiv.

12. Field Horne, ed., *The Diary of Mary Cooper: Life on a Long Island Farm, 1768–1773* (Oyster Bay, NY: Oyster Bay Historical Society, 1981), 24.

13. Lee, *The Cook's Own Book*, xvi.

14. James Deetz, *In Small Things Forgotten: The Archaeology of Early American Life* (New York: Doubleday, Anchor Books ed., 1977), 124–25.

15. Herbert C. Covey and Dwight Eisnach, *What the Slaves Ate: Recollections of African American Foods and Foodways from the Slave Narratives* (Santa Barbara, CA: ABC-CLIO, 2009), 62.

16. Sandra L. Oliver, *Saltwater Foodways: New Englanders and Their Food, at Sea and Ashore, in the Nineteenth Century* (Mystic, CT: Mystic Seaport Museum, 1995), 293–94; Stavely and Fitzgerald, *America's Founding Food*, 182–85; Cox and Jacobs, *Spirit of the Harvest*, 58.

17. Stavely and Fitzgerald, *America's Founding Food*, 95–96; Oliver, *Saltwater Foodways*, 293–94.

18. Oliver, *Saltwater Foodways*, 294–96.

19. Oliver, *Saltwater Foodways*, 294–95.

20. Fannie Merritt Farmer, *The Boston Cooking-School Cook Book* (Boston: Little, Brown, & Co., 1896), 127–29.

21. Karen Hess, *The Carolina Rice Kitchen: The African Connection* (Columbia: University of South Carolina Press, 1992), 111–12.

22. Marcie Cohen Ferris, *Matzoh Ball Gumbo: Culinary Tales of the Jewish South* (Chapel Hill: University of North Carolina Press, 2005), 88.

23. Ferris, *Matzoh Ball Gumbo*, 133–35.

24. William Woys Weaver, *A Quaker Woman's Cookbook: The Domestic Cookery of Elizabeth Ellicott Lea,* rev. ed. (Mechanicsburg, PA: Stackpole Books, 2004), 312–13. Present-day apple dumplings are usually baked, although sometimes a boiled sugar sauce is prepared and spooned over them. Cathi Mazaika, personal communication, November 2, 2010.

25. Mary Rockwood Powers, *A Woman's Overland Journal to California* (Fairfield, WA: Ye Galleon Press, 1985), 53, quoted in Williams, *Wagon Wheel Kitchens,* 132.

26. Stavely and Fitzgerald, *America's Founding Food*, 13–14.

27. Stavely and Fitzgerald, *America's Founding Food*, 14.

28. Karen Hess, ed., *Martha Washington's Booke of Cookery* (New York: Columbia University Press, 1981), 103.

29. Harold McGee, *On Food and Cooking: The Science and Lore of the Kitchen,* rev. ed. (New York: Scribner, 2004), 296–97.

30. McGee, *On Food and Cooking,* 298.

31. One of the highlights of my family's Thanksgiving celebrations is the cranberry sauce. Every year it is prepared and poured into a squirrel-shaped mold. We wait anxiously to see if it will unmold into a squirrel shape to grace

the Thanksgiving table, or if it will be a shapeless, but still delicious, sauce served in a bowl.

32. Weaver, *A Quaker Woman's Cookbook*, 311–12.

33. Hess, *The Carolina Rice Kitchen*, 10–15.

34. Hess, *The Carolina Rice Kitchen*, 17–21.

35. McGee, *On Food and Cooking*, 472–73.

36. Clara Sue Kidwell, "The Northeastern Coast and Woodlands," in Cox and Jacobs, *Spirit of the Harvest*, 55–56.

37. McGee, *On Food and Cooking*, 279–80.

38. Williams, *Wagon Wheel Kitchens*, 126–31.

39. Catharine E. Beecher and Harriet Beecher Stowe, *The American Woman's Home: or Principles of Domestic Science* (New York: J.B. Ford & Co; Boston: H.A. Brown & Co, 1869), 185–86.

40. Andrew F. Smith, "Tomatoes," in *The Oxford Companion to American Food and Drink*, ed. Andrew F. Smith (New York: Oxford University Press, 2007), 591; Andrew F. Smith, *The Tomato in America: Early History, Culture, and Cookery* (Champaign: University of Illinois Press, 2001), 181.

41. McGee, *On Food and Cooking*, 78–79.

42. Sandra L. Myres, ed., *Ho for California! Women's Overland Diaries from the Huntington Library* (San Marino, CA: Huntington Library, 1980), 77, quoted in Williams, *Wagon Wheel Kitchens*, 98. Physical chemist and chef Hervé This spends 15 pages discussing and explaining the science behind cooking a "good" hard-boiled egg in his book, *Building a Meal: From Molecular Gastronomy to Culinary Constructivism* (New York: Columbia University Press, 209), 13–28.

CHAPTER 4
Braising

Braising even may have played a critical role in the development of homo sapiens, and I would argue that it belongs in the pantheon of greatest human achievements, up there with the invention of the wheel and the secret formula for WD40.

—Howard Yoon, "In Praise of Braise,"
Kitchen Window, NPR, January 31, 2007

Braising is a cooking method in which the main ingredient is first browned in oil or fat and then slowly simmered in a small amount of liquid. Although the technique is often associated with meat and poultry dishes, such as pot roast, osso buco, and coq au vin, the technique can also be used to prepare firm fish, vegetables and fruit, and tofu and tempeh. Water, broth, wine, and beer are typically used in Western braised dishes, but soy sauce, tea, yogurt, and coconut milk are commonly found in Asian braised dishes. The cooking technique of braising overlaps with stewing. Some stews are braised, that is, the meat or poultry is first browned and then slowly simmered, but not all braises are stews. Stews usually contain small pieces of meat and/or vegetables in a broth. In contrast, the main ingredient of a braise might be large and should be cooked in a minimal amount of liquid.[1]

The technique of braising is ancient, but the term, from the French word *braiser*, is not commonly found in early American cookbooks. One of the first uses of the term in English printed sources was in Elizabeth Raffald's highly popular book, *The Experienced English Housekeeper*, first published in London in 1769, in which she tells her

Coq au vin, or chicken braised in red wine, is a French
dish that became very popular in the United States in
the 1960s after Julia Child prepared it on her television
show *The French Chef*. Pictured here is a simplified and
kosher version of the dish. (AP Photo/Larry Crowe)

readers to "use some of the braize liquor" to complete "A Neck of
Veal à-la-royal."[2] Braising pans had deep covers that could hold coals,
so that the cooking was done from the top as well as from underneath. Now braising is usually done in a Dutch oven or large casse-
role dish. Braised dishes can be prepared on a stovetop or in the oven.
Braising can also be done in a slow cooker. In that case, the main ingredient would be browned first, and then placed in the slow cooker
with the other ingredients.

The braising liquid should not be allowed to come to a boil, since
that will make the meat tough. Instead, it should be kept at a simmer
(not above 185°F), or if the dish is in the oven, the oven temperature
should not be above 350°F. A braised dish should cook slowly, and
there should be just enough liquid to barely cover the ingredients.

BRAISE, WHAT'S THAT?

Braised dishes can be gourmet delicacies, homey comfort food, or something in between. Throughout American history, many home cooks have prepared braised dishes—essentially one-pot meals—without using the word *braise*.

Chef and author Rick Moonen for example, commented on the meals his mother prepared during his childhood:

> There were seven of us kids growing up in my grandmother's house in New York City's Flushing, Queens, and my mother would get home from work every day and put "that pot" on the stove. We called it "that pot" because we took turns doing the dishes and no one wanted to get stuck having to wash it. It was a big, heavy cast-iron thing, and there was always something delicious inside that would feed all of us: pot roast, fish simmered over vegetables, or my favorite, osso buco. It was years later that I learned the technical term for what Mom was doing by simmering those ingredients in a little liquid was braising—and it's since become one of my favorite techniques. But back then I just knew that something special was going on in that pot, something that produced meats so tender and moist, they flaked off the bone.[3]

Like Moonen's mother, thousands of Americans over the centuries have prepared pot roast. Although the technology and cookware have changed over the centuries, the basic technique is the same. The pot roast recipe that Mrs. L. Rawlings contributed to the 1907 cookbook compiled by the Building Fund Association of the First Baptist Church of Albany, Georgia, is typical of a plain pot roast that could

---

POT ROAST

Five lb. beef roast, 1 qt. boiling water, 1 pod red pepper, 1 tb. salt. Place meat in kettle over a good fire, brown on one side, turn and brown on the other. Now, add the boiling water, salt and pepper; cover and cook slowly 15 min. to every lb. After the water evaporates add no more, as there should be fat enough to finish cooking the meat. Serve with brown sauce.

——

Source: Mrs. L. Rawlings, *The Baptist Cook Book,* compiled by a Committee from the Building Fund Association of the First Baptist Church of Albany, GA, May, 1907 (Columbus, GA: Gilbert Printing, 1907), 21.

be made today. Many cooks would add additional vegetables, such as carrots and potatoes, and perhaps use wine and additional seasonings, such as garlic, parsley, and pepper, but the recipe can be prepared by following the directions as they appeared in this church fund-raiser cookbook using a modern stovetop or stove and oven.

Mrs. Rawlings did not use the word *braise* in this recipe. She may or may not have known that she was braising the beef roast. Yet Angelina Maria Collins wrote of this new technique more than 60 years earlier. Collins, the author of the first cookbook published in Indiana, *Mrs. Collins' Table Receipts: Adapted to Western Housewifery* (1851), opined, "Braising is a mode of cooking decidedly French, as the article, or pan, used for the purpose, was invented and first used by them." Collins continued, "A braised chicken, or turkey, is thought to be delicious by many, and is unrivaled when it makes its appearance at a city hotel. We shall, no doubt, soon, in the West, adopt this process of preparing roasts." She then provided a recipe for braised turkey and braised chicken "from a work just published."[4]

Mary Newton Foote Henderson, well educated, fluent in French, and considered an exceptional hostess in both Saint Louis (her husband, John Henderson, had been a senator from Missouri) and Washington, DC, was well aware of both the term and the technique. She wrote a guide to cooking and entertaining in 1877, *Practical Guide and Dinner Giving*. In her description of braising, she wrote, "A braising-kettle has a deep cover, which hold coals; consequently,

---

VEAL CUTLETS, BRAISED

Professional cooks usually braise veal cutlets. They lard them (an easy matter) all on the same side, the flavor of pork well suiting veal. To proceed then: Mince some onions and carrots; put them in the bottom of a stew-pan; put the cutlets on this layer; cover well with stock (add wine if you choose), and let them cook until thoroughly done.

If you wish to be particular, boil down the stock and glaze them; or make a gravy of the stock with flour, roux, pepper and salt, and strain it; or serve them with tomato-sauce; or make a little round hill of mashed potatoes, and put the cutlets around; or serve with them, instead, beans, pease, or flowerets of cauliflowers.

———

Source: Mary Newton Foote Henderson, *Practical Cooking and Dinner Giving* (New York: Harper & Brothers, 1877), 148.

the cooking is done from above as well as below. It is almost air-tight, thus preventing evaporation, and the article to be cooked imbibes whatever flavor one may wish to give it." Nevertheless, she did not consider a braising pan a necessity.[5]

Nearly every recipe in Henderson's book includes tips on how the dish should be presented at the table. Her recipe for Veal Cutlets, Braised is a typical example.

VENISON

Venison is the term usually used for the flesh of a deer, although sometimes it refers to other game. To prepare it, cooks often larded it—covered it with fat—or braised it. In England, only the gentry normally ate venison because they were the only ones permitted to hunt deer in private game parks. In colonial America, however, deer could be hunted by anyone. Venison was served at the wedding feast of Plymouth Colony's Governor Bradford in 1623. Although colonists were undoubtedly grateful for the bounty of their new homeland, they did not mention venison very often in written accounts. Some scholars speculate that this is because venison, like maize, became associated with Native Americans. By the end of the 17th century, however, overhunting of deer led New England authorities to restrict deer hunting to one season of the year. After deer was not so easily obtained in New England, it once again became the food of elite gatherings.[6]

In a memoir of her life growing up in 19th-century Salem, Massachusetts, Caroline Howard King described a typical menu for one of her parents' dinner parties:

> the piece de resistance, a haunch of venison cooked in claret wine, or partly cooked only, for each guest had a plated silver chafing dish standing before him, on which he was expected to cook his slice or slices according to his own taste. These chafing dishes were really a handsome decoration to the table. They were round, about the size of a large dinner plate, with pretty open work rims and with lion's head handles. They were warmed by iron heaters which fitted into the inside.[7]

The popular English cookbook *A New System of Domestic Cookery, Formed Upon Principles of Economy, and Adapted to the Use of Private Families* was written by Maria Eliza Rundell and contained several recipes for venison. The 1807 edition was the first American edition, but it did not attempt to revise the book for American readers. Nevertheless, the book was popular on both sides of the Atlantic, and it went through several editions. Rundell advised readers to roast a haunch of venison, but noted that stewing was better for the shoulder, "unless it is very fat, and then it should be roasted." Rundell rolled the shoulder in mutton fat that had been marinated in port wine and seasoned with pepper and allspice. Then the meat was simmered in a mixture of port wine, beef or mutton gravy, pepper, and allspice. Rundell stated, "Simmer close-covered, and as slow as you can, for three or four hours."[8]

Deer lived in the American Southwest as well as the rest of the continent. Hopi and other Pueblo men hunted deer until the deer and other game animals became scarce because white settlers raised livestock, which reduced the size and number of wooded areas. As one author has noted, however, deer and other animals such as antelope and mountain sheep "remain alive in the winter animal dances of many Pueblo tribes." A modern-day adaptation of a Hopi venison stew features lightly floured cubes of venison browned in vegetable oil. Chopped onions, celery, and chilies are then sautéed and added to the stew pot, along with water and oregano. Then, after the stew simmers for about 1-1/2 hours, cubed carrots, potatoes, and rutabaga and are added and cooked until tender.[9]

SHIKA SHIRO (POT-ROASTED VENISON)

Three pounds of venison steak; one cupful of syou sauce; one cupful of vinegar; two tablespoonfuls of sugar; one quarter of fresh pork (fat); one quarter pound of miso paste; one onion.

Place the meat in an earthenware bowl and cover with one cup of vinegar, two tablespoons of sugar and the same amount of salt, one tablespoonful of mixed spices, and one onion, sliced. Cover, and put away to pickle for two or three days in a cool place. When ready to cook, remove meat from the juices, cut up the pork in small strips, and fry a light brown in deep iron pan. Add the venison meat, and fry well on both sides until brown, taking care not to burn it. Add the syou sauce, cover tight, and let simmer for one hours, or two, if necessary. Mix the miso paste with a little cold water, and stir it until it thickens. Remove the platter, and garnish with slices of lemon sprinkled with chopped parsley.

Source: Sara Bosse and Onoto Watanna [pseudo.], *Chinese-Japanese Cook Book* (Chicago: Rand McNally, 1914), 80.

The remarkable 1914 *Chinese-Japanese Cook Book* by Sara Bosse and Onoto Watanna (pseudonym of Winnifred Eaton) features a more unusual version of braised venison. Winnifred Eaton, the daughter of an English man and a Chinese woman, took the Japanese pen name Onoto Watanna and assumed a Japanese persona during a period when American sentiments were intensely anti-Chinese, but Japanese culture and styles were popular. She became a successful fiction writer, and her novels, short stories, and screenplays were very popular. Most likely, she did most of the writing for the cookbook; her sister, Sara Eaton Bosse, was an artist, but her name lent credibility to the claim that the cookbook was Japanese and Chinese, since presumably Onoto Watanna would know only Japanese cooking. This was the sisters' only cookbook.[10]

FOWL FARE

Both American Indians and European colonists consumed much of the wildfowl that filled the forests, fields, and marshes of early America. Pigeons were particularly plentiful and popular. Try to imagine a scene from Alfred Hitchcock's *The Birds* (1963), but substitute people dressed in Puritan garb for Rod Taylor, Tippi Hedren, and the rest of the cast. Then you will get an idea of how many passenger pigeons existed in previous centuries. In the 1630s, William Wood, who lived in the Massachusetts Bay Colony, wrote one can see "neyther beginning nor ending, length, or breadth" of passenger pigeon flocks during the spring and fall. In autumn 1813, the artist and naturalist John James Audubon recalled, "[T]he air was literally filled with Pigeons; the light of noon-day was obscured as by an eclipse." Audubon observed people filling the woods of Kentucky to shoot the birds, killing tens of thousands in a few hours. Eventually passenger pigeons became extinct. In 1914, Martha, the last passenger pigeon, died in the Cincinnati Zoo.[11]

Pigeon recipes appear in many 18th- and 19th-century cookbooks. Hannah Glasse, author of *The Art of Cookery Made Plain and Easy*, first published in London in 1747, included several recipes for pigeon. Glasse's cookbook went through many editions and was published in the United States in the 19th century.

One recipe in the 1796 edition of the book is called To fricassee Pigeons the Italian Way. As one culinary historian writes, " 'The Italian way' did not mean literally 'as the Italians do it' but rather as the English imagined they did it. . . . By osmosis through English books and English cooks, such impressions were planted in distant American minds." In this recipe, the pigeons are quartered and fried in oil. Peas are then added to the oil and fried. Then boiling water and seasonings, including salt, pepper, onions, garlic, parsley, and vinegar, are added. The mixture is then thickened with egg yolks.[12]

Americans today are more likely to eat chicken than pigeon. As discussed in other chapters in this book, chicken can be roasted, boiled, fried, or stewed, but it can also be braised. One unusual braised chicken dish from the 1920s is Braised Chicken with Coconut Milk and Spinach. In the 1920s, exotic fare often featured pineapple, coconut, or banana. Many of these dishes consisted of quite ordinary ingredients such as baked ham, but were then topped with pineapple to make it exotic. Yet in November 1928, *Ladies' Home Journal* published a menu for a luncheon that included authentic Hawaiian dishes. The magazine did assure its readers, however, that the Hawaiian food was "delicate and quickly digested." This braised chicken dish is prepared by cutting a chicken into serving pieces, dredging the pieces in flour, and sautéing them in peanut oil or lard until browned. Water is then added to the pan, and the chicken simmered in it for about 20 minutes. The chicken is then removed, coconut milk is added to pot, simmered, and then one pound of spinach leaves are added. When the sauce thickens, the chicken is returned to the pot and simmered until done.[13]

Coq au vin, or chicken braised in red wine, is a French dish that started to become popular in the United States in the 1950s, and then became more popular when Julia Child prepared it on her television show *The French Chef* in the 1960s and on her subsequent shows. Although a sort of French comfort food, which originally was meant to cook an old rooster until tender, it is an elaborate dish that involves blanching salt pork or bacon (to remove extra salt and smoky flavor). The finished dish is garnished with small braised onions and mushrooms.

Some home cooks wanted to prepare gourmet food that did not involve as many steps as dishes such as coq au vin required. Simplified gourmet recipes using canned soups became popular in the 1960s. One such recipe was called Golden Gourmet Chicken. After browning chicken thighs in butter, they were braised in Campbell's condensed Golden Mushroom soup and white wine. When cooked through, the chicken was removed from the pan, and sour cream was added to the pan juices. Then the mixture was poured over the chicken and served.[14]

OTHER BRAISED DISHES

Braising is good way to prepare vegetables. Vegetables such as asparagus, carrots, and green beans can be "quick braised" by browning them in a pan and then simmering them in broth, wine, juice, or cider. Potatoes, sweet potatoes, other root vegetables, and apples are particularly good braised. They can be cut into quarters, sautéed in oil or butter, and the covered with vegetable broth and simmered until tender.[15]

A Vietnamese technique of braising involves caramelizing sugar instead of browning the meat. It is also a good technique for braising winter squash, sweet potatoes, or potatoes. Cook sugar with tablespoon or two of water over medium heat until the sugar liquefies. (This will take about ten minutes.) Then continue cooking until the sugar gets darker. Mix in vinegar and water, being careful not to get burned from steam, then continue to cook until the mixture turns to liquid again. At this point, chopped onion and garlic can be added and cooked until they soften. Then the chopped squash or potatoes should be added. Sprinkle with salt and pepper. Cover and cook on low for a few minutes, then uncover, stir, and cook until the squash is tender and the sauce has thickened. Fresh chilies or hot red pepper flakes can be added to produce a hot and sweet flavor.[16]

Many Indian dishes involve braising meat, poultry, fish, and/or vegetables. Spices, a blend that might include turmeric, cumin, chili powder, coriander, pepper, and cinnamon, are mixed and cooked in ghee (clarified butter). Vegetables, meat, and/or fish are browned in the seasoned ghee. After that, a liquid is added, and the mixture is simmered and usually served with rice.

Korma is an Indian dish that can be meat based or vegetarian. The meat or vegetables are braised with water or broth and yogurt or cream, and seasoned with many of the spices mentioned above. Sometimes coconut milk is used, and vegetable korma might include paneer, a soft Indian cheese. Korma originated in the 16th-century Mughal incursions into northern Indian and present-day Pakistan.

Nineteenth-century American cookbooks often included recipes for curried dishes. The following recipe for a chicken curry involves braising the chicken in butter and then simmering it in a spiced sauce. It is from an unusual cookbook based on temperance principles, and written by Ann Allen, about whom little is known. In her preface, the author writes that as she was "deprived by death of the fostering hand of a kind mother . . . she wishes to be the Orphan's Friend." *The*

ANOTHER [RECIPE FOR CURRY]

2 fat young fowls,
4 large onions,
1 table spoon of curry-powder,
1/2 lb. of butter

Carve the fowls as if for the table, dust them with flour, fry them in butter till they are well browned, lay them in a stew-pan with the onions cut in slips, cover with boiling water; cover the pan and set on to coals. In half an hour take out a cup of the gravy, mix it well with a table spoon of curry-power, and throw it again into the stew-pan, stir it well round, taste and see if your gravy is warm, if not add Cayenne. Bubble the whole until the fowls are tender, serve in a deep dish, with boiled rice.

Curry Powder

3 oz. of coriander seed, 5 oz. of turmeric, 1 oz. of black pepper, 1 oz., of mustard-seed, 1 oz., of ginger, 1/2 oz. Cayenne pepper, 1/2 oz. of lesser cardamom, 1/4 oz. of cinnamon, 1/4 oz., of cumin seed

Dry all well by the fire, then reduce them separately to a powder, pass them through a fine sieve, and mix them well. It should be bottled, and well corked, and kept in a dry place, and labeled. Order saves much time.

———

Source: Ann Allen, *The Housekeeper's Assistant, Composed Upon Temperance Principles* . . . (Boston: James Munroe and Company, 1845), 80–81.

Housekeeper's Assistant, published in 1845, provides many useful hints for cooking and housekeeping.[17]

NOTES

1. For a detailed book on braising that covers all the basics, see Molly Stevens, *All about Braising: The Art of Uncomplicated Cooking* (New York: Norton, 2004). This is not a book for vegetarians, since even the vegetable recipes contain chicken broth or meat. On not browning first, see John Willoughby, "Deep Flavor, No Browning Required," *New York Times,* March 28, 2011, http://www.nytimes.com/2011/03/30/dining/30braise.html.

2. Elizabeth Raffald, *The Experienced English Housekeeper, for the Use and Ease of Ladies, Housekeepers, Cooks, & co.,* 10th ed. (London: R. Baldwin, 1786), 93.

3. Rick Moonen, "Braising," *Saveur,* January 14, 2011, http://www.saveur.com/article/kitchen/saveur-100–2011-Braising.

4. The book title was changed to *The Great Western Cook Book, or Table Receipts, adapted to Western Housewifery* by Mrs. A.M. Collins (New York: A.S. Barnes & Co., 1857), 89.

5. Mary Newton Foote Henderson, *Practical Cooking and Dinner Giving* (New York: Harper & Brothers, 1877), 47.

6. Sandra L. Oliver, *Food in Colonial and Federal America* (Santa Barbara, CA: Greenwood, 2005), 47–48; Keith Stavely and Kathleen Fitzgerald, *America's Founding Food: The Story of New England Cooking* (Chapel Hill: University of North Carolina Press, 2004), 170, 171.

7. Caroline Howard King, *When I Lived in Salem, 1822–1866*, with a preface by Louisa L. Dressel (Brattleboro, VT: Stephen Daye Press, 1937), 25.

8. A Lady [Maria Eliza Rundell], *A New System of Domestic Cookery, Formed Upon Principles of Economy, and Adapted to the Use of Private Families* (Boston: W. Andrews, 1807), 30.

9. Beverly Cox and Martin Jacobs, *Spirit of the Harvest: North American Indian Cooking* (New York: Stewart, Tabori, & Chang, 1991), 178.

10. Biography of Sara Bosse and Onoto Watanna, pseudonym of Winnifred Eaton, Feeding America: The Historic America Cookbook Project, http://digital.lib.msu.edu/projects/cookbooks/html/authors/author_bosse.html; Diana Birchall, *Onoto Watanna: The Story of Winnifred Eaton* (Chicago: University of Illinois Press, 2001).

11. William Wood, *New England's Prospect* (London, 1634; Boston[?]: Reprinted for E.M. Boynton, 1898[?]), 30, quoted in Stavely and Fitzgerald, *New England Cooking*, 154; Audubon quoted in John P. O'Grady, "Clouding," in David Rothenberg and Wandee J. Pryor, eds., *Writing on Air* (Cambridge, MA: MIT Press, 2003), 101.

12. William Woys Weaver, *Thirty-Five Recipes from "The Larder Invaded"* (Philadelphia: The Library Company of Philadelphia and The Historical Society of Pennsylvania, 1986), Recipe 6, 23–24. Weaver includes a modern interpretation and directions for the dish.

13. Sylvia Lovegren, *Fashionable Food: Seven Decades of Food Fads* (Chicago: University of Chicago Press, 2005), 271–74.

14. Lovegren, *Fashionable Food*, 248–49.

15. Mark Bittman offers "Braised Potatoes, Ten Ways" in his cookbook *How to Cook Everything Vegetarian: Simple Meatless Recipes for Great Food* (New York: John Wiley & Sons, 2007), 346–47.

16. Adaptation of "Braised Winter Squash in Caramel Sauce," in Bittman, *Everything Vegetarian*, 368.

17. An Old Housekeeper [Ann Allen], *The Housekeeper's Assistant, Composed Upon Temperance Principles, With Instructions in the Art of Making Plain and Fancy Cakes, Puddings, Pastry, Confectionery, Ice Creams, Jellies, Blanc Mange, Also for Cooking of all the Various Kinds of Meats and Vegetables; With Variety of Useful Information And Receipts Never Before Published* (Boston: James Munroe & Co., 1845), 1.

CHAPTER 5
Broiling and Grilling

> Grilling, broiling, barbecuing—whatever you want to call it—is an art, not just a matter of building a pyre and throwing on a piece of meat as a sacrifice to the gods of the stomach.
> —James Beard, *Beard on Food* (1974)

Grilling is an ancient technique of cooking food that has become increasingly popular in the United States. Outdoor grills come in a range of sizes and models and can be found in a variety of locations all over the country. People grill food on their apartment balconies, in sports arena parking lots, at backyard get-togethers, at picnic sites, and even at the White House. Television chefs and websites provide grilling tips to thousands of viewers. Even popular cartoon character Homer Simpson has extolled the joys of outdoor grilling.[1]

Many people use the term *barbecuing* when they actually mean grilling, but barbecuing is a different cooking method. As discussed in chapter 2, barbecuing is a slow method of cooking in which the food cooks for several hours at a low temperature away from the heat source. Grilling and broiling, however, rely on high temperatures to cook food quickly. The words *grilling* and *broiling* are also often used interchangeably, although they are considered technically different techniques in the United States, where grilling refers to placing food *over* a dry heat source (for instance over charcoal), and broiling means to place the food *under* a dry heat source, such as an oven broiler. Nonetheless, old cookbooks generally use either term without distinction, and in many recipes food can be either broiled or grilled with

Grilled steak and a grilled spring vegetable
salad. (AP Photo/Matthew Mead)

similar results. In addition, whereas the slow cooking and smoking
technique of barbecuing is used mainly to prepare large and tough
cuts of meat, grilling and broiling can be used to cook smaller and
more tender pieces of meat, chicken, and fish, as well as vegetables,
fruit, and tofu.

HISTORY

People have grilled food since prehistoric times; in fact, most likely
grilling has been a method of food preparation ever since humans
first began to cook meat and fish. In North America, European explorers observed the people of many different tribes grilling the food
they caught. The eastern woodland Indians, for example, ate many
types of fish. They grilled fish directly on the coals, on flat stones over
the coals, and on wooden racks placed over a frame. The well-known
17th-century engraving by Theodor de Bry, *How They Cook Their Fish*,

illustrates the last method of grilling fish. This grilling was done soon after catching the fish. They did not smoke the fish for later use, as some tribes did.[2]

Tribes throughout the northeast region of what became the United States traveled to follow game animals and fish. In the spring, they often moved closer to the coast, where they could follow the fish runs in nearby rivers and bays. Shad runs occurred in April, and in May, bluefish swam along the coastline, where they found other fish to eat. Indians caught a great number of fish during these seasonal migrations. American Indians sometimes ate fish right after they caught it, but they also dried or smoked it for later use. Northeastern Indians often combined the game and fish they caught with plants and berries they had gathered. Although there are few actual 17th-, 18th-, and 19th-century American Indian recipes in existence, there are modern adaptations of food and techniques that have been passed down through generations. For example, one cookbook on North American Indian cooking features a modern version of a northeastern Indian recipe that is made by dipping bluefish fillets in maple sugar (also produced by northeastern Indians), then sprinkling the fillets with dried spicebush berries or allspice before grilling or broiling them.[3]

American Indians grilled their food over open fires. Indians of the Great Plains, for example, often grilled trout and small game animals by placing them on spits or forks made of green wood held over a fire. Green onions and ground spicebush berries were favorite seasonings. A traditional method of cooking buffalo used by the Plains Indians, however, was to place the meat directly on red-hot coals. In the West, Native Americans grilled Canada goose over a wood fire by using a branch made of green alder wood or applewood as a spit.[4]

In contrast, in the 18th and early-19th centuries, New England housewives used gridirons when they wanted to grill in their kitchen fireplaces. A gridiron was generally made of wrought iron parallel bars attached at each end to another bar, forming a square or rectangle. There were legs attached to it, so that the frame could be placed over a bed of coals, and a long handle enabled the cook to move the gridiron around the hearth. In the early-19th century, some versions of the gridiron featured shorter legs in the front so that the gridiron sat at a tilt, and it included grooves in the bars and a trough for collecting the melted fat and juices of the cooking meat. These juices could then be used to make a gravy or sauce.[5]

Grilling was a popular method of cooking fish in early America. In New England, most white households consumed fish once a week,

TO BROIL SHAD, MACKEREL, AND SALMON

Have the bars of the gridiron well greased with lard; lay your fish on, flesh side down; when half done, turn it and finish, skin down; when done, pour over sweet cream, if you have it, or spread over a little butter.

Source: E. A. Howland, *The American Economical Housekeeper, and Family Receipt Book* (Cincinnati, OH: H. W. Derby, 1845), 62.

more often for those who lived along the coast. As with the Indians, those who lived close to rivers where fish, such as shad and salmon, spawned enjoyed fresh fish during the spawning season but consumed dried fish during much of the year. In the cookbook *The American Economical Housekeeper,* published in 1845, Esther Allen Howland provided the above recipe for grilling fish.

Howland also gave her readers advice on broiling meat, much of which is still useful today. She noted, for example, the necessity of keeping the gridiron clean. She also cautioned that the meat should not be more than three-quarters of an inch thick or it "will be done too much on the outside before the inside is done through." She further advised cooks to "[t]ake care to prepare your fire in time, so that it may burn quite clear; a brisk, clear fire is indispensable, or you cannot give your meat that browning which constitutes the perfection of this mode of cookery, and gives a relish to food it cannot receive in any other way." Finally, she warned her readers to watch the meat carefully and to bring the food "to table as hot as possible" in a warmed dish.[6]

TO BROIL BEEF-STEAK

Cut slices of beef as thick as your hand, put each on the gridiron, and set it over a bed of live coals free from any smoke, and broil ten minutes; when done, take it up on a platter or deep plate, and put pieces of butter over the meat; it should be broiled the last thing before the family sit down, and brought to the table hot; pour a very little hot water over the meat.

Source: E. A. Howland, *The American Economical Housekeeper, and Family Receipt Book* (Cincinnati, OH: H. W. Derby, 1845), 57.

Howland reiterates these directions in her recipes, which reflect the sensibilities of the time. Most of her recipes contain little seasoning but do use more butter than most 21st-century Americans would be comfortable using.

With a few exceptions, broiling techniques and recipes for broiled food varied little throughout the 19th century in American cookbooks. Fannie Farmer's influential 1896 *Boston Cooking-School Cook Book,* for example, explained that broiling "is cooking over or in front of a clear fire. The food to be cooked is usually placed in a greased broiler or on a gridiron held near the coals. . . . [T]ender meats and fish may be cooked this way." Farmer's recipes provided step-by-step directions as well as additional information, such as the Table Showing Composition of the Various Fish Used for Food, which indicated the amount of protein, water, and other components of common fish, such as haddock.[7]

Some 19th-century broiled recipes did depart from the simple broiled meat and fish seasoned with salt and butter and brushed with butter. Author and reformer Mary A. Livermore contributed one such recipe to the *Woman Suffrage Cook Book* (2nd ed.), edited by Hattie A. Burr. Livermore's recipe for broiled chicken used whole chickens that were cut open in the back and pounded to lie flat. The chicken was then "broiled over hot coals." The recipe then directed the cook

---

TO BROIL FISH

Cod, haddock, bluefish, and mackerel are split down the back and broiled whole, removing head and tail or not, as desired. Salmon, chicken halibut, and swordfish are cut in inch slices for broiling. Smelts and other small fish are broiled whole, without splitting. Clean and wipe fish as dry as possible, sprinkle with salt and pepper, and place in well greased wire broiler. Slices of fish should be turned often while broiling; whole fish should be first broiled on flesh side, then turned and broiled on skin side just long enough to make skin brown and crisp.

To remove from broiler, loosen fish on one side, turn and loosen on other side; otherwise flesh will cling to broiler. Slip from broiler to hot platter, or place platter over fish and invert platter and broiler together.

Source: Fannie Merritt Farmer, *The Boston Cooking-School Cook Book* (Boston: Little, Brown, & Co., 1896), 146.

to boil the liver, heart, and gizzard and chop them finely. This gravy was thickened with a flour-and-butter roux and "a cup of sweet cream if you have it." When the chickens were cooked through, they were supposed to be dipped in the gravy and placed back on the grid-iron over the coals for a minute, with the cook "taking care that they do not burn." Then the chicken was once again placed in the gravy, "allowing it to boil up once, and send to the table hot."[8]

Ardashes H. Keoleian's *Oriental Cook Book* (1913) featured more exotic recipes of the Middle East "adapted to American tastes and methods of preparation." The title page of his cookbook announced that he was "formerly of Constantinople." He noted that "in the Ori-ent" broiled meats were generally cooked on wooden or metal spits over a charcoal fire. His cookbook included a great variety of broiled meats, including whole lambs and rabbits. The shish kebabs often featured broiled cubes of meat served with a sauce of vegetables and spices.[9]

Grilling remained an indoor cooking technique for most white Americans throughout the 19th century and halfway through the 20th. (In frontier areas and on the Overland Trail, of course, men and women cooked outdoors. Southern barbecues and clambakes featured outdoor cooking, too.) In the early-20th century, however, there were several cookbooks that focused on outdoor grilling. Horace Kephart's *Camp Cookery,* published in 1910, was one of them. Kephart's book was aimed primarily at groups of men on hunting or fishing trips. He provided detailed advice on what provisions to bring, step-by-step instructions on building fires, and other practical sugges-tions. Simple grilling over the fire was only one method of cooking featured in this cookbook. Kephart also included directions for more elaborate dishes, and advised his readers to bring Dutch ovens and frying pans on their hunting trips.[10]

Camping was also a popular activity for young people, especially in groups such as the Boy Scouts, Girl Scouts, and Campfire Girls. First published in 1940 in *The Outdoor Book* by the Campfire Girls, S'Mores are still popular. Called Heavenly Crisp in this publication, the treat is made by toasting marshmallows on sticks over a fire then sandwiching the toasted marshmallows between two graham crackers and a chocolate bar. After eating them, people want "s'more!"[11]

By the 1930s, outdoor grilling had become very popular in the western United States.[12] After World War II, it became a national trend. Makers of charcoal briquettes reported a great increase in the production and sale of their products in the early 1950s, and as one historian has reported, "Kingsford increased production by 35 percent and added thousands of retail outlets, typically gas stations," but limited advertising "for fear of not being able to meet the demand."[13] The popularity of outdoor grilling was due to a number of factors, such as the increased popularity of outdoor activities, the postwar growth in housing, particularly in the suburbs, and a new emphasis on family togetherness.[14]

After World War II, as soldiers returned to civilian life, married, and started families, American factories turned from manufacturing bombers and war munitions and toward manufacturing cars, kitchen appliances, and other consumer goods instead. In order to meet the increasing demand for affordable housing, builders constructed millions of new homes in the decade following the end of the war. Many of these houses were located in new suburban communities that had become possible with the construction of new roads and the growth of car ownership. Although these suburban houses were often smaller than their prewar counterparts, they often came with picture windows, patios, breezeways, and lawns. Consequently, there was plenty of outdoor space in which to put grills and hold backyard cookouts. Moreover, backyard cookouts meshed perfectly with the suburban family lifestyle that developed during the postwar baby boom. While children played in the yard, men socialized around the grill, and women gathered the accompanying side dishes, plates, and utensils. As one scholar notes, "Because outdoor grilling was generally seen as being a masculine activity it allowed men to take part in an event that straddled the line between male activity and family activity . . . but it put the family into a topsy-turvy world where dad cooked with enormous utensils and everyone ate outside with their hands."[15]

The kitchens of 1950s homes with their modern appliances and packaged convenience foods were women's domains, but the backyard grill belonged to men.[16] Manufacturers produced large tools designed specifically for outdoor cooking—they could not be confused with the indoor tools used by women in their kitchens. Cookbooks and cooking magazines assumed men would do the outside grilling, while all other chores from planning to cleaning up would be done by women.

Steak was the ideal "manly" food, but hamburgers, hot dogs, and chicken were also popular grilled foods. Less likely choices, such as Spam and bologna, also made it to the backyard grill. For example, a Crisco cookbook, *Praise for the Cook*, published in the 1950s, included a recipe titled, Barbecued Bologna for Men à la Crisco. It consisted

of a two-to-three-pound bologna sausage spread with a mixture of
Crisco and Kitchen Bouquet (a seasoning sauce made mainly of caramel coloring and a vegetable base that is used primarily to impart a
brown color to an item being cooked.) The bologna was then grilled
and served sliced on rye bread or hamburger buns.[17]

Popular side dishes to go with the grilled meats included garlic
bread wrapped in aluminum foil, which could then be placed on the
grill; corn, cooked on the grill or boiled in a pot in the kitchen; Three
Bean Salad, using canned beans; and baked beans, also usually from
a can. Potatoes were popular, too, and they were sometimes wrapped
in foil and baked on the coals. A more dangerous method of cooking
potatoes was created in the mid-1950s and became a fad for a brief
time. This method involved cooking potatoes in rosin, which is highly
flammable.[18]

Cooking on skewers was another trend of the 1950s. The traditional kebab consisted of lamb or steak chunks, which were marinated before grilling. However, recipes published during this time
featured all types of combinations. One recipe suggested for parties
included chunks of suet, cubes of ham, and canned, spiced crabapples
in a sweet soy-sauce glaze.[19]

Food manufacturers marketed their products to capitalize on the
barbecue fad. They advertised condiments, such as ketchup and mustard, and produced steak and barbecue sauces. They also emphasized
the ease with which their canned products, such as baked beans,
could be prepared to accompany foods cooked on the grill. An advertisement in *Life* magazine is one example of a new food item that
combined the love of barbecue with the popularity of convenience
foods. This advertisement was for Oscar Mayer's Sack O' Sauce in a
Can O' Meat. Consumers could buy beef, pork, or wieners, which
came in a can along with the packaged barbecue sauce. The meat was
then quickly heated with the sauce on top, and a busy family could
pretend they were enjoying a barbecued meal without the time or
mess.[20]

Nevertheless, actual grilling was very popular, and although grills
were readily available for purchase, some people desired to build their
own. Cookbooks included chapters on grill construction, and magazines regularly featured articles giving step-by-step directions on
how to build a grill. Many of these were constructed from cinder
blocks and wire. There were also brick fireplace-type grills. Some do-
it-yourself grills transformed discarded objects into grills. One man
wrote to *Look* in 1954 to describe the grill he had made from an old

refrigerator. Even odder was the Incin-O-Grill, a permanent grill that could also be used as a backyard incinerator.[21]

In the mid-1950s, using a hibachi to prepare grilled foods became a craze, along with the Polynesian and Asian food fad. The hibachi was often used at parties, sometimes indoors, which is not recommended because of smoke and dangerous fumes. Since the war, people were more familiar with Hawaii and Asia, and with Hawaiian and Asian food, or at least Americanized versions of it. Popular culture contributed to the Polynesian fad. The 1949 musical *South Pacific*, based on stories from James Michener's 1947 book *Tales of the South Pacific*, won several Tony awards and a Pulitzer Prize. The popular movie version of the musical premiered in 1958. In 1959, Michener's episodic novel *Hawaii* was published and soon became a bestseller.

Polynesian restaurants became increasingly popular in the 1950s and 1960s, and people wanted to make the Polynesian dishes at home. People had Hawaiian-themed parties, and luaus were also popular themes for schools and clubs. Although a luau did not feature a menu of all grilled foods, it might include some grilled items. For example, rumaki—bite-sized chicken livers marinated in a soy-sauce-based mixture, combined with water chestnuts, and wrapped in a piece of bacon—were broiled or cooked over the hibachi. Often they were considered an essential feature of a pu-pu platter.[22] They were also popular at the ubiquitous cocktail parties of the 1950s and 1960s. Often the addition of pineapple or pineapple juice served to make a dish Hawaiian.

Since that time, Americans have become more familiar with other Asian foods. Korean Barbecued Short Ribs, or *kalbi*, for example, are very popular at Korean restaurants. The short ribs are marinated in a mixture of soy sauce, garlic, sesame oil, sesame seeds, and green onions, with a bit of sugar. They are then cooked on a grill over a medium-hot flame. As one "designated *kalbi* griller" from a Korean family writes, *kalbi* is "best served the way Korean restaurants do: cut into pieces right over the grill . . . and then wrapped inside a fresh leaf of lettuce with a finger of steaming white rice, a dollop of spicy red bean paste (gochichang), a few slivers of raw or grilled garlic, and shredded strips of fresh green onion." More recently, Korean barbecue has merged with Mexican cuisine in the form of Korean tacos made with Korean barbecued beef wrapped in a corn tortilla and topped with typical Mexican taco condiments, such as salsa, onions, lettuce, and cilantro. Some Korean taco places also serve tacos with Korean barbecued chicken or pork.[23]

GRILLS

As the popularity of backyard grilling increased in the 1950s, some people looked at ways to improve grills. George Stephen invented a kettle-type grill in 1951. One feature of this grill was its ventilated lid, which controlled the smoke and flames that ruined many outdoor meals cooked on brick grills. The grill became so popular that Stephen was able to buy out Weber Brothers Metal Works, where he was part owner. He renamed his grill the Weber grill.[24]

Kamado grills have become popular, especially in the Atlanta, Georgia, area, where they can be found in restaurants and neighborhood backyards. The popular grills sold in the United States are called Big Green Eggs because of their shape and color. Fans cook entire meals on them, including cakes and pizzas, and believe the grills use less charcoal but cook faster and more evenly.[25]

The first gas grill was created by Modern Home Products (founded by Walter Koziel) in the 1950s and first marketed in 1960. This first gas grill was a round steel grill, but the more popular rectangular grills were introduced in 1964. Gas grills have become very popular and now come with extra features that many consumers want. These features include side burners, rotisseries, and even infrared burners. The use of grilling accessories, such as fish and vegetable baskets, poultry roasters, and pizza stones, has also increased. In a 2009 survey commissioned by the Weber-Stephen Company, 35 percent of those surveyed admitted that they own two or more grills. One in five own both a charcoal and a gas grill.[26]

Although hamburgers, steak, hot dogs, and chicken remain the most popular foods cooked on backyard grills, Americans grill—and want to grill—many other foods. A 2010 New York Times column titled "101 Fast Recipes for Grilling" provided just that. It listed simple recipes for grilled fruit and vegetables, meat, fish and shellfish, sandwiches, and desserts. Vegetables such as zucchini and eggplant are delicious when sliced, brushed with garlic-infused olive oil, and grilled, a fruit salad can combine lightly charred fruits, and a real grilled cheese sandwich can be made on the grill.[27]

Charcoal and gas grills never should be used inside. Restaurants have special ventilation systems to permit grilling inside, and there are specially vented gas grills that can be installed in home kitchens. An oven broiler can be used to produce a grilled effect indoors. The broiler door should be kept open to maintain the temperature and to keep the food from baking instead of broiling. It is helpful to use a broiler pan. A broiler pan consists of two parts. The top pan is slotted to allow grease to drip into the deeper pan it rests on. Smoke, of course, will go into the kitchen, so meat should be trimmed of excess fat when broiling, and marinated foods should be drained first to eliminate dripping and smoking in the oven.

Electric grills can be also be used to grill inside. There are two main types, the open grill and the contact model. The open grill is somewhat similar to an outside grill. The grill sits over the burner of the stove and the food cooks on a grill. As with an outdoor grill, the food needs to be flipped to cook both sides. A contact model cooks the food from above and below at the same time, making it much faster method of grilling. Contact model grills are similar to sandwich grills or panini makers. Indoor grills do not produce the authentic flavor of an outside grill, but they are an alternative for people who cannot or do not want to cook outdoors.

HEALTH

Many people watch their weight and cholesterol levels by eating lean cuts of broiled or grilled meat, fish, or poultry. Unfortunately, charring meat also produces carcinogens. Some, called polycyclic aromatic hydrocarbons (PAHS), are in the charred areas, which can be scraped off or avoided by not charring the meat. Heterocyclic amines (HCAs), however, form when meat is cooked at high temperatures. They form beneath the surface of the meat and thus cannot be scraped off.

It is not clear what cancers can result from these compounds, and scientists are not sure how big a risk it is to consume them. Therefore, it is probably wise to avoid consuming charred meat too often. Marinating the meat, eating less meat, eating leaner cuts, and eating lightly grilled vegetables along with or instead of meat can also help reduce the risks involved in consuming grilled meat.[28]

NOTES

1. President Obama received grilling tips from chef Bobby Flay at the Fatherhood Barbeque Town Hall Meeting at the White House on June 19, 2009, AP Photo/Haraz N. Ghanbari, http://www.examiner.com/examinerslideshow.html?entryid=328235; "Homer's 6 Best Grilling Tips," *Parade Magazine*, May 23, 2010, http://www.parade.com/food/2010/05/23-homer-simpson-grilling-tips.html.

2. Theodor de Bry, *How They Cook Their Fish, c.1590,* http://www.loc.gov/pictures/item/2001696970/?sid=d73cfb88f2c88caf57d245fa45233643.

3. Beverly Cox and Martin Jacobs, *Spirit of the Harvest: North American Indian Cooking* (New York: Stewart, Tabori, & Chang, 1991), 54–56, 78.

4. Cox and Jacobs, *Spirit of the Harvest,* 128, 129, 217.

5. Frank G. White, "Gridiron Wars: or Here's the Beef," *Old Sturbridge Visitor,* Summer 2003, 10–11, https://osv.org/explore_learn/document_viewer.php?DocID=2071. White observes that the modern-day George Forman Grill has similar features to collect the melted fat from cooking meat; however, these features are intended to keep fat away from health-conscious consumers.

6. Esther Allen Howland, *The American Economical Housekeeper, and Family Receipt Book* (Cincinnati, OH: H.W. Derby, 1845), 47; Feeding America: The Historic American Cookbook Project, http://digital.lib.msu.edu/projects/cookbooks/html/books/book_14.cfm.

7. Fannie Merritt Farmer, *The Boston Cooking-School Cook Book* (Boston: Little, Brown, & Co. 1896), 22, 147.

8. Hattie A. Burr, *The Woman Suffrage Cook Book* (Boston: Hattie A. Burr, 1890), 35.

9. Ardashes H. Keoleian, *The Oriental Cook Book* (New York: Sully & Kleinteich, 1913), 101.

10. Horace Kephart, *Camp Cookery* (New York: Outing Publishing Co., 1910).

11. Mark H. Zanger, *The American History Cookbook* (Santa Barbara, CA: Greenwood, 2003), 348.

12. My mother, Sylvia Schreiber, remembers one time sometime in the early 1930s when her father cooked kosher hot dogs on the ledge of the coal heater in the basement for a Saturday night visit of some cousins. Although it is now impossible to know why my grandfather decided to cook using the basement coal heater, perhaps he was inspired by discussions of outdoor cooking. Because my grandmother usually did the cooking, this change in cook and cooking venue made this meal similar to many backyard grilling parties. Sylvia Schreiber, conversation with the author, June 21, 2010.

13. Laura Shapiro, *Something from the Oven: Reinventing Dinner in 1950s America* (New York: Penguin, 2004), 173.

14. Tim Miller, "The Birth of the Patio Daddy-O: Outdoor Grilling in Postwar America," *Journal of American Culture* 33, no. 1 (2010), 6, http://www3.interscience.wiley.com/cgi-bin/fulltext/123326799/HTMLSTART.

15. Carolyn M. Goldstein, *Do It Yourself: Home Improvement in 20th-Century America* (New York: Princeton Architectural Press, 1998), 36–37; Lawrence Culver, *The Frontier of Leisure: Southern California and the Shaping of Modern America* (New York: Oxford University Press, 2010), 213; Miller, "The Birth of the Patio Daddy-O," 7.

16. This seems just as true in the early-21st century. The television show character Dexter Morgan, a newly devoted family man and serial killer, commented on the masculine features of the backyard cookout with this wry

observation: "The backyard barbecue, it's a holdover from the last Ice Age when food was scarce and men had to work together to take down a large beast. Those who worked well with others survived and their genes have been passed down through the centuries until they landed here, in this . . . my community." Said by Dexter (Michael C. Hall) Off Voice, *Dexter,* season 4, episode 3, "Blinded by the Light," 2009.

17. The recipe is included in Sylvia Lovegren, *Fashionable Food: Seven Decades of Food Fads* (Chicago: University of Chicago Press, 2005), 172.

18. Lovegren, *Fashionable Food,* 176.

19. Lovegren, *Fashionable Food,* 178–79.

20. "Oscar Mayer's Great New 'Sack O' Sauce in a Can O' Meat,'" *Life,* January 16, 1950, 74.

21. Lovegren, *Fashionable Food,* 174; Miller, "The Birth of the Patio Daddy-O," 9.

22. Lovegren, *Fashionable Food,* 174, 276–83.

23. Howard Yoon, "A Hard-to-Kick Habit: Korean Barbecue Short Ribs," *Kitchen Window,* NPR, August 10, 2005, http://www.npr.org/templates/story/story.php?storyId=4793091; John T. Edge, "The Tortilla Takes a Road Trip to Korea," *New York Times,* July 27, 2010.

24. Weber-Stephens Company History, http://www.fundinguniverse.com/company-histories/WeberStephen-Products-Co-Company-History.html.

25. John T. Edge, "Green Eggs and Hamburgers," *New York Times,* July 13, 2011.

26. Colleen Joyce Pontes, "Gas Grill," in *The Oxford Companion to American Food and Drink,* ed. Andrew F. Smith (New York: Oxford University Press, 2007), 253; The 21st Annual Weber GrillWatch Survey, Weber-Stephen Products Co, http://weber.mediaroom.com/index.php?s=41&cat=1.

27. Mark Bittman, "101 Fast Recipes for Grilling," The Minimalist, *New York Times,* June 29, 2010. One of my daughters and I particularly enjoy the recipe for tahini tofu steaks, which involves basting slices of tofu with tahini thinned with lemon juice and mixed with garlic.

28. The findings are summarized in Deborah Franklin, "Summer Hazards: Sunburn . . . and Barbecue?" NPR, May 25, 2006, http://www.npr.org/templates/story/story.php?storyId=5428963.

CHAPTER 6
Frying

> The frying-pan has awful sins to answer for. What untold horrors of dyspepsia have arisen from its smoky depths, like the ghost from witches' caldrons! The fizzle of frying meat is a warning knell on many an ear, saying, "Touch not, taste not, if you would not burn and writhe!"
>
> —Catharine E. Beecher and Harriet Beecher Stowe,
> *The American Woman's Home* (1869)

Frying is a quick method of cooking food in hot oil or fat. Frying has a long history, and fried food has always been popular in America. In the passage quoted above, the nineteenth-century domestic reformers Catharine Beecher and Harriet Beecher Stowe were not actually condemning fried food, only poorly prepared fried food. As they rightly noted, when done well, frying results in food that is crispy and delicious.[1]

Almost a century after the Beecher sisters made their assertions about frying, Peg Bracken offered her opinion on the subject. Bracken, who had been an advertising copywriter before achieving celebrity status with her 1960s bestseller, *I Hate to Cook Book,* provided the following advice on how to *talk* about frying:

Never say "fry" if you don't mean "deep-fat fry." You can say

"pan fry"
"pan broil"
"sauté"

Fried chicken, an American classic, can be
found throughout the United States, although
it is often associated with the South. (AP
Photo/Larry Crowe)

"brown in butter"
"sizzle in butter"

or you may go all the way and say "cook it *à la pôele*," which is a
French phrase meaning "stew in butter at such a low temperature that
the object is cooked before it starts to brown." But "fry" means the
way you would cook doughnuts, if you ever did, which you don't, because you can buy perfectly lovely doughnuts all made.[2]

Despite Bracken's humorous claims, frying can refer to several
techniques of cooking food in fat or oil. The Beecher sisters, in *The
American Woman's Home,* explained the two basic methods of frying.
The first, deep-frying, totally immerses the food in boiling fat. The
second method is pan-frying, which uses only enough oil to coat a
pan. Deep-frying is used to prepare food such as doughnuts, French
fries, and fried chicken. Pan-frying, however, can be subdivided into

shallow pan-frying, sautéing, and stir-frying. These methods can be used to cook a variety of food items, from fish fillets to tofu.

Deep-frying differs from other methods of frying in that it requires a cooking pot that is deep enough to submerge the food under at least two inches of oil. A large saucepan or kettle, a Dutch oven, or an electric deep-fryer can be used for deep-frying. The temperature of the oil is usually kept between 350°F and 375°F. One method of testing the temperature of the oil is to drop a cube of bread into the hot oil. The bread should quickly float to the surface of the oil and then turn golden brown. If it sinks, the temperature needs to be raised a little bit, or the food will absorb too much oil and will be soggy. If the bread cooks too quickly, the temperature should be lowered to prevent the food from burning. The goal is produce food that has a golden-brown crispy exterior and a tender cooked interior. As a noted food columnist and cookbook author has declared, "The result [of deep-frying] is either the crispest, most ethereal delights you can imagine or a soggy, greasy mess."[3]

In contrast to deep-frying, sautéing uses only a small amount of fat or oil. Sauté comes from the French word *sauter*, meaning "to jump." To sauté, the oil is heated and the food is placed in it, but not moved until it is begins to brown. In stir-frying, however, the food is constantly stirred. Food cooked this way has to be cut into small pieces to allow it to cook quickly and evenly, and the pieces should be about the same size so that they all take about the same amount of time to cook. Pan-frying, or shallow frying, uses less oil than deep-frying, but more oil than sautéing. Pan-fried food can become crispy and brown, as with deep-frying, but the food has to be turned, since it is not completely covered by the hot oil.

THE SCIENCE OF FRYING

Metal is a great conductor of heat. During frying, the metal of the frying pan conducts heat from the fire or stove to the surface of the food. Oil assists in the process by filling in the tiny gaps between the food's surface and the pan; it also keeps the food from sticking to the pan.

For successful frying, the temperature has to remain high enough to cook the food, even though water vapor from the food is present. The sound of sizzling (for example, from meat being fried) is "actually the sound of moisture from the meat being vaporized as it hits the hot metal pan," according to a one well-known food-science author. The moisture comes from inside the food because frying dehydrates the outer surface of the food. To provide some insulation for meat or vegetables, they are sometimes breaded or dipped in batter before frying. This outer surface then becomes crisp and flavorful while the food under it remains moist.[4]

Deep-frying is actually somewhat similar to boiling, since the food is totally immersed in the hot oil, but the temperature of the hot oil in deep-frying is much hotter than the temperature of boiling water. Deep-frying allows the food surface to dry out and become crisp and brown. The hot oil helps to conduct the heat from the pan to the food.[5]

FATS AND OILS

Many different types of fat and oil are used for frying. Butter, margarine, lard, poultry fat, or any one of a number of vegetable oils, including olive oil, peanut oil, and corn oil, can be used to fry food. Eggs, for example, are often fried in butter, but sometimes oil or even bacon fat might be used. Olive oil might be used to sauté vegetables, but it is not suitable for deep-frying because it smokes at high temperatures. Snack foods, such as potato chips, are fried in vegetable oils that can withstand higher temperatures. Fried snack foods are extremely popular in the United States, and it takes billions of pounds of oil to prepare them. "In the United States, nearly 2 billion pounds of oil is used annually for frying salty snack foods," according to one expert on cooking oils.[6] Thus cooking oil is an important matter to consider in any discussion of frying.

The European colonists relied mainly on butter (in areas where there were dairy cows), lard from pigs, beef tallow, and the drippings from roasting meats. One food historian states, "Cooking with butter was characteristic of Tudor cookery, largely replacing the earlier lard and olive oil (being expensive, the latter came to be reserved for salads), but never altogether replacing beef suet and marrow among the wealthy." The family book of recipes that Martha Washington received in 1749 when she married Daniel Custis, and which she gave to her granddaughter, Eleanor Parke Custis, in 1799, when she married Lawrence Lewis, originated during the Tudor period. This recipe book and others of the period reveal a continuance of this Tudor style of cooking and food preferences in Virginia centuries later. The recipes in Washington's book often use fresh or sweet butter, but they also call for clarified butter for frying.[7]

One example of food fried in butter from this cookbook is Fryde Pudding, actually a sort of sweet, thick pancake. It contained eggs, cream, grated bread, sugar, nutmeg, cinnamon, currants, and wheat flour. It was fried in "good butter," flipped over, and the other side was then fried. It was served with sugar sprinkled on top.[8]

Cheese Balls are another fried dish included in Martha Washington's book. They were a type of cream cheese fritter, with cinnamon, nutmeg, and sugar, and most likely they were deep-fried in clarified butter. European settlers brought various kinds of cheese fritters with them to America. In St. Augustine, Florida, pastries called Fromajadas are still prepared and enjoyed. Although these pastries are now usually baked, similar 16th-century Spanish versions were fried. St. Augustine was founded by Spain in 1565. Florida went back and forth between Spain and England before Spain sold the colony to the United States in 1821. Consequently, British food preferences might also have influenced how these fritters are prepared.[9]

Mrs. N.K.M. Lee, the author of *The Cook's Own Book,* which is thought to be the first alphabetical culinary encyclopedia in America, preferred olive oil for frying, but she noted, "[T]he best oil is expensive, and bad oil spoils every thing that is dressed with it. For general purposes, and especially for fish, clean, fresh lard is not near so expensive as oil or clarified butter, and does almost as well. Butter often burns before you are aware of it; and what you fry will get a dark and dirty appearance."[10]

Lard, or fat rendered from pigs, was the most commonly used shortening in early America. It was used for both frying and for baking. Europeans brought both pigs and cows to their settlements in North America, but cows were more often found in New England and the mid-Atlantic areas. Although cows were valued for butter and other dairy products and for beef, beef fat never became as popular with early Americans as lard for use in cooking and baking.

Late fall was the traditional time to butcher pigs. Housewives or their daughters, servants, or slaves then rendered the fat from pigs (or other animals). Farmwife Mary Cooper of Long Island recorded in her diary entry for December 19, 1772, "Our people very buese dressing hogs and beaf. . . . I am up most of this night trying tallow." On December 21, she noted that she was "up all this night trying fat." Farmwives such as Mary Cooper stored the fat in a cool place within their larders, where they could keep it for many months. In the South, pigs and hogs were a major source of food and fat for both the black and white populations. Beef was more commonly eaten in Africa because of Islamic prohibitions against eating pork, but in America, African and African American slaves were generally given pork to eat. After slaughtering the pigs, slaves rendered the fat into lard. The solid pieces left in the pot were called cracklins', and they were eaten by themselves or mixed with cornmeal to make cracklin' bread. As more people moved away from farms in the 19th century, they lost their access to lard. Lard was mass-produced in the 19th century, but it became too expensive for poor and working-class people to use in large quantities.[11]

The dietary laws of Judaism prohibit observant Jews from using lard because it is made from pigs. Jews can use butter, but not for meals with meat because dietary laws also prohibit the mixing of meat and dairy in one meal. Mediterranean Jews have traditionally cooked with olive oil, but olive oil was expensive and therefore not a staple in northern European or in American kitchens until fairly recently. Northern European Jews, the Ashkenazim, used goose fat, or schmaltz, and they brought the practice of raising geese to North America when they emigrated in large numbers during the late-19th and early-20th centuries.

In New York's Lower East Side, pigs owned mainly by Irish immigrants roamed the streets as late as the 1850s. In the 1860s, the recently created sanitary police, along with other reform groups, helped to reduce the city's pig population. Despite the attempts by reformers to decrease the livestock population in New York, poultry farms sprang up in the tenements of the Lower East Side in the 1870s, mainly among the Jewish immigrants. Unlike the pigs, however, geese, chicken, and other poultry remained inside the buildings. Although inspectors raided and fined poultry farmers, immigrants continued to raise poultry as long as it remained profitable. (In the 1920s, one historian notes, "[T]he kosher poultry trade was lucrative enough to attract organized crime, and a racketeering operation grew up around the city's kosher slaughterhouses.")[12]

Jewish housewives gathered at these poultry farms to select the fattest birds, particularly for Sabbath and holiday meals. They diced and cooked the fat-filled skin to produce schmaltz. Eventually, chickens replaced geese, and chicken fat replaced goose fat in Jewish kitchens.

French chemist Hippolyte Mège-Mouriès created margarine from beef suet and milk in 1869, and into the 20th century other types of artificial butter were made from animal fats. At first, margarine was marketed as a cheap alternative to butter. Later many believed it to be a healthy alternative to butter. In the early-20th century, new forms of cooking fat made from vegetable oils appeared. These were hydrogenated vegetable oils. Crisco is the most famous of these products. Proctor & Gamble, which manufactured Ivory and other soaps, created this vegetable shortening and introduced it in 1911. P & G marketed

Crisco as an inexpensive alternative to butter and lard, but they also emphasized its purity. The first advertisements also stressed that Crisco could be used over and over because it did not absorb odors from food cooked in it, and it could be heated to higher temperatures than other fats and oils. In addition, because Crisco was neither meat nor dairy (pareve), Jewish cooks could use it to prepare any type of food, and it could also be used in baking or frying. It was packaged with kosher certificates on the label. In 1933, Proctor & Gamble published *Crisco Recipes for the Jewish Housewife* with recipes written in both English and Yiddish. More recently, the Crisco brand has been used for vegetable oils, sprays, and sticks that do not contain trans fats.[13]

Some present-day cooks have gone back to using chicken schmaltz for cooking, although generally they do so as a special treat, and not for everyday cooking. During the Jewish holiday of Hanukkah, when it is traditional to eat fried foods, some fry the latkes (potato pancakes) in chicken schmaltz for a nostalgic culinary experience. Vegetable oil works just as well to fry these tasty treats, however, and it is more appealing to vegetarians and those who are concerned about their cholesterol intake.[14]

QUICK AND EASY

Eggs, pancakes, French toast, sausage, bacon, and similar breakfast foods are commonly prepared in a fry pan or lightly greased griddle. As well as being easily prepared, such foods cook quickly. Cooking sprays, nonstick pans, and electric or gas stove tops make cooking these types of dishes almost foolproof. It was a little more challenging, however, to cook them over an open fire, as 17th- and 18th-century cooks did, although the quick cooking time meant the cook did not have to spend a long time at a hot fire. Early American cast iron frying pans were called spiders. They had long handles, and some had three legs to allow them to rest in the fireplace. Dishes quickly prepared in a fry pan could be served at breakfast while other dishes simmered, or they could be prepared during hot days so the oven did not have to be heated.

Sometimes food was fried because ovens were not available. On the Overland Trail, for example, emigrants traveling west usually prepared quick breads in frying pans. Although they sometimes baked bread in Dutch ovens, they did not often have time to let dough rise and bake. The quick breads were usually made of flour and water, and then fried in buffalo grease, lard, or other available fat. Missionary

Narcissa Whitman, who was traveling west with her husband, described this bread in a letter she wrote to her mother and sisters in 1836. After weeks in which she had no bread at all, Whitman was happy to have this bread, even if it might have seemed unpalatable to those back home.

> Girls, If you wish to know how they (fried cakes) taste, you have the pleasure of taking a little flour & water & make some dough roll it thin, cut it into square blocks, then take some beef fat and fry them! You need not put either salt or pearl ash in your dough. Believe me I relish these as well as I ever did any made at home.[15]

American Indians prepared similar fried breads of wheat or corn, but the popular American Indian Fry Bread, served at festivals and gatherings of American Indians, is a relatively recent invention. It is usually deep-fried in a cast iron skillet. Fry bread originated in the 19th century, when the U.S. government forced many tribes to leave their homelands. To prevent them from starving, the U.S. government provided the Indians with flour, sugar, and lard. Fry bread is prepared and served at most tribal festivals, often with honey or powdered sugar, or as the base for an Indian taco, which is topped with ground beef, cheese, lettuce, tomatoes, and salsa. (Alluding to the popularity and pervasiveness of fry bread within American Indian culture, a character in the 1999 movie *Smoke Signals,* written by Sherman Alexie, wears a Frybread Power T-shirt.)

Welsh cookies, a type of cookie similar to a teacake or sweetened biscuit, are cooked on a griddle, not baked in an oven. The cookies are popular in the Scranton, Pennsylvania, area. They are made by cutting shortening (old versions used lard, newer ones use Crisco and/or butter) into flour, lightly seasoning the mixture with nutmeg, and adding milk, eggs, and currants (or raisins).

Small pieces of meat and fish can also be prepared quickly in a frying pan. For example, lightly breaded fried fish has been popular throughout American history. Mrs. Lee discussed the frying of "soles" in great detail in *The Cook's Own Book*. She informed her readers that the fish must be dry, completely and evenly coated with egg, then coated completely with breadcrumbs. She explained how the fish should be cut, if it was too large for the pan, how the cooking fat should be clean, and how to make certain the temperature of the fat was hot enough. She then discussed the actual frying process and how the fish should be dried afterward. As she observed, "[W]e have been very particular and minute in our directions; for, although a fried sole is so frequent and favorite a dish, it is very seldom brought to table in perfection."[16]

Fried fish has been a popular dish among campers and fishermen and -women. Author Ernest Hemingway included a recipe for fried trout in an article he wrote for the *Toronto Star* in 1920, "Camping Out: When You Camp Out, Do It Right." In this recipe, the cook is instructed to gut the trout and remove its gills, if necessary, then to coat it in cornmeal. After that it was fried in Crisco and bacon fat over a campfire. The bacon was partially cooked first in the pan, and then draped over the fish as it finished cooking.[17]

Stir-frying is also a quick method of cooking food; some time must be spent in chopping and preparing the ingredients before the cooking begins, however. Chinese immigrants brought stir-frying to America, but the technique can be used to prepare non-Asian foods, as well. Stir-frying is often done in a wok; a large skillet that can withstand high temperatures can also be used.

Cooking should not begin until all of the food is sliced and diced and the sauces prepared. All of the food should be dry before it is cooked, or the oil will splatter and the food will not cook properly. The wok should be heated first, and the oil added to it. In an essay on stir-frying, in which she describes the drama of her parents' stir-frying "performance," Chinese American Grace Young declares, "The moment the wok is hot, turn on the exhaust fan, swirl in the oil, and immediately add the food." She further notes, "[G]arlic, ginger, and vegetables require immediate stir-frying; but poultry, meat, and seafood should cook undisturbed for a minute or two, so that the ingredients sears slightly before stir-frying." Sauces should be added by swirling them "down the sides of the wok to prevent the temperature of the pan from dropping." Once cooked, a stir-fried dish should be placed on a warmed platter and brought to the table to be consumed immediately. A stir-fry should evoke *wok hay,* the breath of a wok, "that elusive seared taste that only lasts for a minute or two."[18]

THE POPULARITY OF DEEP-FRIED FOOD

The popularity of deep-fried food goes back to the early years of American history. Deep-fried oysters were a popular dish in 19th-century Philadelphia. The Philadelphia style of preparing them—which resulted in perfectly crisp, not greasy oysters—was kept a secret by professional chefs in the city, although the technique goes back to at least the 1820s. In 1879, James Parkinson published L. F. Mazzetti's recipe for Philadelphia Fried Oysters in the *Confectioner's Journal*. Mazzetti was chef de cuisine at the trendy West End Hotel in Philadelphia. Trained in Milan and Paris, he was considered to be an extremely talented chef, and he became the White House chef during President Ulysses S. Grant's administration.[19]

To prepare oysters in the Philadelphia style, fresh oysters were sprinkled with salt and allowed to drain in a colander for an hour. They were then covered lightly with cracker dust, allowed to sit for ten minutes, and then dipped in beaten eggs and coated with breadcrumbs. The oysters were then fried in "frying hot" lard. Culinary historian William Woys Weaver advises home cooks to follow Mazzetti's directions, but adds that they should then "allow one bottle of Dom Perignon for each dozen oysters. Lock the doors, disconnect the phone and invite absolutely no one until you are certain all the oysters are gone."[20]

Croquettes were popular in both the North and the South in the 19th century and into the 20th. They often were made as a way to use up leftover meat, poultry, or vegetables. Almost every cookbook included recipes. *The Blue Grass Cook Book* included a short chapter with a variety of croquettes, including brain, egg, fish, rice, and one titled Very Fine Croquettes.

VERY FINE CROQUETTES

1 pound of cooked turkey or chicken,
3 teaspoons of chopped parsley,
1 pint of cream,
1 large onion,
1/4 pound of butter,
1/4 pound of bread-crumbs,
Salt, pepper, and cayenne pepper to taste.
Sprinkle the parsley over the meat and run through grinder twice. Boil the onion with the cream and strain onion out, and when cool pour cream over bread-crumbs, add the butter, and make a stiff mixture, then add salt, etc. Beat in the meat and mix all together.

If too stiff, add a little cream and make as soft as can be handled. Put on ice to get stiff. Then roll and shape. Dip in egg, and roll in bread-crumbs, and fry in hot lard.

———

Source: Minnie C. Fox, *The Blue Grass Cook Book,* with an introduction by John Fox Jr. (New York: Fox, Duffield, & Co., 1904), 80–81.

Deep-fried snack foods, appetizers, and finger foods are extremely popular in the United States. The snack-food industry is a billion-dollar industry in the United States. One company notes on its website that it in 2011, it produced over one million pounds of potato chips each week.[21] According to legend, George Crum, the American Indian chef at Moon's Lake House in Saratoga Springs, New York, invented potato chips in 1853. As the story goes, a customer (sometimes said to be Cornelius Vanderbilt) was displeased with the fried potatoes Crum had prepared and sent them back, perhaps more than once. Annoyed, Crum sliced potatoes extra thin, deep-fried them, and covered them with salt. He expected the customer to be upset, but instead, the customer loved the potatoes. In all likelihood, Crum was not the only person accidentally to create potato chips, and some earlier recipes for fried potatoes seem to be potato chips.[22]

French fries, which are potatoes cut into thin strips and then deep-fried, are also very popular. Americans consume approximately 600 million servings of French fries every month—from fast-food restaurants alone. French fries, however, have a long history, and recipes for frying potatoes were included in most 19th-century cookbooks.

A visit to a food court or street fair often reveals a multiethnic cavalcade of fried foods. At many such places or events, one can find egg rolls, tacos and tortilla chips, and falafels, as well as French fries, onion rings, and funnel cakes. The fried food served at many ethnic restaurants appeal to Americans who might hesitate to eat less familiar looking food. Before sushi became almost ubiquitous in America, Americans in a Japanese restaurant might have chosen tempura, meat or vegetables coated in a light batter and fried. Chinese restaurant menus feature egg rolls, fried wontons, and sometimes even chicken fingers. Most Indian restaurants serve pakora, deep-fried vegetable fritters, a popular street food in India, and falafels, fried chickpea balls that are very popular in Israel and Lebanon, are served at most Middle Eastern restaurants.

Two of the most popular fried foods with a long cultural history in the United States are doughnuts and fried chicken.

DOUGHNUTS

Doughnuts are one of the most popular fried treats in America. Most scholars believe Dutch immigrants introduced them to America in the 17th century. In the Netherlands, the Dutch used oil to fry the doughnuts, which were made from yeast dough, but in America, they switched from oil to lard, since it was more readily available. Other immigrant groups carried recipes and traditions for their own doughnuts to America. For example, Moravians and other German groups brought *faschnauts,* which are traditionally made and eaten on Shrove Tuesday or Fat Tuesday, the day before Lent begins. They were made to use up the fat in the house before Lenten fasting began. The French contributed *beignets,* the official state doughnut of Louisiana, and Jewish immigrants brought *sufganiyat,* jelly doughnuts traditionally eaten during Hanukkah. Jelly doughnuts have become popular as year-round treats in the United States.

Mid-19th-century cookbooks included recipes for doughnuts made with both yeast and quick-raised dough. The anonymous author of *The Cook Not Mad, or Rational Cookery,* provided recipes for crullers, which used only eggs to make them light, and for doughnuts, made with yeast. The word *cruller* comes from the Dutch word *krulle,* a twisted cake, and describes many different types of doughnuts, but in the 1840s, one culinary historian explains, "it was generally a doughnut with a hole." These cakes were usually rolled in sugar after frying.[23]

Nineteenth-century American whaling ships customarily treated their crews to doughnuts fried in whale oil each time they filled one thousand barrels with oil. Mary Brewster, the wife of a ship's captain, wrote of one such event, "At 7 PM boats got fast to a whale and at 9 got him to the ship Men all singing and bawling Doughnuts

---

NO 118. CRULLERS, SOMETIMES CALLED MIRACLS OR WONDERS

Six ounces of butter, twelve ounces sugar, one pound twelve ounces of flour, six eggs, one nutmeg; fry in hot lard.

NO 120. TO MAKE DOUGHNUTS

One quart of milk, three eggs, one pound and a quarter of sugar, three quarters of butter, a little ginger, one tea cup of yeast, let it rise, then fry in hot lard. [The recipe is missing flour. Presumably one adds enough until a dough forms.]

Source: Anonymous, *The Cook Not Mad, or Rational Cookery* (Watertown, NY: Knowlton & Rice, 1831), 35, 36.

Doughnuts to morrow as this will certainly make us 1,000 barrels."
She noted the next day, "This afternoon the men are frying doughnuts in the try pots and seem to be enjoying themselves merrily."[24]

Early doughnuts did not have holes. They could be cut into different shapes, but they were always deep fried, and as one author states,
"[They] were considered an economical sweet suitable for filling up
small boys or eating for tea." Doughnuts cooked on ships might have
had to adjust the recipes to the ingredients they had available. A whaling ship might not have had milk or eggs, and doughnuts prepared
onboard most likely used pearl ash or saleratus for leavening. Molasses or brown sugar would probably have been used as a sweetener.
Doughnuts would have been a special treat because oil was too valuable to use it for frying foods very often.[25]

The popularity of doughnuts spread throughout the nation after
Red Cross and Salvation Army volunteers provided servicemen with
these homey, tasty treats during World War I. Adolph Levitt, a
Russian Jewish immigrant living in New York City, developed an au-
tomated doughnut machine in the 1920s, and five years later he created a standardized doughnut mix for it. Doughnuts were billed as
The Hit Food of the Century of Progress at the Chicago World's
Fair in 1934. That same year, Frank Capra's delightful screwball com-
edy, *It Happened One Night,* featured a scene in which Peter Warner (Cary Grant) teaches runaway heiress Ellie Andrews (Claudette
Colbert) how to properly dunk a doughnut, "Dunking's an art," he
tells her. "It's all in the matter of timing. I ought to write a book
about it." In 1948, William Rosenberg opened a doughnut shop in
Quincy, Massachusetts, that featured 52 varieties of doughnuts. More
stores opened, and the chain later became Dunkin' Donuts. Krispy
Kreme, another major doughnut chain, began in 1937, when Vernon
Rudolph started selling his hot doughnuts to local grocery stores in
Winston-Salem, North Carolina. According to the company's website, Krispy Kreme was "recognized as a 20th century icon" in 1997,
and the company donated artifacts to the National Museum of American History.[26]

FRIED CHICKEN

Fried chicken might be considered the quintessential American food,
but it has a long history that can be traced back to late-medieval
chicken dishes that were prepared by frying pieces of chicken and
then braising them in a sauce. Such dishes became known as *fricassee.*

Martha Washington's *Booke of Cookery* includes a recipe for Frykacy of Chikin Lamb Ueale or Rabbits; however, the use of cloves, mace, and nutmeg, along with other herbs, indicates this recipe originated in an earlier time period.[27]

In 1824, Mary Randolph published *The Virginia Housewife: or, Methodical Cook,* which many consider the first true American cookbook, and definitely the first American regional cookbook. The book was republished at least 19 times before the Civil War, and even present-day southern cooks refer to it. The cookbook includes the first published recipe for Fried Chickens. Randolph came from an aristocratic Virginia family, related to the Jeffersons and other elite planter families. She was known for her knowledge of food and for the excellent meals served at her table. Her husband, David Meade Randolph, a cousin, was appointed the U.S. marshal of Virginia, a federal post, during George Washington's presidency, but Thomas Jefferson removed him from his position in 1801 because of their political differences. (Randolph was a Federalist and open critic of Jefferson.) To supplement the family's income, Mary Randolph opened a boarding-house in Richmond in 1807.

This recipe could be followed today to produce the typical southern fried chicken with gravy. The fried mush, to which Randolph refers, is corn fritters. They would have been made from a cornmeal batter, dropped by spoonfuls into the hot fat, and fried.

Slaves did the actual cooking in Mrs. Randolph's kitchen, as they did throughout the kitchens of the South. After the Civil War, fried chicken became part of the regional southern cuisine eaten by both whites and African Americans. It can be found throughout the United States, and it helped to spawn a fast-food empire, Kentucky Fried Chicken.

FRIED CHICKEN

Cut them up as for the fricassee, dredge them well with flour, sprinkle them with salt, put them into a good quantity of boiling lard, and fry them a light brown; fry small pieces of mush and a quantity of parsley nicely picked, to be served in the dish with the chickens; take half a pint of rich milk, add to it a small bit of butter, with pepper, salt, and chopped parsley; stew it a little, and pour it over the chickens, and then garnish with the fried parsley.

———

Source: Mary Randolph, *The Virginia Housewife: or, Methodical Cook* (Baltimore: Plaskitt & Cugle, 1838), 75–76.

Harlan Sanders of Kentucky (made an honorary Kentucky colonel in 1936) opened a small restaurant in the front room of a gas station in 1930. He developed a method of using pressure cookers to fry chicken in 1939. In 1952, he began selling franchises for his Kentucky Fried Chicken chain. By 1964, there were more than 600 Kentucky Fried Chicken franchises in the United States and Canada and 1 in England. To address present-day health concerns, KFC, now owned by Tricon Global Restaurants, Inc., which also owns Pizza Hut and Taco Bell, modified the recipe and replaced the cooking oil in 2007 so that there are zero grams of trans fat per serving. In 2009, KFC introduced Kentucky Grilled Chicken.[28]

Fried chicken evokes strong feelings from many people. Novelist William Styron, for example, insisted that for "Southern fried chicken," only young, tender birds were suitable; they should be coated with flour, not dipped in batter, and they should be fried in bacon fat in a shallow pan. He emphasized that this delicacy is "best eaten with rice and giblet gravy and *always,* as I have pointed out, conveyed to the mouth with the fingers."[29]

Although often associated with the South, fried foods cross national, international, and cultural lines. In the post–World War I era cookbook *The Italian Cook Book,* Maria Gentile remarked that "for patriotic reasons and for reasons of economy, more attention has been bestowed upon the preparing and cooking of food that is to be at once palatable, nourishing and economical." She then explains that Italian cuisine has all of these qualities. Although some of the dishes in the cookbook would seem unusual and perhaps too foreign to many American women at that time, the book also includes a recipe for fried chicken.

FRIED CHICKEN (POLLO FRITTO)

Wash a spring chicken and keep in boiling water for one minute. Cut into pieces at the joints, roll them in flour, season with salt and pepper and dip in two whole beaten eggs. After leaving the pieces of chicken for half an hour, roll them in bread crumbs, repeating the operation twice if necessary. Put into a saucepan with boiling oil or fat, seeing that the pieces of chicken are well browned on both sides. Keep the fire low, Serve hot with lemon.

Source: Maria Gentile, *The Italian Cook Book: The Art of Eating Well* (New York: Italian Book Co., 1919), 29.

Fried chicken is prepared throughout the United States, not just the South, and with all sorts of adaptations, including various marinades for the chicken and different types of coatings. Although purists would not consider them to be true versions of fried chicken, variations of fried chicken include boneless versions, called chicken nuggets and chicken fingers (and even vegetarian chickenless versions), fried chicken wings, often called Buffalo chicken wings or hot wings, and oven-baked fried chicken.

A food scholar who traveled the country eating and learning about fried chicken commented on the way the dish has been adapted by cooks who have brought their own ideas to preparing it, just as they have changed and adapted other foods. He explains that "each cook arrives at the stove with his or her own palate, his or her own cultural inclinations, and no matter how closely that cook might follow an established recipe, they are predisposed to refashion a dish to reflect, at least in part, their own traditions. And so it is with chicken as fried in my America."[30] And so it is with fried foods in general.

NOTES

1. Catharine E. Beecher and Harriet Beecher Stowe, *The American Woman's Home: or Principles of Domestic Science* (New York: J.B. Ford & Co, 1869), 181–82.

2. Peg Bracken, "Good Cookmanship, or How to Talk a Good Fight," in *The I Hate to Cook Book* (New York: Harcourt, Brace, & World, 1960), 150–56, in Molly O'Neill, ed., *American Food Writing: An Anthology with Classic Recipes* (New York: Penguin Books, 2009), 321–22.

3. Mark Bittman, *How to Cook Everything Vegetarian: Simple Meatless Recipes for Great Food* (Hoboken, NJ: John Wiley & Sons, 2007), 26.

4. Harold McGee, *On Food and Cooking: The Science and Lore of the Kitchen*, rev. ed. (New York: Scribner, 2004), 159–62, 786.

5. McGee, *On Food and Cooking*, 162, 786.

6. Monoj K. Gupta, Introduction to *Frying Technology and Practices*, by Monoj K. Gupta, Kathleen Warner, and Pamela J. White (London: Taylor and Francis, 2004), 1.

7. Karen Hess, editor, *Martha Washington's Booke of Cookery* (New York: Columbia University Press, 1981), 9.

8. Hess, *Martha Washington's Booke*, 111–12.

9. Hess, *Martha Washington's Booke*, 152; Mark H. Zanger, *The American History Cookbook* (Santa Barbara, CA: Greenwood, 2003), 16–17.

10. N.K.M. Lee, *The Cook's Own Book: Being a Complete Culinary Encyclopedia Comprehending all Valuable Receipts for cooking Meat, Fish, and*

*Fowl, and Composing every kind of Soup, Gravy, Pastry, Preserves, Essences, &c.
that have been Published OR Invented During The Last Twenty Years particularly the very best of those in the Cook's Oracle, Cook's Dictionary, and other
systems of Domestic Economy with Numerous Original Receipts, and a complete
system of Confectionary* (Boston: Munroe & Francis, 1832), xx–xxi.

11. Michael Krondl, "Lard and Shortening," in *The Oxford Companion
to American Food and Drink*, ed. Andrew F. Smith (New York: Oxford University Press, 2007), 352–53; Field Horne, ed., *The Diary of Mary Cooper:
Life on a Long Island Farm, 1768–1773* (Oyster Bay, NY: Oyster Bay Historical Society, 1981), 46; Herbert C. Covery and Dwight Eisnach, *What
the Slaves Ate: Recollections of African American Foods and Foodways from the
Slave Narratives* (Santa Barbara, CA: ABC-CLIO, 2009), 99.

12. Jane Ziegelman, *97 Orchard: An Edible History of Five Immigrant
Families in One New York Tenement* (New York: Smithsonian Books, 2010),
111–15.

13. Ziegelman, *97 Orchard*, 118. Also see the Crisco website's account of
its history at http://www.crisco.com/About_Crisco/History.aspx.

14. Linda Morel, "Schmaltzy History: A Nostalgic Look at Fats for
Frying Latkes," *JTA: The Global News Service of the Jewish People*, November 28, 2010, http://www.jta.org/news/article-print/2010/11/28/2741378/
schmaltzy-history-a-nostalgic-look-at-fats-for-frying-latkes?TB_iframe=true&
width=750&height=500 http://www.jta.org/news/article-print/2010/11/28/
2741378/schmaltzy-history-a-nostalgic-look-at-fats-for-frying-latkes?TB_if
rame=true&width=750&height=500.

15. Clifford Drury, ed., *First White Women over the Rockies* (Glendale,
CA: Arthur H. Clarke Company, 1963), 78, quoted in Jacqueline Williams,
Wagon Wheel Kitchens: Food on the Overland Trail (Lawrence: University
Press of Kansas, 1993), 139. Also see the entry for August 11, 1836, "The
Letters and Journals of Narcissa Whitman, 1836–1847," *New Perspectives
on the West*, PBS, http://www.pbs.org/weta/thewest/resources/archives/
two/whitman1.htm#080536.

16. Lee, *The Cook's Own Book*, 199.

17. Zanger, *The American History Cookbook*, 347.

18. Grace Young, "The Breath of a Wok," in *The Wisdom of the Chinese
Kitchen: Classic Family Recipes for Celebration and Healing* (New York: Simon
& Schuster, 1999), 20–23, in O'Neill, *American Food Writing*, 657–61.

19. William Woys Weaver, *Thirty-Five Receipts from "The Larder Invaded"* (Philadelphia: The Library Company of Philadelphia and The Historical Society of Pennsylvania, 1986), 65.

20. Weaver, *Thirty-Five Receipts*, 66.

21. Utz, http://www.utzsnacks.com/about_history.html.

22. For example, see the recipe To Fry Sliced Potatos, in *The Virginia
Housewife: or, Methodical Cook*, by Mary Randolph (Baltimore: Plaskitt &
Cugle, 1838), 97.

23. William Woys Weaver, *A Quaker Woman's Cookbook: The Domestic Cookery of Elizabeth Ellicott Lea*, rev.ed. (Mechanicsburg, PA: Stackpole Books, 2004), 326.

24. Joan Druett, ed., *She Was a Sister Sailor: The Whaling Journals of Mary Brewster, 1845–1851* (Mystic, CT: Mystic Seaport Museum, 1992), quoted in Sandra L. Oliver, *Saltwater Foodways: New Englanders and Their Food, at Sea and at Shore, in the 19th Century* (Mystic, CT: Mystic Seaport Museum, 1995), 103 [no date/page no. given for Brewster's journal entry].

25. Oliver, *Saltwater Foodways,* 104, 117.

26. Gil Marks, "Doughnuts," in *Encyclopedia of Jewish Food* (Hoboken, NJ: John Wiley & Sons, 2010), 163–64; Krispy Kreme, http://www.krispykreme.com/about-us/history.27. Hess, *Martha Washington's Booke,* 44–45.

28. KFC, http://www.kfc.com/about/history.asp.

29. William Styron, "Southern Fried Chicken," in *The Artists' & Writers' Cookbook,* ed. Beryl Barr & Barbara Turner Sachs (Sausalito, CA: Contact Editions, 1961), 87–92, in O'Neill, *American Food Writing,* 330–34.

30. John T. Edge, *Fried Chicken: An American Story* (New York: G. P. Putnam's Sons, 2004), 169.

CHAPTER 7
Roasting

The roasted turkey took precedence on this occasion, being placed at the head of the table; and well did it become its lordly station, sending forth the rich odor of its savory stuffing, and finely covered with the froth of the basting . . . like the celebrated pumpkin pie, an indispensable part of a good and true Yankee Thanksgiving.
—Sarah J. Hale, *Northwood: or Life North and South* (1827)

Roasting is a dry method of cooking that can be done over an open fire, in the ashes, or in an oven. Because roasting can dry and toughen meat, it should be used for cuts that can withstand cooking with dry heat. Often such meat is more expensive than less choice cuts, which can be pot roasted or braised. Meat that is roasted over a fire needs constant watching and turning to prevent scorching. Roasting also requires a steady, hot fire or a constant oven temperature. This could be a problem for cooks in previous decades who needed firewood for hearth cooking or wood or coal to heat their ovens. Although roasting in an oven requires less vigilance than open-hearth roasting, it still requires some time and attention (although certainly less than frying or boiling). Moreover, a hot oven can make a kitchen extremely uncomfortable on a warm summer day. Even today a cook might choose not to use the oven in order to keep the house cooler on a sweltering day. Roasting often takes longer than frying, broiling, and boiling, and time might be an issue for people who work long hours outside of the home and who might not want to begin roasting when they

Vegetables, as well as meat, can be roasted.
Pictured here is roasted squash with almonds
and cranberries. (AP/Wide World Photo)

arrive home. Dishes such as roast beef and turkey are thus often prepared and served for special meals or on weekends or when people
have the time and do not mind the expense. They are often associated
with holidays, such as Thanksgiving, as depicted by the 19th-century
author and editor Sarah Josepha Hale in the passage quoted at the
beginning of this chapter.

Although roasting is frequently thought to be a cooking technique
used for meat and poultry, such as roast beef or turkey, roasting is
also used to prepare vegetables and fruit, such as potatoes and apples.
Beans, seeds, nuts, and legumes are also roasted to enhance their flavor or to make them palatable. For example, coffee beans—they are
actually the seeds of the coffee plant—must be roasted before they are
ground and brewed with water to make the beverage. Roasted coffee
beans are also coated with chocolate and eaten as candy.

Roasted meat develops a deeply flavored browned surface due to
the Maillard reaction, also called the "browning reaction." When

meat is cooked between 300° F and 500°F, the denatured proteins that exist in the outer layers of the meat recombine with sugars, producing the browning (it is different from but similar in effect to caramelization, which involves sugars only). In addition to its appealing look and flavor, meat cooked this way develops a "roasted aroma." As one food scientist describes it, this aroma can be of "a generic 'roasted' character," but roasted meat can have many other aromas, such as "grassy, floral, oniony or spicy, and earthy." According to this authority, "Several hundred aromatic compounds have been found in roasted meats!"[1]

This browning technique can also be used for roasting fish and vegetables. For example, to give a salmon fillet a brown roasted appearance and taste, it should be placed in a pan in which butter or oil has been preheated in a hot oven (475°F). The fish will sizzle in the hot fat, which helps it to brown without overcooking.[2]

Roasting has been a method of cooking meat since prehistoric times. The simplest and oldest method is spit-roasting, in which the meat is impaled on a spike made of wood or metal and then cooked over a fire. The spit is kept turning so that no section of the meat is exposed to the high heat for long. Large cuts of meat, or even whole animals, can be cooked this way, getting thoroughly browned without being overcooked.[3]

The Moravian missionary John Heckewelder lived among and wrote about the Delaware, Mohican, and other American Indian tribes that lived in what is now western Pennsylvania and Ohio. The men of the tribes hunted, but as Heckewelder observed in a book first published in 1818, "The Delawares, Mohicans, and Shawanos are very particular in their choice of meats, and nothing short of the most pressing hunger can induce them to eat of certain animals, such as the horse, dog, wild cat, panther, fox, muskrat, wolf, & c." He further observed that they roasted, boiled, or broiled the meat that they caught. "Their roasting is done by running a wooden spit through the meat, sharpened at each end, which they place near the fire, and occasionally turn."[4]

Indians in the southwestern part of the United States often favored roasting over other methods of preparing food because the scarcity of water there made it difficult to boil or cook with water very often. Roasted maize, however, was popular with American Indian tribes throughout what is now the United States. A common method of roasting maize was simply to place the ears in trenches over hot coals. Buffalo Bird Woman, a Hidatsa Indian born in North Dakota around 1839, recalled that individuals in her family used to roast green corn whenever they wanted it.

> When I wanted to roast green corn I made a fire of cottonwood and prepared a bed of coals. I laid the fresh ear on the coals with the husk removed. As the corn roasted, I rolled the ear gently to and fro over the coals. When properly cooked I removed the ear and laid on another.
>
> As the ear roasted, the green kernels would pop sometimes with quite a sharp sound. If this popping noise was very loud, we would laugh and say to the one roasting the ear, "Ah, we see you have stolen that ear from some other family's garden!"[5]

American Indians frequently roasted root vegetables by setting them over still-hot coals or by placing them in hot ashes. Sometimes, particularly in the Southwest, American Indians used pit roasting to cook large pieces of meat. The roasting pit took time to prepare. First, the men of the tribe dug a deep pit. Then they placed rocks at the bottom of the pit and started a fire. The fire was allowed to burn brightly until it burned out. Then the meat was placed in the pit on a layer of branches over the smoldering fire. After the meat was covered with more branches, it was left to roast in the pit all day.[6]

Roasting on a spit, barbecuing, and grilling are similar cooking techniques that do overlap. Grilling (or broiling) is a quick method of cooking that uses a direct source of heat; barbecuing uses indirect heat and smoke. It is a slow cooking technique, and often the food being cooked is marinated first, with a sauce added before it is served. Roasting requires the food to be surrounded by heat. To accomplish this in 17th- and 18th-century America, cooks had to use spits and various other devices to cook meat over a fire. Sometimes the spits were supported on hooks or cords that made it easier for the cook to turn them. One scholar states, "Much ingenuity was dedicated to designing roasting devices throughout the Colonial and Federal eras. One device . . . looks like a small brass barrel on legs with part of the side cut away. A spit installed vertically was driven by a clockwork device at the top, which was wound up and turned the spit until it ran down." Roasting used a great deal of wood, since the fire had to be big and bright and without much smoke. When meat was being roasted, the cook put a pan underneath it to catch the fat and juices to prevent them from dripping into the fire. These juices were then used to make gravies.[7]

Kitchen appliances called *tin kitchens* appeared in the late 1700s, but only the wealthy could afford them at first because they were imported from England. As American tinsmiths began to produce them, however, the cost decreased, and they became more affordable for middling American households. Tin kitchens were roasting ovens made of tin that fit into the fireplace. The interior was curved and one side was open to the fire. There was a spit inside for the meat. The reflective interior helped to cook the meat faster and with less fuel, and the drippings fell onto the curved bottom, where they could be collected to make gravy or added to other dishes.[8]

In the detailed directions for roasting beef she provided in her 10th edition of *Directions for Cookery, In Its Various Branches* (1840), cookbook author Eliza Leslie stated, "The best apparatus for the purpose [of roasting beef] is the well-known roaster frequently called a tin-kitchen." Before roasting, however, the cook had to prepare the fire "at least half an hour before the beef is put down, and it should be large, steady, clear, and bright, with plenty of fine hot coals at the bottom." Leslie advised cooks to "wash the meat in cold water, and then wipe it dry, and rub it with salt. Take care not to run the spit through the best parts of it." She noted that some cooks also covered the fat with paper. After the meat was placed in the roaster, she cautioned that it should not be set "too near the fire, lest the outside of the meat should be burned before the inside is heated."

Her precise directions are worth quoting at length because they give such a vivid picture of hearth cooking with a tin oven.

> Put some nice beef-dripping or some lard into the pan or bottom of the roaster, and as soon as it melts begin to baste the beef with it; taking up the liquid with a long spoon, and pouring it over the meat so as to let it trickle down again into the pan. Repeat this frequently while it is roasting; after a while you can baste it with its own fat. Turn the spit often, so that the meat may be equally done on all sides.
>
> Once or twice draw back the roaster, and improve the fire by clearing away the ashes, bringing forward the hot coals, and putting on fresh fuel at the back. Should a coal fall into the dripping-pan take it out immediately.
>
> An allowance of about twenty minutes to each pound of meat is the time commonly given for roasting; but this rule, like most others, admits of exceptions according to circumstances. Also, some persons like their meat very much done; others prefer it rare, as it is called. In summer, meat will roast in a shorter time than in winter.
>
> When the beef is nearly done, and the steam draws towards the fire, remove the paper that has covered the fat part, sprinkle on a little salt, and having basted the meat well with the dripping, pour off nicely

(through the spout of the roaster) all the liquid fat from the top of the gravy.

Lastly, dredge the meat very lightly with a little flour, and baste it with fresh butter. This will give it a delicate froth. To the gravy that is now running from the meat add nothing but a tea-cup of boiling water. Skim it, and send it to table in a boat. Serve up with the beef in a small deep plate, scraped horseradish moistened with vinegar.

Serving roast beef (and sometimes other meat) with a froth produced by dredging the meat with flour and melted butter was a typical 19th-century practice. Providing additional advice, Leslie informed her readers that "pickles are generally eaten with roast beef, and "French mustard is an excellent condiment for it."[9]

In the last couple decades of the 19th century, Americans roasted food in both tin ovens and in wood or coal ovens. Maria Parloa was the principal of the Boston Cooking School, the author of several cookbooks, and a magazine journalist who wrote for *Good Housekeeping Magazine* and the *Ladies' Home Journal.* Her 1882 cookbook, *Miss Parloa's New Cook Book,* stated, "There are two modes of roasting: one is to use a tin kitchen before an open fire, and the other and more common way is to use a very hot oven. The former gives the more delicious flavor, but the second is not by any means a poor way, if the meat is put on a rack, and basted constantly when it is the oven." She provided directions for roasting beef either way. In both versions, she instructs home cooks to dredge the beef with salt, pepper, and flour, and then to add hot water to the pan. The meat was then basted with the gravy that formed. She instructed her readers to "*Never* roast meat without having a rack in the pan. If meat is put into the water in the pan it becomes soggy and looses its flavor."[10]

Hearth cooking—and roasting meat in the fireplace—has often been romanticized. In her nostalgic look back upon her girlhood, 19th-century author Lucy Larcon described how "[p]otatoes were roasted in the ashes, and the Thanksgiving turkey in a 'tin-kitchen,' the business of turning the spit being usually delegated to some of us, small folk, who were only too willing to burn our faces in honor of the annual festival." As she recalled, "[C]ooking-stoves were coming into fashion, but they were clumsy affairs, and our elders thought that no cooking could be quite so nice as that which was done by an open fire. . . . There is no such home-splendor now."[11]

Nineteenth-century cookbook authors contributed to the debate over roasting on spits, in tin kitchens, or in ovens. Assuring her readers that she would provide directions for all three methods, Virginia novelist Mary Virginia Terhune entered the fray in her popular cookbook, *Common Sense in the Household: A Manual of Practical Housewifery*, first published in 1871. Terhune (who used the pen name Marion Harlan) wrote,

> In this day of ranges and cooking-stoves, I think I am speaking within bounds when I assume that not one housekeeper in fifty uses a spit, or even a tin kitchen, for such purposes. It is in vain that the writers of receipt-books inform us with refreshing *naïveté* that all our meats are baked, not roasted, and expatiate upon the superior flavor of those prepared upon the English spits and in old-fashioned kitchens, where enormous wood-fires blazed from morning until night. . . . I am not denying the virtues of spits and tin kitchens—only regretting that they are not within the reach of every one.[12]

Modern electric rotisserie ovens combine spit roasting and oven roasting. The spit rotates automatically within the rotisserie oven. These ovens are used most frequently for roasting chicken. Sometimes the chicken is positioned upright so that the fat drains down. Home cooks might use a small automatic rotisserie oven, whereas larger rotisserie ovens are used in commercial establishments.

TURKEY

Roast turkey holds a special place in the hearts and minds of many Americans because it is often seen as the centerpiece of Thanksgiving dinner, a traditional meal for the most traditional of holidays. As Sarah Josepha Hale noted in the quotation that began this chapter, it is an "indispensable" part of the feast. British observer Charles Mackay stated that roast turkey was "*the piece de rigueur*" at Thanksgiving. "As roast beef and plum pudding are upon Christmas-day in Old England, so is turkey upon Thanksgiving-day among the descendants of the Puritans in New England."[13]

Wild turkeys inhabited most of North America when Europeans first arrived. Wild turkeys are omnivores, and although they prefer to eat nuts, acorns, and seeds, they will forage and eat a variety of plants and berries, as well as insects, snails, slugs, and even small snakes. They are easily domesticated, however, and by the time the first Spaniards arrived in the American Southwest, turkeys had been domesticated for hundreds of years, even though wild turkeys remained plentiful throughout the continent. One scholar has stated, "Turkeys have been associated with humans in North America for millennia."

Many American Indian tribes hunted turkeys, but not all of them actually ate turkeys. Some valued their feathers or bones; some consumed turkey eggs but not turkey flesh. Some prepared the birds by boiling and others by roasting. The Navajo, according to one authority, "only ate the birds roasted, believing that boiling destroyed their flavor."[14]

Among the Pueblo of the American Southwest (which include the Zuni, Hopi, and Taos, among others), turkey feathers were used for ceremonial purposes and for warmth. The Spanish explorer Francisco Vásquez de Coronado wrote to the Viceroy Antonio de Mendoza in 1540 and observed, "The Indians tell me that they do not eat these [turkeys] in any of the seven villages but they keep them merely for the sake of procuring feathers. I do not believe this because they are very good, and better than those of Mexico."[15]

The turkey is an important character in both Pueblo and Navajo mythology. In a book on North American Indian cooking, the author remarks, "At Cochiti Pueblo, a pregnant woman may wear a turkey feather in her belt to ensure her child will be born with luxuriant hair. By taking the hair of little children in their beaks and pulling it, turkeys have the power to make hair grow." The recipe that follows this observation is Pueblo Roast Turkey with Piñon-Raisin Stuffing. The turkey in this modern-day American Indian recipe is roasted in the oven after being brushed with a butter-chili mixture and stuffed with a bread stuffing that includes piñon nuts, pine nuts that are found primarily in New Mexico.[16]

When English colonists settled in New England, they hunted and ate several types of wild fowl, including turkeys. Although the Pilgrims hunted and ate turkeys, as did the Wampanoag, there is no evidence that they ate turkey together during their 1621 gathering, which is often depicted as the first Thanksgiving. Wild turkeys continued to be a target for hunters, but American farmers began to raise turkeys, too, along with other poultry. For example, in 1792, Maine midwife Martha Ballard recorded in her diary the success she had in raising turkeys. On April 7 of that year, she discovered one of her turkeys had laid an egg. For the next several weeks, she recorded "setting" turkeys on eggs. On May 25, an egg began to hatch. On May 26, she reported, "[M]y Black Turkey Brot out 14 chicks." On June 2, she had 43 young turkeys in her yard, and more hatched in August.[17]

Roast turkey appears to have been a frequent meal for the Ballards, particularly when they had company. On September 7, 1792, her family "Dind on a Turkey." On October 14, "we had a Turkey roasted." Her diary reminds modern-day readers that turkey—and

indeed, nearly all of the food consumed by Ballard and her family—
was grown, raised, or prepared in her household or grown, raised, or
prepared by neighbors. On October 21, Ballard killed and roasted
a turkey. On October 29, she killed three young turkeys. On November 10, she reported that she had "stript Turkey feathers." On
November 29, she roasted a turkey for her family, and gave another
turkey to Mr. Densmore, a neighbor, probably in barter for tending
his wife or because Mrs. Densmore was instructing Ballard's daughter
in dressmaking.[18]

Recipes for both wild and domesticated turkey appear in some
19th-century cookbooks. Because a wild turkey is generally leaner
than a domesticated bird, and may also be old and tough, some authors suggested first boiling the bird before roasting, then roasting
the bird with broth in the pan. In *Housekeeping in Old Virginia,* compiled by Marion Cabell Tyree, granddaughter of Patrick Henry, from
"Two Hundred and Fifty Ladies in Virginia and her Sister States,"
there are recipes for Wild Turkey, in which Tyree instructs her readers to wash the turkey thoroughly with soda and water, then to boil it
for five minutes before stuffing it and roasting it in broth. The cookbook also contains a Simpler Way to Prepare Wild Turkey, in which
the directions say to "prepare the turkey as usual," and then to place
it "in the baking-pan, with water enough to make gravy." In addition to being lean, stringy, or tough, a wild turkey might have un-
digested food in its crop (a pouch in the throat where food is stored
before digestion), which can become foul smelling. In contrast, food
is often withheld from domesticated birds for several hours to allow
their crops to empty before they are slaughtered.[19]

So how did roast turkey become associated with Thanksgiving?
Colonies and later states declared days of thanksgiving throughout
the 17th, 18th, and early-19th centuries. These were religious holidays that were often celebrated with church attendance, prayers, and
fasting. Because the holiday was always celebrated in the fall—and
most frequently in New England—it became conflated with fall harvest festivals featuring the food that would be found in New England.
Moreover, pigs and cattle were usually butchered early in the winter,
so it is possible that in many households fresh beef and pork were not
available at Thanksgiving.[20] At the same time, wild turkeys are usually
hunted in the late fall and winter, when they are fatter. By the 19th
century, turkey (usually roasted, but sometimes boiled) was the centerpiece of most Thanksgiving dinners. For example, in 1806, William
Bentley, pastor of the East Church in Salem, Massachusetts, noted,

"[A] Thanksgiving is not complete without a turkey."[21] During the Civil War, there were public appeals and collections of food and money to supply Union soldiers with turkeys for their Thanksgiving dinners.

One scholar has suggested, "Turkey is consumed at Thanksgiving feasts because it was native to America, and because it is a symbol of the bounteous richness of the wilderness." Another has put forward the notion that turkey "became the symbol of the dominant culture, and the stuffing and side dishes, and desserts the immigrants' contribution."[22]

Thanksgiving became a national holiday in 1863. Sarah Josepha Hale spent 17 years lobbying for the holiday by writing to members of Congress and state and territorial governors. She also wrote editorials promoting the idea of a national thanksgiving holiday in *Godey's Lady's Book*. She finally appealed directly to President Abraham Lincoln, and he proclaimed the last Thursday of November a national holiday. President Franklin D. Roosevelt moved the holiday to the next-to-the-last Thursday in November to extend the Christmas shopping season and add a boost to the economy during the Great Depression, and in 1941 Congress declared the fourth Thursday in November as Thanksgiving.

Of course, Thanksgiving is celebrated throughout the United States, and the meal often reflects the ethnic and regional traditions of those preparing it. In the South, cornbread stuffing is often served with the turkey. Because the United States has so many different ethnic groups with their own styles and beliefs about cooking and food, it is not unusual to find several different ethnic cooking traditions merged in a single Thanksgiving dinner. One Louisiana cook, for example, prepares an annual Thanksgiving cornbread dressing that combines Louisiana and Russian Jewish cuisines. The dressing is made with cornbread, schmaltz, chicken broth, and oysters.[23]

ROAST BEEF AND ITS VARIATIONS

In the United States, meat has traditionally been an important and popular part of most diets. Beef and pork, as well as wild game, were plentiful throughout the continent. Eliza Leslie's directions for roast beef were quoted in length earlier in the chapter. Most 19th-century cookbooks include similar, if not always as detailed, instructions for this dish. Rufus Estes, who was born a slave, then worked for the Pullman Company, and then became chef for "the subsidiary companies of the United States Steel Corporations in Chicago," included roast beef in his 1911 compilation *Good Things to Eat*. In Roast Beef, American Style, the directions stated to "[l]ay the meat on sticks in a dripping pan, so as not to touch the water which is placed in the bottom of the pan." The meat was seasoned with salt and pepper and roasted for three or four hours, with frequent basting. Before serving, Estes suggested garnishing the beef with browned cracker crumbs and parsley. Estes also included Roast Beef on Spit, which gave instructions for cooking the beef over a brisk fire. The meat was served with gravy prepared from the drippings and garnished with horseradish.[24]

In the 1960s, Beef Willington became the in party dish. As one scholar notes, "[I]t was rich, dramatic, expensive, and seemed difficult and time-consuming to prepare. In short, it was everything a gourmet dish should be." Recipes for Beef Wellington appeared in a range of magazines, and even ethnic restaurants included the dish on their menus. Betty Crocker's 1967 *Hostess Cookbook* included a meal entitled Betty Crocker's Extra-Special Dinner Party Starring Beef Wellington, which used canned and frozen convenience foods for the side dishes. As this cookbook declared, "Dramatic, delicious Beef Wellington demands all the cook's time and talent. . . . This stunning main dish is accompanied by canned and frozen vegetables chosen to ease the preparation and to color complement the meat." Beef Wellington usually consists of a beef fillet, which is roasted and cooled, although sometimes other cuts of beef—or even other types of meat are used. Then it is sometimes coated with pâté de foie gras and mushrooms and enclosed in puff pastry and baked. Many complain that the beef gets overcooked and steams inside the pastry. The 1975 edition of *Joy of Cooking* opined about the dish, "If time is no object and your aim is to out-Jones the Joneses, you can serve this twice-roasted but rare beef encased in puff paste—but don't quote us as devotees."[25]

CHESTNUTS, CORN (AND OTHER VEGETABLES), AND COFFEE

For many people, "The Christmas Song," commonly known as "Chestnuts Roasting on an Open Fire," evokes a cozy winter scene from the past.[26] Most chestnuts in the United States now come from China or Europe because the chestnut blight fungus destroyed nearly all American chestnut trees early in the 20th century. It is not necessary to roast chestnuts over an open fire, however; they can be roasted in an oven. Chestnuts should have an X cut into the peel with a sharp knife before cooking to allow steam to release. Many advise boiling chestnuts for several minutes and then roasting them. Chestnuts have to be peeled while they are still warm.

Anyone who has looked at recent cookbooks, recipes, and menus knows that roasted vegetables are popular. *Roasted* in this context can mean in the oven or over a grill. Roasted red peppers, for example, can be prepared in the oven, over a grill, under a broiler, or even held to a gas flame until charred. Peppers should then be wrapped in foil until they are cool enough to peel off the skin.

Fruits, such as grapes, tomatoes, and strawberries, can also be roasted. Slow roasting at a low temperature (about 250°F) makes the water evaporate and produces a more concentrated flavor. Lightly toss fruit with oil, add a little bit of sugar and salt, and arrange the cut fruit on a parchment-paper-lined cookie sheet. Roast for an hour or more until the fruit is transformed. It should shrink. In the case of strawberries, syrupy juices will form around the berries.[27]

Even easier is roasted corn on the cob. One scholar of African and African America foodways says, "Roasted ears of corn on the cob were a traditional treat during the period of enslavement, when they were roasted in the dying embers of a fire. Today they can be done on a barbecue grill." The corn can be roasted in its husk. An alternate method is to husk the corn and wrap it in foil. Sometimes the corn is first coated with butter or oil. Then the foil-wrapped corn is placed on the grill. With either method the corn should be turned so that it cooks evenly. It takes about five to seven minutes to roast an ear of corn.[28]

Other vegetables can also be roasted in an oven or over a grill. Potatoes, for example, can be roasted whole or sliced, chopped, and roasted in an oven with onions, garlic, olive oil, and herbs. Grains such as quinoa can be roasted, too. One cookbook author suggests first boiling quinoa for a few minutes with potatoes and garlic, and then pouring them into an oiled pan. The mixture is then drizzled with oil, sprinkled with salt and pepper and roasted. After roasting, chopped red peppers, scallions, and cheese can be added.[29]

Although most people probably do not think about the roasting process when they drink a cup of coffee, coffee beans have to be roasted before they can be ground and brewed. Many people purchase already roasted beans or, more commonly, already roasted and ground coffee, but some home cooks today do desire to roast their own coffee. One popular method is to use old popcorn poppers. Directions can be found on numerous websites and food blogs. Freshly roasted beans produce especially flavorful, rich coffee.

In the 19th century, coffee beans were often sold green. The Quaker widow Elizabeth Ellicott Lea advised the readers of her 1853 cookbook, *Domestic Cookery,* to pick out stones and dirt from the green coffee beans before roasting them. She suggested using a Dutch oven for roasting, but noted that coffee could also be roasted in the "dripping pan in a brick oven." This could be done after the bread was removed because the oven would still be warm. "Put about two pounds in a pan; stir it a few times—it will roast gradually, and if not sufficiently brown, finish in a stove or before the fire." Because it took time and fuel to heat a brick oven for bread baking, it made sense not to waste the heat that remained in the oven when it could be used to cook other foods after the bread was baked. Lea also suggested placing several pans of coffee in the oven at the same time, if preparing coffee for a large family.[30]

Those without access to ovens, such as travelers on the Overland Trail, had to use a skillet to roast the green coffee beans. Yet on the Overland Trail simply preparing a pot of coffee required someone to find fresh water, gather fuel, and make a fire before roasting and grinding the beans. Arbuckles' Coffee claims John Arbuckle was the "first coffee roaster to package whole bean coffee in sealed one pound packages" in 1864. Its motto claims Arbuckles' Coffee is "the coffee that won the West."[31]

Once coffee was roasted, ground, and boiled, however, probably nothing equaled its restorative powers, as one 19th-century traveler to Oregon recalled:

> We still had coffee, and making a huge pot of this fragrant beverage, we gathered round the crackling camp fire—our last in the Cascade Mountains—and, sipping the nectar from rusty cups and eating salal berries gathered during the day, pitied folks who had no coffee.[32]

NOTES

1. Harold McGee, *On Food and Cooking: The Science and Lore of the Kitchen,* rev. ed. (New York: Scribner, 2004), 148. The Maillard effect is also responsible for toast, popcorn, French fries, and many other foods. Some scientists believe the Maillard effect is responsible for the antioxidants in roasted coffee; see Yazheng Liu and David D. Kitts, "Confirmation That the Maillard Reaction Is the Principal Contributor to the Antioxidant Capacity

of Coffee Beans," *Food Research International* 44, no. 8 (October 2011), 2411–22.

2. Mark Bittman, "Salmon Roasted in Butter," Diner's Journal: Notes of Eating, Drinking and Cooking, *New York Times,* July 23, 2008.

3. Yes, grilling and roasting overlapped in the centuries before ovens existed, but it requires time to cook whole animals and large cuts of meat, as opposed to the quick grilling of a small fish or small cut of meat. Unlike grilling and barbecuing, a smoky flavor is not desirable in roasting, and unlike barbecue, roasting meat is a dry technique.

4. Rev. John Heckewelder, *History, Manners, and Customs of The Indian Nations Who Once Inhabited Pennsylvania and the Neighbouring States,* rev. ed., with an introduction by Rev. William C. Reichel (Philadelphia: Historical Society of Pennsylvania, 1881), 196.

5. Gilbert Livingstone Wilson, ed., Buffalo Bird Woman's Garden, recounted by Maxi'diwiac (Buffalo Bird Woman) of the Hidatsa Indian Tribe (ca.1839–1932), http://digital.library.upenn.edu/women/buffalo/garden/garden.html#IV.

6. Linda Murray Berzok, *American Indian Food* (Santa Barbara, CA; Greenwood, 2005), 112–13.

7. Sandra L. Oliver, *Food in Colonial and Federal America* (Santa Barbara, CA: Greenwood, 2005), 109–10.

8. Oliver, *Food in Colonial and Federal America,* 110.

9. Eliza Leslie, *Directions for Cookery, In Its Various Branches,* 10th ed. (Philadelphia: E.L. Carey & A. Hart, 1840), 69–71.

10. Maria Parloa, *Miss Parloa's New Cook Book: A Guide to Marketing and Cooking* (New York: Charles T. Dillingham, 1882), 132–33.

11. Lucy Larcon, *A New England Girlhood: Outlined from Memory* (Boston: Houghton, Mifflin, 1889), 22.

12. Marion Harland, *Common Sense in the Household: A Manual of Practical Housewifery* (New York: Scribner, Armstrong, & Co., 1873), 83–84.

13. Charles Mackay, *Life and Liberty in America: or Sketches of a tour in the United States and Canada in 1857–8* (New York: Harper and Brothers, 1859), 65.

14. Andrew F. Smith, *The Turkey: An American Story* (Urbana: University of Illinois Press, 2006), 5, 7, 10–12.

15. Quoted in Beverly Cox and Martin Jacobs, *Spirit of the Harvest: North American Indian Cooking* (New York: Stewart, Tabori, & Chang, 1991), 182.

16. Cox and Jacobs, *Spirit of the Harvest,* 182–83.

17. Laurel Thatch Ulrich, *A Midwife's Tale: The Life of Martha Ballard, Based on Her Diary, 1785–1812* (New York: Knopf, 1990), 133; "Martha Ballard's Diary, May 24–30, 1792," www.dohistory.org.

18. Martha Ballard's Diary, September 7–November 29, 1792, www.dohistory.org; Ulrich, *A Midwife's Tale,* 132.

19. Marion Fontaine Cabell Tyree, *Housekeeping in Old Virginia, Containing Contributions from Two Hundred and Fifty Ladies in Virginia and Sister States, Distinguished for Their Skill in the Culinary Art and Other Branches of Domestic Economy* (Richmond, VA: J.W. Randolph & English, 1878), 110; Smith, *The Turkey*, 48.

20. Jane C. Nylander, *Our Own Snug Fireside: Images of the New England Home, 1760–1860* (New Haven, CT: Yale University Press, 1994), 268–69.

21. William Bentley, *The Diary of William Bentley, D.D.* (Salem, MA: Essex Institute, 1905), 3:264, quoted in Smith, *The Turkey*, 69.

22. James Robertson, *American Myth, American Reality* (New York: Hill and Wang, 1980), 15, quoted in Smith, *The Turkey*, 82.

23. Shirley Ettinger Orlansky, "Thanksgiving Cornbread Oyster Dressing," in *Matzoh Ball Gumbo: Culinary Tales of the New South*, by Marcie Cohen Ferris (Chapel Hill: University of North Carolina Press, 2005), 218.

24. Rufus Estes, *Good Things to Eat as Suggested by Rufus* (Chicago: Published by the Author, 1911), 29.

25. Sylvia Lovegren, *Fashionable Food: Seven Decades of Food Fads* (Chicago: University of Chicago Press, 2005), 231–36; Irma S. Rombauer and Marion Rombauer Becker, *Joy of Cooking* (Indianapolis, IN, and New York: Bobbs-Merrill, 1975), 455.

26. Mel Tormé and Bob Wells, "The Christmas Song" (1944).

27. For complete recipes, see Joy Manning, "Out-of-Season Produce Can Be Turned from Sad to Succulent with an Oven Stint," *Philadelphia Inquirer*, March 1, 2012.

28. Jessica B. Harris, *High on the Hog: A Culinary Journey from Africa to America* (New York: Bloomsbury, 2011), 255.

29. Mark Bittman, "Roasted Quinoa with Potatoes and Cheese," in *How to Cook Everything Vegetarian: Simple Meatless Recipes for Great Food* (Hoboken, NJ: John Wiley & Sons, 2007), 561.

30. William Woys Weaver, ed., *A Quaker Woman's Cookbook: The Domestic Cookery of Elizabeth Ellicott Lea*, rev. ed. (Mechanicsburg, PA: Stackpole Books, 2004), 183.

31. Jacqueline Williams, *Wagon Wheel Kitchens: Food on the Oregon Trail* (Lawrence: University Press of Kansas, 1993), 38, 40, 50; Arbuckles' Coffee, http://www.arbucklecoffee.com.

32. Leslie Scott, Diary, in *Covered Wagon Women: Diaries and Letters from the Western Trails*, ed. Kenneth L. Holmes (Glendale, CA: Arthur C. Clark Co., 1983), 5:134.

CHAPTER 8
Smoking

What's a New York deli without a spread of whole smoked fish and slabs of salmon to admire?
—Michael Stern, Editor, Roadfood.com, in a review of Tal Bagels in New York City

Smoking is an ancient method of preserving food. It is most often used to preserve meat and fish, but smoking is also used to cure some cheeses. Chipotle peppers, paprika, and lapsang souchong tea are smoked, as well as malt for whiskey and beer, some nuts, and tofu. The technique of smoking can impart flavor to foods, as in barbecue and in some of the above-mentioned foods, rather than preserve them (see chapter 2). There are also artificial smoke products that can be added to foods to give them a smoky flavor.

To preserve food, smoking is often combined with salting and/or drying. Some Native Americans dried meat over fires or even in the sunlight. For nomadic tribes, it was necessary to be able to pack up and travel efficiently; consequently they dried meat both to preserve it and to make it less bulky to carry.

In the mid-18th century, Nicholas Cresswell, an Englishman who traveled through the American colonies and kept a diary of his experiences, described the technique of drying buffalo meat. He was traveling with a group through the backcountry area along the Ohio River when a member of the group shot a buffalo, a bull, that Cresswell was certain "weighed a thousand." The next day he wrote:

Sliced smoked pork loin with broiled raspberry chipotle glaze. (AP Photo/Larry Crowe)

> All hands employed in curing our Buffalo meat, which is done in a peculiar manner. The meat is first cut from the bones in thin slices like beefsteaks, then four forked sticks are struck in the ground in a square form, and small sticks are stuck in the ground in a square form, and small sticks laid on these forks in the form of a gridiron about three feet from the ground. The meat is laid on this and a slow fire is put under it, and turned until it is done. This is called jerking the meat. I believe it is an Indian method of preserving the meat. It answers very well, where salt is not to be had, and will keep a long time if it be secured from the wet.[1]

The Plains Indians, such as the Lakota, also dried buffalo meat. Sometimes they dried the meat in the sunlight, a process that could take several days. After mass-produced salt became readily available in the latter half of the 19th century, drying buffalo meat to make jerky took less time. The meat was dipped in a solution of salt and water, which also protected it from flies. It was then kept hanging over the heat of a cookstove until the meat dried completely, which probably took a day or two. The drying takes 8 to 10 hours if done in an oven set at 150°F. The traditional flavoring for the buffalo jerky made by Plains Indians is salt. Southwestern Indians add chili powder, and some tribes near the Canadian border add wild ginger.[2]

SMOKED FISH: RED HERRINGS AND SUNDAY BRUNCH

One food scientist has observed that in past centuries the techniques used to preserve fish could be extreme, although they were effective. "The medieval Yarmouth red herring was left ungutted, saturated with salt and then smoked for several weeks, leaving it capable of lasting as long as a year, but also odiferous enough to become a byword for establishing—or covering up—a scent trail." Modern transportation, refrigeration, and canning techniques have eliminated the necessity for such drastic methods. Today, most fish are soaked in a salty brine for a few hours to a few days; then they are hung to dry before smoking. Salting draws some of the proteins within the fish to the surface. As the fish dries, the protein deposits on the surface form "a shiny gel or pellicle that will give the smoked fish an attractive golden sheen." The next step for most fish is to smoke it at a relatively cool 85°F, which dries the flesh without cooking it but prevents the surface from becoming too hard. After this first smoking, the fish is then either cold smoked or hot smoked. Cold smoking permits the fish to retain a delicate texture. Hot smoking cooks the fish and gives it a flaky texture.[3]

In the Pacific Northwest of the 18th and 19th centuries, salmon was so abundant that when they returned to the rivers to spawn, some American Indians said, "[Y]ou could walk across their backs." Many observed special rituals when the salmon returned. Among the Kwakiutl, the wife of the fisherman who caught the first salmon each year said this prayer: "O supernatural one! O swimmers! I thank you that you are willing to come to us. Protect us from danger that nothing evil may happen to us when we eat you. . . . For that is the reason you come here that we may catch you for food. We know that only your bodies are dead here, but your souls come to watch over us."[4]

The People of the 'Ksan who lived along the 'Ksan river in north-central British Columbia collected and preserved the memories of their elders in a book called *Gathering What the Great Nature Provided*. They lived by hunting fish and game and gathering berries, greens, and roots. Fish was sometimes eaten fresh, but most often it was smoked for later use.

'Ksan women smoked fish, and to do so, they declared a woman

has to be a hard worker, very clean. She's up early and to bed late. If she's not actually preparing fish for the smokehouse, she's watching those fish already in the smokehouse, seeing that no flies get at the fish, tending the tiny smoke-making fires; cleaning off any specks of soot; moving the fish again and again to see that they dry evenly and do not sour. She's got to be patient. If you're in a hurry nothing will be done right.[5]

The Eastern Woodland Indians were also hunters and gatherers. As soon as the ice began to break in March, the men began fishing, first in the rivers and then, later in the year, in the ocean. One French observer in the 17th century exclaimed over how plentiful the fish were and how easily the Native Americans caught them. "From the month of May to the middle of September, they are free from all anxiety about their food; for the cod are upon the coast, and all kind of fish and shellfish."[6] Like their Northwest Pacific counterparts, Eastern Woodland Indians smoked some of the fish they caught. Sometimes they smoked it on sticks over fires, but to smoke large numbers of fish they built tepees from crossed sticks covered with birch bark. In these tepees, they hung the fish head down over the smoky fire. Today some people who want to re-create this method of smoking fish use canvas coverings instead of bark for the tepees. In a modern recipe for Eastern Woodland Indians style Maple Sugar Smoked Fish, brook trout is rubbed with salt, pepper, bay leaves, and maple sugar before air drying. Then it is smoked over damp wood chips.[7]

Although fish was plentiful in the waters off the New England coast, and fishing was of great importance to the economy of the area, fish was not popular with most 19th-century New Englanders. As one scholar notes, "[F]ish suffered from what modern people consider bad public relations—some of it deserved but most of it a matter of habit and prejudice." Many considered fish the food of the poor, Roman Catholics, and immigrants, and there were scores of white, Protestant New Englanders who did not want to be associated with these groups. Moreover, 19th-century Americans did not believe fish was as filling or nutritious as meat. One 19th-century authority even declared, "It is not desirable that fish should be the sole kind of animal food eaten by any nation; and even if milk and eggs be added thereto, the vigor of such people will not be equal to that of flesh-eating nations."[8]

Fish is highly perishable. Since ancient times, humans have used salting, drying, smoking, and pickling to preserve food. Sometimes the methods are combined, which keeps food preserved for a longer period of time. For example, cod is almost fat free, and when it is salted and then dried, it lasts for a particularly long time. Many prefer the taste of salted, dried cod that has been soaked and restored to that of fresh cod.[9] Most of the cod that was caught by early-19th-century New England fishermen was salted and dried. The best fish was "merchantable," and it went mainly to Spain, Portugal, and other Catholic nations. The refuse salt cod was sold primarily to feed the slave population in the West Indies. Later in the 19th century, many commercial fisheries began to prefer preserving fish by pickling it rather than by salting it.[10]

Smoking, as well as the above methods of salting and drying, is also an ancient method for preserving fish. As one authority has observed, it "works especially well on oily-fleshed fish such as herring, mackerel, or salmon, although watery-fleshed fish, like haddock as well as salted or pickled fish, could also be smoked." Smoking alone is not effective for long-term preservation, however, and smoked fish made up only a small part of 19th-century New England's trade.[11]

Some people did (and do) smoke small batches of fish at home. Sarah Josepha Hale, the 19th-century author and editor of *Godey's Lady Book,* included a recipe for smoking meat or fish in her 1857 book, *Mrs. Hale's Receipts for the Million.*

In the 19th century, commercially smoked fish was targeted to particular groups; smoked salmon was considered the most superior of smoked fish by the English and their descendants. Those of German descent enjoyed smoked sturgeon and eel. Finnan haddie, or

---

TO SMOKE HAMS AND FISH ON A SMALL SCALE

Drive the ends out of an old hogshead or barrel; place this over a heap of sawdust of green hard wood, in which a bar of red-hot iron is buried; or take corn-cobs, which make the best smoke; place them in a clean iron kettle, the bottom of which covered with burning coals; hang the hams, tongues, fish, & c, on sticks across the cask and cover it, but not closely, that the cobs or sawdust may smoulder slowly, but not burn.

Source: Sarah Josepha Hale, *Mrs. Hale's Receipts for the Million: Four Thousand Five Hundred and Forty-Five Receipts, Facts, Directions, etc. in the Useful, Ornamental, and Domestic Arts* (Philadelphia: T. B. Peterson, 1857), 324.

smoked haddock, first produced in Scotland, was sold to the Canadian Maritime Providences, where many were of Scots descent.[12]

In Scotland, finnan haddie is traditionally a breakfast food, usually served grilled.[13] It is also prepared in a cream sauce. Indicating that audiences of the 1930s were probably familiar with the dish, Cole Porter made a suggestive reference to finnan haddie in his song, "My Heart Belongs to Daddy," sung by Mary Martin in the musical *Leave It to Me*. Mary Martin made her Broadway debut in the 1938 musical. *Finnan haddie* is one of the phrases Porter used to rhyme with *daddy* in the song, which Martin sings with mock innocence. Daddy referred to her sugar daddy, and Martin does a striptease while surrounded by men in Siberian attire at a Siberian railroad station. The scene from the musical was re-created in the movie *Night and Day* (1946), with Martin playing herself and Cary Grant portraying Cole Porter.

Most Americans today are probably much more familiar with smoked salmon than they are with other smoked fish. There are different styles of smoked salmon produced by using various methods of smoking and a variety of spices, sugar, and salt. Scottish-style smoked salmon is coated with a mixture of salt, sugar, and spices. This dry brine is then rinsed off, and the salmon is cold smoked. Kippered salmon is hot smoked, which produces a cooked fish with a firmer texture and smokier flavor.

Jewish immigrants from Russia brought the technique for producing lox, a type of salted and smoked salmon, to London and New York. *Lox* comes from the Yiddish word *lachs,* which means "salmon." The Jews of Eastern Europe were used to preserving food by drying, salting, smoking, and pickling to have it during times of scarcity, but smoked salmon would have been eaten only on special occasions because it was expensive. Lox was first pickled in brine, then the surface salt was rinsed off, and the salmon was lightly smoked. The fish remained very salty, and it was eaten with cream cheese to tone down the saltiness. It is usually served with bagels. Nova is a newer invention that originally came from Nova Scotia. A cookbook author describes it as "cured in salt and brown sugar, then washed and cold-smoked over smoldering hardwood. It is silky-soft and mild-tasting." Often it is served on sliced rye or pumpernickel bread.[14]

Smoked salmon is also featured in appetizers and cocktail food. For example, it can be placed on cream-cheese-covered baguette slices or cocktail size black bread and topped with a mixture of dill, capers, and mustard, or it can be baked in phyllo dough or encased in wonton wrappers. Smoked salmon is often added to scrambled eggs, omelets, and pasta.

SMOKED MEAT

From the 17th century on, pork has been extremely popular in the American South. The Spanish explorer Hernando de Soto brought the first domesticated hogs to America when he arrived in Florida in 1540. One rare breed of swine descended from these hogs still lives on Ossabaw Island, off the coast of Georgia, and they are in great demand at historic sites, such as Colonial Williamsburg, because they do not look like the modern-day pink pigs.[15] Subsequent explorers and settlers brought more hogs to the New World because they could be eaten during the long sea journey but were not difficult to care for after reaching land, because they are omnivores and skilled foragers. In the 17th-century Chesapeake, hogs were permitted to run wild. In the South particularly they flourished, although they also did well even in the colder areas of the northern colonies, while cattle left to fend themselves were often thin and stringy.

Pigs and hogs were traditionally slaughtered late in the fall once the temperature became cooler.[16] For the warmer southern colonies/states, pig slaughtering often did not take place until December, because to preserve the meat properly it had to be cool before salting. Colonel William Rhodes Estill in his recipe for curing hams in *The Blue Grass Cook Book,* further declared, "Kill your hogs when the wind is from the northwest." In her romanticized remembrance of antebellum foodways in the South, Martha McCulloch-Williams states, "Plenty in the smokehouse was the cornerstone of the old time southern cookery. Hence hog-killing was a festival as joyous as Christmas—and a little less sacred." According to one scholar, "[S]moking pork was a procedure dating back to the Middle Ages that sealed in fat and protected freshly cut meat from spoilage." It was heavy work. McCulloch-Williams wrote with complete sincerity that although there was usually sufficient labor on plantations to take care of slaughtering the hogs, "owners indulged their slaves by asking help of each other—of course returning the favor at need." The large sides of pork were tossed into large containers of salt and turned until they were completed coated. The meat was then hung up to dry for a couple days. After that, colonists in the early-17th century or those without smokehouses hung the salted slabs of pork in the chimney. As one historian has described this early smoking technique, "[W]ith the pork hanging in the shaft, the wood smoke clogged the chimney and slowly coated the meat's surface, enhancing its flavor while extending its shelf life."[17]

Ham is a cut of meat that comes from the thigh of a pig's hind leg. Early colonial Americans used the same method of curing ham as Europeans of the time. It is sometimes referred to as the *threes method*: salt, saltpeter (potassium nitrate, a type of rock salt that keeps the smoked meat red), and smoke. After sugar became more readily available, due to the success of sugarcane production in Brazil and the growth of the transatlantic trade in goods and spice, it became the fourth *s* in the curing technique. According to one scholar, "[S]ugar-cured hams became the bedrock of American porcine cuisine."[18]

Traditional Virginia hams came from hogs that were permitted to forage on acorns and roots. (Early in the 20th century, Virginia farmers began feeding their hogs peanuts instead.) The meat was then dry cured and smoked, as described above, with the ham salted and packed into barrels or casks. The salt was then rinsed off, and the ham was smoked, usually over green hickory chips. During the colonial period, one authority notes, spices, such as pepper, red pepper, and sugar, were rubbed into the ham after the salting. "While sugar boosted flavor, pepper boosted the survivability of the ham" and made it less susceptible to infestation by insects.[19]

Smithfield hams, which can be produced only in and around the town of Smithfield, Virginia, are dry cured, smoked, and aged.

TO CURE HAMS

For every ham, half a pound each of salt and brown sugar, half an ounce each of cayenne pepper, allspice, and saltpeter; mix and rub well over the hams, laying them in the barrel they are to be kept in with the skin side down; let them remain a week; make a pickle of water and salt strong enough to bear an egg, add to it half a pound of sugar, pour over the hams till they are thoroughly covered, let them remain four weeks, take out and hand up to dry for at least a week before smoking; smoke with corn-cobs or hickory chips. An old but a good way.

—Mrs. S. M. Guy

———

Source: Estelle Woods Wilcox, *Buckeye Cookery, and Practical Housekeeping: Compiled from Original Recipes* (Minneapolis, MN: Buckeye Publishing Co., 1877), 380.

McCulloch-Williams states, "Hams perfectly cured and canvassed [securely covered in a canvas] keep indefinitely in the right sort of smokehouse—but there is not much gain in flavor after they are three years old."[20] Other country hams are usually produced the same way. Some hams are aged for a number of years. They are covered with mold, dust, salt, and spices, which must be scrubbed off before the ham is prepared for eating. After that, the ham has to be soaked and cooked in water before baking.

Wet curing is another technique for preserving meat, such as ham. In this method, the ham is salted, then pickled, and then smoked. Or it could be pickled only and then smoked. Wet curing produces sweeter, moister hams than the traditional dry cured hams. They are sometimes called *city hams.*[21]

Many 19th-century cookbooks include directions for salting and curing a variety of meat, such as ham, beef hams, beef tongue, bacon, and even rabbit, venison, and other game. The above recipe for curing ham from the popular 19th-century cookbook *Buckeye Cookery* is one of many included in the book. This one calls for salting, brining, and then smoking.

Beef hams can be produced using a similar method. McCulloch-Williams wrote, "Beef hams are troublesome—but worth the trouble."

McCulloch-Williams declared of beef hams, "Properly cured meat is salt but not too salt, of a deep blackish-red, and when sliced thin, partly translucent, also of an indescribable savoriness."[22]

Before modern-day ready-to-eat hams came into existence, most hams, as described above, had to be boiled before baking. The

Take them from small but well fatted animals, cut off the shank, also part of the top round. Rub over very scantly with powdered saltpeter, mixed well though moist sugar, then lay down in salt for a fortnight, else cover with brine made thus. Pint pickling salt to the gallon of cold water, teaspoon sugar, and pinch of whole cloves. Boil and skim. Pour cold over the hams in a clean barrel. Let stand a fortnight, take out, drain and wipe, rub over with dry salt, and hang high in cold air. Smoke lightly, but not too much, for a month. Cover all over with ground black pepper, mixed to a paste with molasses, canvas and leave hanging.

Source: Martha McCulloch-Williams, *Dishes and Beverages of the Old South* (New York: McBride, Nast, 1913), 68–69.

BOILED HAM

For a twelve-pound Columbia ham. Cover ham with cold water and add two bay leaves, four cloves and six peppercorns. Let come to boil slowly, and boil four hours, or until the small bone pulls out. Let cool in that water, take ham out and remove skin. Cover ham with brown sugar, and press a few whole cloves into the ham. Then pour over one cup cooking sherry, bake in a moderate over about forty minutes.

———

Source: The Neighborhood Cook Book, compiled under the Auspices of the Portland Section in 1912, Council of Jewish Women, rev. and enl. (Portland, OR: Bushong and Co, 1914), 128.

following recipe comes from the second edition of a community cookbook compiled by the Council of Jewish Women in Oregon. The cookbook is nonkosher, containing recipes for shellfish as well as the ham recipe above.[23]

Today, most store-bought hams need only to be baked. Ham can also be purchased already cooked and sliced for sandwiches. Some dry-cured hams, such as prosciutto, do not need to be cooked before eating.[24]

Bacon has been ubiquitous throughout American history. Although eaten by all classes, it was often the food that was given to soldiers, slaves, and travelers, as well as the standby food for when nothing else was available. For example, 18th-century Philadelphia Quaker Elizabeth Drinker recorded in her diary on August 3, 1794, "[D]iscover'd another theft this morning of a large piece of beef fine roasting ribs, brought last evening for our dinner to day, and two pounds of exellint Butter, so that we must put up with the old resource, of Bacon and Chicking, for which may we be thankful."[25]

Forty-niner Luzena Stanley Wilson recalled in her memoir a time on the Overland Trail when the oxen pulling the wagon belonging to her and her husband seemed to be failing. Her husband told her they had to lighten the load.

We looked over our load, and the only things we found we could do without were three sides of bacon and a very dirty calico apron which we laid out by the roadside. We remained all day in camp, and in the meantime I discovered my stock of lard was out. Without telling my husband, who was hard at work mending the wagon, I cut up the bacon, tried out the grease, and had my lard can full again.

The resourceful Wilson also managed to clean and mend her apron. During all this, the oxen had time to graze and rest. Her husband told her it was good they had "left those things; that the oxen seemed to travel as well again." A long time after the couple laughed over the memory, Wilson says, "and his belief that the absence of the three pieces of bacon and the dirty apron could work such a change."[26]

Although many people who eat pork refrain from eating bacon or limit how much they eat because of the high salt and fat content and concerns about nitrates and nitrites, bacon and bacon products have become very popular. In addition to bacon and eggs, BLTs (bacon, lettuce, and tomato sandwiches), and bacon-wrapped shrimp, bacon is also added to cookies, cakes, and other dishes. There are products such as "bacon bits," bacon flavored vodka, and Baconnaise, a bacon-flavored mayonnaise, which talk show host Jon Stewart declared was "for people who want heart disease but are too lazy to actually make the bacon." (The product is actually kosher and vegetarian.) In the ultimate artery-clogging concoction, the people behind the BBQ Addicts website created a recipe they call Bacon Explosion: The BBQ Sausage Recipe of All Time. It consists of thick bacon strips woven together with a layer of Italian sausage spread on top. They add barbecue rubs and sauce, roll the mixture up, and cook it in a smoker "in a constant cloud of hickory smoke."[27]

SMOKEHOUSES

The earliest known use of the term *smoak house* occurred in 1716 plantation records from York County, Virginia. Most likely 17th-century Virginians used their chimneys or less permanent structures for smoking meat. By the mid-18th century, however, smokehouses were commonplace on plantations in Virginia, Maryland, and surrounding areas. In general, the structures were square structures with sharply pitched roofs and were made of wood. Thomas Cooper, an Englishman who published a 1795 account in London of life in the United States, described a smokehouse of Archibald M'Allister in Lancaster County, Pennsylvania:

> His smokery for bacon, hams, etc. is a room about twelve feet square, built of dry wood a fireplace in the middle, the roof conical, with nails in the rafters to hang meat intended to be smoaked. In this case a fire is made on the floor in the middle of the building in the morning, which it is not necessary to renew during the day. This is done for four or five days successively. The vent for the smoke is through the crevasses of

the boards. The meat is never taken out 'till it is used. If the walls are of stone, or greenwood, the meat is apt to mould.[28]

Nineteenth-century writer and reformer Lydia Maria Child recognized that although it was "good economy" to preserve pork, beef, and other meat, not all of her readers had smokehouses. The 1844 edition of her popular cookbook *The Frugal Housewife* gave instructions for salting, pickling, and smoking ham, beef, mutton, and tongue. After providing directions for "an old-fashioned way for curing hams," which was a dry cure of salt, saltpeter, and molasses rubbed into the meat "every day for six weeks," she directed her readers to "hang them [the hams] in a chimney, or smoke-house, four weeks."[29]

McCulloch-Williams recalled "old southern smokehouses had for the most part earthen floors, trenched to make the smoke fires safe. . . . Whatever the floor, eternal vigilance was the price of safe bacon—you looked at the smokehouse fires first thing in the morning and last at night." It was also important to have the meat hanging high enough and to have merely smoke and not flames, so that the meat did not cook or develop a foul taste.[30]

Juliet Corson, who founded the New York Cooking School, remarked, "The salting and smoking of meat can be accomplished on a small scale, and sometimes is very desirable." Her 1885 cookbook, *Miss Corson's Practical American Cookery and Household Management,* included directions and illustrations for constructing a pickling or salting trough, a pickling tub, and a smoking closet or furnace. The smoking furnace was a wooden box with a stove underneath with a funnel connection to the closet. There was pipe at the top to allow the smoke to escape. "The closet is about three feet by five, with strong iron rods running through the top to hold the meat." Corson advised using oak for smoking meat, but she also admitted green hickory, maple, and corncobs "made good smoke." For a smoking closet, Corson instructed, a fire should first be made of charcoal, a layer of sawdust should be spread over that, and then bay leaves, dried thyme, and "twenty juniper-berries." The fire was to be kept smoldering and the herbs replaced every other day.[31]

There seems to be a renewed interest in curing and smoking meat, in addition to smoking it for flavor, as in barbecue. There are many types of smokers on sale, including electric ones with digital controls. Numerous websites provide instructions for building smokehouses and smokers.[32]

Smoking food at the table is a technique used by chefs who have been inspired by molecular gastronomy (see chapter 11) or by the New Nordic cuisine. This smoking is done with cool smoke, so the dishes are flavored with smoke but not cooked. They are often smoked under glass. One Spanish chef takes the smoke theme literally. He offers his patrons a dark chocolate "cigar" filled with smoke-infused ice cream. Dipping spices served on the side resemble ashes.[33]

NOTES

1. Nicholas Cresswell, *The Journal of Nicholas Cresswell, 1774–1777* (New York: Dial Press, 1924), 75–76.

2. Beverly Cox and Martin Jacobs, *Spirit of the Harvest: North American Indian Cooking* (New York: Stewart, Tabori, & Chang, 1991), 99, 121.

3. Harold McGee, *On Food and Cooking: The Science and Lore of the Kitchen,* rev. ed. (New York: Scribner, 2004), 236–37.

4. Cox and Jacobs, *Spirit of the Harvest,* 200.

5. Quoted in Laura Schenone, *A Thousand Years over a Hot Stove: A History of American Women Told through Food, Recipes, and Remembrances* (New York: Norton), 16. A photograph of a replicated 'Ksan smokehouse can be seen on the website of the 'Ksan Historical Village, http://www.ksan.org/html/village/unique.htm.

6. Quoted in James E. McWilliams, *A Revolution in Eating: How the Quest for Food Shaped America* (New York: Columbia University Press, 2005), 60.

7. Cox and Jacobs, *Spirit of the Harvest,* 76.

8. Todd S. Goodholme, ed., *Goodholme's Domestic Cyclopedia of Practical Information* (New York: C.A. Montgomery, 1885), 202, quoted in Sandra L. Oliver, *Saltwater Foodways: New Englanders and Their Food at Sea and Ashore in the 19th Century* (Mystic, CT: Mystic Seaport Museum, 1995), 343.

9. For a detailed history of cod, see Mark Kurlansky, *Cod: A Biography of the Fish That Changed the World* (New York: Walker and Co., 1997).

10. Oliver, *Saltwater Foodways,* 342–43.

11. Oliver, *Saltwater Foodways,* 343.

12. Oliver, *Saltwater Foodways,* 343.

13. Ann Pringle Harris, "Fare of the Country; Scottish Prize: Finnan Haddie," *New York Times,* December 6, 1987, http://www.nytimes.com/1987/12/06/travel/fare-of-the-country-scottish-prize-finnan-haddie.html?pagewanted=all&src=pm.

14. Claudia Roden, *The Book of Jewish Food: An Odyssey from Samarkand to New York* (New York: Knopf, 1996), 69. Many Jewish communities pair fish and cheese together, and fish is often considered to be dairy under Jewish dietary laws.

15. For more on Ossabaw Island pigs, see Ed Crews, "Ossabaw Island Pigs: Feral American Breed Provides 400-Year-Old Genetic Link between Past and Present," Colonial Williamsburg Foundation, http://www.history.org/foundation/journal/winter10/pigs.cfm.

16. For a thoughtful modern-day account of slaughtering pigs written by a chef, see Edward Lee, "Magnolia 610, Louisville, Kentucky," *Gastronomica, the Journal of Food and Culture* 12, no. 1 (Spring 2012), http://gastronomica.org/content_1201_lee.html.

17. Martha McCulloch-Williams, *Dishes and Beverages of the Old South* (New York: McBride, Nast, 1913), 39; Minnie C. Fox, *The Blue Grass Cook Book* (New York: Fox, Duffield, & Co, 1904), 98. McWilliams, *A Revolution in Eating*, 2.

18. David Shields, "The Search for the Cure: The Quest for the Superlative American Ham," *Common-Place* 8, no. 1 (October 2007), 2, http://www.common-place.org/vol-08/no-01/shields/.

19. Shields, "The Search for the Cure."

20. McCulloch-Williams, *Dishes and Beverages of the Old South*, 50.

21. Shields, "The Search for the Cure."

22. McCulloch-Williams, *Dishes and Beverages of the Old South*, 69.

23. For a discussion of how southern Jews have dealt with nonkosher foods, see Marcie Cohen Ferris, *Matzoh Ball Gumbo: Culinary Tales of the Jewish South* (Chapel Hill: University of North Carolina Press, 2005), esp. 11–13, and 254–55.

24. For more on food safety concerning ham, see "Ham and Food Safety," USDA Fact Sheet, http://www.fsis.usda.gov/Factsheets/Ham/index.asp.

25. Elaine Forman Crane, ed., *The Diary of Elizabeth Drinker* (Boston: Northeastern University Press, 1991), 1:579.

26. Fern L. Henry, *My Checkered Life: Luzena Stanley Wilson in Early California* (Nevada City, CA: Carl Mautz Publishing, 2003), 14–15.

27. http://seattlest.com/2009/02/26/baconnaise_on_the_daily_show.php; "Bacon Explosion: The BBQ Sausage Recipe of All Time," http://www.bbqaddicts.com/blog/recipes/bacon-explosion/. For bacon products, recipes, and everything about bacon, see bacontoday.com. A humorous play written by Cocol Bernal called *Bacon* was performed at Albright College in 2011. The story was about the attraction between a butcher known as The King of Bacon and a female television cooking show host and their love of bacon.

28. Quoted in Michael Olmert, "Smokehouses," *Colonial Williamsburg Journal* (Winter 2004–5), http://www.history.org/foundation/journal/winter04–05/smoke.cfm.

29. Lydia Maria Child, *The American Frugal Housewife*, with a new introduction by Jan Longone (Mineola, NY: Dover, 1999), 41–42.

30. McCulloch-Williams, *Dishes and Beverages of the Old South*, 48, 46.

31. Juliet Corson, *Miss Corson's Practical American Cookery and Household Management* (New York: Dodd, Mead, 1885), 325–29.

32. For example, see the blog Cowgirl's Country Life, http://cowgirls country.blogspot.com/2008/05/my-uds-so-far.html.

33. MolecularRecipes.com, http://www.molecularrecipes.com/category/smoking-2/.

CHAPTER 9
Steaming

Turns out you can steam anything in a normal stainless steel pot, with an inch of water and a lid. But only a bamboo steamer will retain water, so that it grows attractive mold.
In case you want to steam penicillin.

—Lisa Scottoline, "Chick Wit," *Philadelphia Inquirer,*
February 5, 2012

Steaming is a moist heat method of cooking in which food is cooked or heated over boiling water, broth, wine, or other liquids. It is often used to prepare fish and other delicate foods because they are not moved about as they might be when submerged in boiling or simmering fluids. As novelist and newspaper columnist Lisa Scottoline humorously observed in the above quote, food can be steamed in nearly any type of container, as long as the container can be safely placed within a pot that contains an inch of two of water, then covered, and heated. Steamed puddings, for example, are prepared by putting the pudding in a sealed mold, which is then placed in a pot of simmering water. This is usually done in an oven.

Many people associate steaming only with the steamed milk in cappuccino or lattes. To produce the beautiful steamed milk designs in coffeehouse drinks, baristas use expensive espresso machines with steaming wands. Less expensive equipment will steam and foam milk, but it will not produce the microfoam of the professional equipment. In either case, the milk for steamed milk should be cold and fresh—never reheated—and the pitcher should also be cold and large enough to hold the milk when it is steamed.

Mussels are often steamed in their shells with garlic and wine. Pictured here are steamed mussels with garlic and Spanish chorizo. (AP Photo/J. Scott Applewhite)

Meat, poultry, fish, and vegetables are often steamed in metal or bamboo steamer baskets. Bamboo steamers are usually used to make Asian dishes, including steamed dumplings. These steamers may have several compartments stacked on top of each other, and so this technique is sometimes called *compartment steaming*. The food that takes longer to cook is placed in the bottom container. The steamer compartments are all put in a wok that has an inch of two of water in it, and then covered and heated. In this way, a whole meal can be prepared.

Another method of steaming food is by sealing it in paper, foil, or leaves, then placing the sealed food in an oven. The food steams within the wrapping. Shellfish, such as mussels, can be similarly steamed within their own shells. Food can also be steamed in a microwave.

Although it might not be the choice for the environmentally conscious, steaming can also be done in the microwave using specially made plastic bags. The websites of these commercial products often have wide assortment of recipes, and some also include instructions for steaming without using the plastic bags. Consumers can also buy frozen vegetables that can be microwaved in their own bags. Of course, the frozen vegetables can also be placed in glass or ceramic containers that can be used in the microwave.[1]

The 1990 edition of *The Fannie Farmer Cookbook* offers an entire chapter on microwave cooking. Marion Cunningham, the author of the 13th edition, notes, "Steaming or moist-heat cooking is what the microwave does best, so to retain the moisture, cover the dish snugly with plastic wrap, venting the with a hole or two, or cover it with the microwave dish lid if it has one."[2] To prevent chemicals in the plastic from leaching into food when it is microwaved, only plastic wrap and containers that are labeled microwave safe should be used.

A staff chef for the *Cooking Lab of Modernist Cuisine,* the multivolume work based on molecular gastronomy (see chapter 11), explains that he had a problem coming up with a meat recipe that uses the microwave. In general meat does not cook very well in the microwave because it gets too dry. Then he remembered his mother's Six-Minute Microwaved Tilapia recipe, "which mimics a traditional Chinese steamed fish dish." He adapted her recipe for the book. The fish is steamed with ginger, scallions, and rice wine, then covered with fresh ginger, scallions, and cilantro, and drizzled with hot peanut oil, soy sauce, and sesame oil.[3]

Steaming is often considered a particularly healthy method of food preparation because there is no fat involved, as there is in frying, and nutrients do not leach into the water, as they do in boiling and simmering. For example, one source on healthy foods asserts,

> Brussels sprouts can provide you with some special cholesterol-lowering benefits if you will use a steaming method when cooking them. The fiber-related components in Brussels sprouts do a better job of binding together with bile acids in your digestive tract when they've been steamed. When this binding process takes place, it's easier for bile acids to be excreted, and the result is a lowering of your cholesterol levels.[4]

Even 19th-century cooks considered this a benefit. Juliet Corson, who founded the New York School of Cookery, indicated this in her 1885 cookbook, *Miss Corson's Practical American Cookery and Household Management.* She stated, "Steaming is an excellent way of cooking, calculated to prepare food for imparting all its nutriment to the system. It preserves all the flavor of food, and prevents its absorption of water when this is undesirable."[5]

VEGETABLES AND GRAINS

William Alcott, the early-19th-century reformer and advocate of vegetarianism, believed that boiling and steaming was the best method of preparing rice. His recipe for steamed rice directed the cook to boil the rice for "twelve minutes only." The recipe then stated to drain the water and put the container of uncovered rice in front of a fire, turning it frequently, until the water evaporated. He opined, "The rice will then be whole, dry and tender, with the additional benefit of being much better for the stomach than when reduced to a pulp in water."[6]

Many other grains and grainlike products cans be prepared in a similar way. Quinoa, for example, is an ancient food from South America that was rediscovered by Americans only a few decades ago. It has been a staple of people in the Andes region of South America for more than 5,000 years. The Inca considered it to be a sacred grain. For a brief period of time, Spanish conquerors even tried to suppress the cultivation of quinoa.

It is often called a supergrain because it is a complete protein and contains many other valuable nutrients, such as lysine, an essential amino acid, magnesium, folate, and phosphorus. Quinoa, however, is not actually a grain. It is the seed of a plant that is related to spinach and chard. Most recipes advise cooks to rinse and soak the quinoa to eliminate all traces of saponin, which produces a bitter taste. In most cases, commercially available quinoa has already been cleaned, but the rinsing and soaking will not hurt the finished product. The quinoa is then put into a pot of water (or broth), brought to a boil, simmered for about fifteen minutes, and then allowed to sit with the lid (to steam) for about five more minutes. The cooked quinoa can then be eaten with stews, added to casseroles and other dishes, or even eaten as a breakfast cereal.

Couscous is another grain that has only recently become familiar to most Americans, although it is a staple of North Africa. It is made from crushed semolina (the hard grain of hard wheat). Many authorities declare that it should always be steamed. In North Africa, couscous is traditionally prepared in a special steamer called a *couscoussier,* and it is steamed over stews. In the United States, couscous is generally sold in boxes, and it is often served in place of rice or pasta. The boxed couscous is precooked, and the instructions provided on the box usually call for boiling the couscous in water or broth. Cookbook author and columnist Martha Rose Shulman, however, advises readers to ignore these instructions. Instead, she says, the couscous should be reconstituted and steamed. Shulman's directions advise home cooks to mix couscous with a bit of salt, cover it with broth and water, and let it sit until the liquid is absorbed, stirring occasionally so that the couscous does not clump together. She then adds one to two table-spoons of olive oil and rubs the grains between her fingers. After this preparation, she then steams the couscous over a stew for about 20 to 30 minutes. Both quinoa and couscous are rather bland, but they pair well with spicy stews.[7]

Most 19th-century cookbooks recommended the preparation of veg-etables by boiling, stewing, frying, and baking. As the *Boston Cooking-School Cookbook* stated, "Vegetables should be washed in cold water, and cooked until soft in boiling, salted water." Nonetheless, the book included a recipe for Steamed Winter Squash, followed by a recipe for Boiled Winter Squash with the qualification "Unless squash is very dry, it is much better steamed than boiled."[8] William Alcott favored steaming potatoes, placing them over boiling water "for forty to sixty minutes, according to the size of the potatoes; watch them, and as soon as they are soft, (which you will know by trying them with a fork), take them out and peel them."[9]

Many modern-day American cooks prefer crisper, brighter colored vegetables that are lightly steamed or stir fried. Present-day recipes often feature vegetables such as broccoli or green beans that are steamed for a few minutes until just tender, then topped with a sauce or mixed with other ingredients. In a recent edition of *Fine Cooking* magazine, for ex-ample, there is a recipe for Pan-Steamed Asparagus with Lemon-Caper Mayonnaise. The recipe directions call for "pan-steaming" the aspara-gus until "crisp-tender," and then serving it with a sauce of mayonnaise mixed with garlic, capers, lemon zest, mustard, and pepper.[10]

FISH AND SHELLFISH

Fish and shellfish were staple foods for many of the tribes on both the East and West coasts of what is now the United States. Native Ameri-cans cooked fish in a variety of ways and also smoked it for later use (see chapter 10). Bruce Miller, a Skokomish ceremonial leader and chef, grew up on the Skokomish Reservation, located on the Puget Sound in Washington State. In the 1990s, he was one of the few Skokomish who still lived on a traditional diet of native foods. He re-membered the family feasts of traditional Skokomish foods his large, extended family enjoyed, and in a newspaper article he recalled the times when his grandparents "would leave us kids on the beach all day telling us that everything we needed was right there. We'd dig clams and gather oysters and mussels and crabs and build a fire to heat rocks, then bury all that food in seaweed and let it steam." Traditionally this steaming was done in a fire pit called an *imu*. For those who want to re-create the flavors in a modern kitchen, Miller adapted a recipe for Skokomish Steamed Seafood that included clams, oysters, and halibut fillets or steaks. A layer of seaweed is placed on the steamer rack within a large steamer pot. The shellfish is put on top of the seaweed, then covered with more seaweed. The halibut is placed on top of the second layer of seaweed, sprinkled with sea salt, covered, and steamed until the fish flakes and the shells of the clams and oysters have opened.[11]

Accounts from English observers and archaeological evidence indicates 17th-century Indians in what is now New England also steamed shellfish in pits dug into the ground. It is estimated that fish and shellfish made up 9 percent of the diet of New England Indians. Most often, women gathered shellfish on the beaches while the men of the tribe canoed in coastal waters, rivers, and lakes to catch fish, using hooks, nets, or arrows.[12]

According to some authorities, white New Englanders scorned the eating of clams in the 17th and 18th centuries because they associated them with scarce times and savages. Recipes for clams did not appear in American cookbooks until the 1830s, when Lydia Maria Child explained how to steam them "in their own water" in her *American Frugal Housewife*. After steaming the clams, she directed readers to remove them from the shells, strain the water, and cook the clams in it for 10 to 15 minutes. The broth could then be thickened with flour and water, and toasted bread or crackers could be added to it, along with "pepper, vinegar, and butter to your taste." The final result might have been an early version of New England clam chowder.[13]

Later in the 19th century, in *The Boston Cooking-School Cook Book*, Fannie Merritt Farmer admonished her readers to make certain the clams were alive when purchased and kept that way until they were cooked. She further cautioned home cooks to wash and scrub the clams thoroughly. With the preciseness for which she was noted, Farmer instructed readers to place the clams in a large pot, "allowing one-half cup hot water to four quarts clams; cover closely and steam until shells partially open, care being taken that they are not overdone." She suggested serving the clams with "individual dishes of melted butter," but she observed, "some prefer a few drops of lemon juice or vinegar added to the butter." Farmer also included a recipe for clams steamed on seaweed over hot rocks. She called this recipe Roasted Clams and noted that it was how clams "are served at a clam bake."[14]

Other types of shellfish and fish are often steamed. Mussels steamed in garlic and white wine is a classic French dish. Portuguese immigrants in Massachusetts steamed mussels in wine or dry sherry with garlic, chopped tomatoes, peppers, and saffron. Good crusty bread is a must for sopping up the delicious broth.[15] Mussels can also be steamed in beer, broth, or coconut milk. Shrimp can also be steamed in a number of ways. One easy method is to boil water or a mixture of water and beer, and to place shrimp sprinkled with Old Bay seasoning in a steamer basket over the boiling water.

Fanny L. Gillette included recipes for both steamed oysters and steamed fish in her popular cookbook, *The White House Cook Book,* first published in 1887, when she was almost 60 years old. Gillette had no connection with the White House, but Hugo Ziemann, who had been a White House steward and a well-known chef, coauthored later editions of the book.

Steamed fish is also a standard dish in Chinese kitchens and restaurants. For example, one present-day food blogger has a detailed entry with instructions on how to prepare perfect Restaurant Quality Steamed Fish. She includes a few secrets in her recipe. First, the fish should be stuffed with scallions, ginger, and cilantro, and it should also be placed on a bed of these ingredients (over medium heat, not a rolling boil); the herbs and cooking juices should be discarded. Instead, a mixture of mixture of soy, herbs, and spices is heated in the microwave for 30 seconds and poured over the cooked fish. Heated scallion-and-ginger-infused oil is poured on top just before serving.[16]

Steaming is especially effective for cooking thin fillets because they can cook quickly and evenly. Thicker pieces of fish, such as steaks or

---

STEAMED FISH

Secure the tail of the fish in its mouth, the body in a circle; pour over it half a pint of vinegar, seasoned with pepper and salt; let it stand an hour in a cool place; pour off the vinegar, and put it in a steamer over boiling water, and stem twenty minutes, or longer for large fish. When the meat easily separates from the bone it is done.

———

Source: Hugo Ziemann and Mrs. F. L. Gillette, *The White House Cook Book: A Comprehensive Cyclopedia of Information for the Home* (New York: Saalfield Publishing Co., 1913), 54.

whole fish, should be steamed over liquids that are not boiling to prevent overcooking the surface. One food scientist suggests keeping the temperature low to provide gentle cooking of fish by steaming it without the lid, so that the "steam and room air combine to give an effective cooking temperature of 150–160° F."[17]

CHICKEN AND TURKEY

Steamed chicken is not a dish often seen in modern American households. Chicken breasts are sometimes steamed in the microwave to use in other dishes or prepared for those who are dieting or who want or have to eat a bland diet. However, a Japanese recipe for Sake-Steamed Chicken, adapted and published in the *New York Times,* promises a succulent, flavorful dish. The whole chicken is rubbed with salt; then steamed over a mixture of sake and water for about one-to-one-and-one-half hours. After steaming, a sauce of soy sauce, ginger, and orange is poured over it.[18]

In the 19th century, it was not uncommon to find recipes for boiled or steamed chicken or turkey. Mary Lincoln, a teacher at the Boston Cooking School, included a recipe for Boiled or Steamed Turkey in her *Mrs. Lincoln's Boston Cook Book,* published in 1884. She advises her readers to rub the turkey with salt, pepper, and lemon juice. Then the legs and wings are trussed to the body and pinned in a cloth "to keep it whiter and preserve the shape." Lincoln comments, "Turkeys are much nicer steamed than boiled." In keeping with the style of bland, white food favored at this time, she suggests garnishing the turkey "with a border of boiled rice or macaroni, and pour part of the [oyster, celery, lemon, or caper] sauce over the fowl."[19]

PUDDINGS

> Now bring us some figgy pudding.
> —"We Wish You a Merry Christmas," a traditional English
> Christmas carol

Although unfamiliar to most 21st-century Americans, boiled and steamed puddings were very popular with early Americans in both the North and South, and they continued to be popular through the 19th century.[20] Part of the traditional English cookery brought by colonists to the United States, puddings have a long history. Early puddings contained meat, suet, or marrow and other ingredients. They were placed in an animal's intestine and boiled. Black puddings contained blood; white puddings were made of chicken or veal.[21]

By the 17th century, cloth pudding bags were being used in place of animal intestines. (Boiled puddings are also discussed in chapter 3.) In the middle of the 19th century, many cooks began using a metal steamer to prepare their puddings. Juliet Corson stated, "The advantage of steaming puddings over boiling them is that they are less likely to be watery if they are steamed." She explained that any of the recipes in her cookbook for boiled puddings could be steamed instead, "but a little longer time must be allowed for cooking them, and care must be taken to have the cover of the steamer very tight, in order to prevent the escape of steam."[22]

In 2007, Michele Norris, host of NPR's popular show *All Things Considered*, invited baker Dorie Greenspan to explain what figgy pudding is and how it is prepared. Greenspan explained that figgy pudding, also called Christmas pudding or plum pudding, is similar to a fruitcake, "but [figgy pudding] is steamed; it's chockablock with dried fruit; it's so boozy … it's delicious." Although English Puritans banned Christmas revelry, Christmas puddings did not die away. Greenspan's version uses figs, rum, brandy, raisins, and spices. She prepares the pudding in an 8-to-10-cup capacity tube or Bundt pan that is then placed within a large stockpot or lobster pot for the steaming. After steaming, the pudding can be flamed before serving for a dramatic presentation. If the pudding is not to be served immediately, it can be wrapped and refrigerated, and then resteamed before serving.[23]

Most 19th-century cookbooks contain numerous recipes for boiled and steamed puddings, although some, such as Christmas puddings, were made only once a year. In 1893, the Board of Lady Managers of the World's Columbian Exposition, a world's fair held in Chicago, contributed recipes for a cookbook. The plan was to sell the cookbook to raise money to provide funds for poor women who wanted to attend the fair. Each recipe included the contributor's name and signature, and some also wrote brief descriptions of their entries. Mrs. Rollin A. Edgerton, of Arkansas, contributed her recipe for Graham Christmas Pudding, with the following note: "The Christmas pudding which I add was served up this Christmas on my table and pronounced delicious. Dyspeptics need not fear this 'Plum Pudding,' and it is rich enough to please the most fastidious. Wishing your philanthropic efforts every success, I am, Mrs. Rollin A. Edgerton." Unlike most Christmas puddings, this one does not include alcohol.

GRAHAM CHRISTMAS PUDDING

Beat two eggs; take one-half cup of sweet milk; one half-cup of molasses, in which dissolve one-half teaspoon of soda; a lump of butter the size of an egg; one cup of Graham flour (don't sift); two cups of flour, in which a cup of stoned raisins are well rubbed; one small teaspoon of salt; spice with cinnamon, cloves and nutmeg, one teaspoonful all together. Then steam two hours and serve with a hard sauce of butter and fine sugar creamed together, with one well beaten egg and grated nutmeg as finish. Wholesome, delicious, and extremely simple to prepare.

Source: Carrie V. Shuman, comp., *Favorite Dishes: A Columbian Autograph Souvenir Cookery Book* (Chicago: R. R. Donnelly and Sons, 1893), 134.

Nevertheless, Sylvester Graham, the dietary reformer who advocated a bland diet based on whole grains and vegetables without stimulating spices or alcohol, would not have approved of it because it is spiced with cinnamon, cloves, and nutmeg and is served with a rich hard sauce. The use of "Graham" in the title most likely refers only to the inclusion of whole-wheat flour, sometimes called Graham flour, in the recipe.[24]

NOTES

1. Ziploc, http://www.ziploc.com/Recipes/Pages/default.aspx.
2. Marion Cunningham, *The Fannie Farmer Cookbook,* 13th ed. (New York: Knopf, 1990), 449.
3. "Microwaved Tilapia"; the website also has a video demonstration, http://modernistcuisine.com/cook/recipe-library/microwaved-tilapia/.
4. "What's New and Beneficial about Brussels Sprouts," The World's Healthiest Foods, George Mateljan Foundation, http://whfoods.org/genpage.php?pfriendly=1&tname=foodspice&dbid=10.
5. Juliet Corson, *Miss Corson's Practical American Cookery and Household Management* (New York: Dodd, Mead, & Co., 1885), 47.
6. William A. Alcott, *The Young House-keeper or Thoughts on Food and Cookery* (Boston: George W. Light, 1838), 406.
7. Martha Rose Shulman, "Couscous: Just Don't Call It Pasta," *New York Times,* February 24, 2009, http://www.nytimes.com/2009/02/24/health/23recipehealth.html.
8. Fannie Merritt Farmer, *The Boston Cooking-School Cook Book* (Boston: Little, Brown, & Co., 1896), 269, 270.

9. Alcott, *The Young House-keeper,* 421.

10. "Pan-Steamed Asparagus with Lemon-Caper Mayonnaise," *Fine Cooking,* April–May 2012, 73.

11. Schuyler Ingle, "The Time of Food: Preserving the Past: Dining with a Living Treasure," *Los Angeles Times,* November 24, 1991, http://articles.latimes.com/print/1991–11–24/food/fo-378_1_happy-time; Beverly Cox and Martin Jacobs, *Spirit of the Harvest: North American Indian Cooking* (New York: Stewart, Tabori, & Chang, 1991), 222–23.

12. Keith Stavely and Kathleen Fitzgerald, *America's Founding Food: The Story of New England Cooking* (Chapel Hill: University of North Carolina Press, 2004), 78.

13. Lydia Maria Child, *The American Frugal Housewife,* with a new introduction by Jan Logone (Mineola, NY: Dover, 1999), replication of the 29th ed. of *The American Frugal Housewife* (New York: Samuel S. & William Wood, 1844), 58–59.

14. Farmer, *The Boston Cooking-School Cook Book,* 165.

15. For one recipe, see "Portuguese Mussel Stew," in *Moosewood Restaurant Daily Special: More than 275 Recipes for Soups, Stews, Salads, and Extras,* by the Moosewood Collective (New York: Clarkson Potter, 1999), 169.

16. "Chinese Steamed Fish Recipe," *Steamy Kitchen,* 2007, http://steamykitchen.com/132-chinese-steamed-fish.html.

17. Harold McGee, *On Food and Cooking: The Science and Lore of the Kitchen,* rev. ed. (New York: Scribner, 2004), 216.

18. "Sake-Steamed Chicken with Ginger and Scallions, Adapted from Harris Salat, *New York Times,* March 4, 2011, http://www.nytimes.com/2011/03/09/dining/09apperex.html?ref=dining.

19. Mary Johnson Bailey Lincoln, *Mrs. Lincoln's Boston Cook Book: What to Do and What Not to Do in Cooking* (Boston: Roberts Brothers, 1884), 257.

20. Damon Lee Fowler, *Classical Southern Cooking* (Layton, UT: Gibbs Smith, 2008), 366.

21. Karen Hess, ed., *Martha Washington's Booke of Cookery* (New York: Columbia University Press, 1981), 101–11.

22. Corson, *Miss Corson's Practical American Cookery,* 457–58.

23. "Now, You Can Bring Us Some Figgy Pudding," *All Things Considered,* NPR, December 18, 2007, http://www.npr.org/templates/story/story.php?storyId=17356371.

24. "Graham Christmas Pudding," in *Favorite Dishes: A Columbian Autograph Souvenir Cookery Book,* comp. Carrie V. Shuman (Chicago: R. R. Donnelly and Sons, 1893), 134.

CHAPTER 10
Stewing

This was after stew. But then, so is everything. When the first
man crawled out of the slime and went to make his home on
land, what he had for dinner that night was stew.
                              —William Goldman, *The Princess Bride*

Stewing is a moist heat method of preparing food by slowly simmering meat, poultry, fish, and/or vegetables in a liquid until they are
tender. Stew is not quite as old as William Goldman claimed it to be
in the above quote, but stewing is an ancient technique for preparing food. It is likely that before the invention of pottery or bronze,
prehistoric people used large shells or animal stomachs as cooking
containers to boil food. Later documents describe stews prepared this
way. For example, Herodotus wrote of nomad Scythians in the fifth
century BCE who "put the flesh into an animal's paunch, mix water
with it, and boil it like that over the bone-fire." American Plains Indian tribes also used an animal hide or stomach as a pot in which
to stew game. Heated stones were placed in the paunch to cook
the food.[1] Stews can be found in most cuisines of the world. *De Re
Coquinaria (The Art of Cooking),* the oldest surviving collection of
ancient Roman recipes (often called *Apicius* and attributed incorrectly
to Marcus Gavius Apicius) contains several recipes for stews.

Although the word *stew* might frequently conjure images of steaming pots of beef, chicken, or fish stew, it can also refer to vegetable
dishes, such as ratatouille. Sometimes meat, vegetables, and fruit are
stewed together. Such combinations are found in a variety of dishes
from Moroccan tagines to German veal stew with dried pear.[2]

Irish stew was traditionally made with mutton in 18th-century Ireland. In America, it was often prepared with other types of meat, such as beef or veal. The meat is usually combined with root vegetables, and it is often cooked until the separate ingredients break down, forming a thick broth. (AP Photo/Larry Crowe)

WHAT IS A STEW?

To some extent, the term *stew* is open to interpretation. *Stew* is both a noun and a verb, and perhaps that is why there are so many variations in what it means. In fact, *stew* was used almost exclusively as a verb in 17th- and 18th-century recipes.[3] Even today, tomatoes, vegetables, or dried fruit are often prepared by stewing, but a dish such as stewed tomatoes is not called usually called a stew—unless other ingredients are added to it, and it is served as a main course. As discussed in chapter 4, the techniques of stewing and braising overlap, and so some, but not all stews, are braised. To add to the confusion, stews and soups have much in common. Many stews are simply thickened soups. Or soups are stews that have been thinned with water, broth, or milk. Chowders and gumbos, for example, can be classified as soups or stew.

Sometimes stew has been made by people who have combined whatever is on hand in an attempt to stretch meager supplies. "One of our dishes was composed of anything that we could get hold of," recalled Civil War soldier Alfred Bellard. "Pork or beef, salt or fresh, was cut up with potatoes, tomatoes, crackers, and garlic, seasoned with pepper and salt, and stewed. This we called Hish and Hash or Hell fired stew."[4]

Similarly, a World War I–era cookbook exhorts housewives to "[h]ave stews at least once a week. They can be made appetizing and in varied ways. Select some particular vegetable for the chief flavor, subordinating the others to it. Thicken it one week with rice, the next with barley, next with macaroni." Curiously, although the book includes many recipes for meat substitutes, meatless soups, and economical ways to cook or extend pieces of meat, it does not actually include any stew recipes.[5]

Many stews are associated with particular regions of the United States. Gumbo and chowder, for example, discussed in chapter 3, are usually associated with Louisiana and New England, respectively. Both Georgia and Virginia claim Brunswick Stew as their own. This stew is often made with leftovers or available meat, such as squirrel, along with bacon, corn, lima beans, tomatoes, and potatoes. Booyah is a thick chicken and vegetable stew that is popular in Wisconsin. Cioppino is a fish stew that Italian fishermen made popular in San Francisco.

Many stews require a long simmering time. Cholent, the traditional Jewish Sabbath stew, is required to cook far longer than most stews. Those who follow traditional Jewish customs do not work on the Sabbath—sundown Friday night to sundown Saturday night. Cooking, building a fire, or turning on an oven is considered work. Thus, cholent was prepared on Friday, before the start of the Sabbath, and then allowed to simmer overnight to be eaten as the midday meal on Saturday.

In medieval Europe—and even later—women would seal their pots of cholent with a flour and water paste before taking them to the village baker's oven to cook overnight. The men of the town, along with the children, collected the cooked cholent on the way home from synagogue. Cholent, as well as some other traditional Jewish dishes, is being revived in the United States by cooks who want to reclaim their heritage by preparing the types of food eaten by their ancestors in Eastern Europe.[6]

Stews have been popular with many immigrant groups because the slow cooking of such dishes is suited to—in fact, often demands—the use of cheaper cuts of meat.[7] The slow simmering of the less choice pieces of meat, fish, or poultry with vegetables and spices can produce a mouth-watering aroma and taste. Such dishes, developed because of dietary, cultural, or monetary restrictions, often later become the longed-for treats, the comfort food and tangible representations of a bygone time.

Throughout the centuries, immigrant groups coming to America have attempted to re-create the dishes of their homelands. Often, however, the needed ingredients are unavailable or too expensive. Moreover, in the early-20th century, dietitians and reformers frequently looked upon the food choices and dishes of immigrants with alarm and disdain. Many of these reformers and educators believed spicy foods were dangerous and unhealthy. Dietitian Bertha M. Wood wrote a cookbook that conveyed many of the then-prominent beliefs and stereotypes about immigrants to the United States. Yet she also expressed some sympathy toward the various groups of people who arrived, often penniless, in America. For example, in contrast to the opinion often given by other Americans that immigrants "should learn to eat American food if they are to live here," she countered, "[W]hen a person is ill and needs a special diet, it is no time to teach him to eat new foods. It is like hitting a person when he is down. Our milk soups are nutritious, but so are theirs; why not learn what they are and prescribe them. The same is true of other foods."[8]

Wood's cookbook examined the foods and nutritional practices and needs of several different immigrant groups. Each chapter includes recipes, sometimes modified to present "healthier" options. This Bean Stew (Greek) is from the chapter on the Near East.

Home economists of the late-19th and early-20th centuries also believed that American food would help to unite the nation. As one scholar notes, "The Italian garlic, furry Bohemian mushrooms, Jewish

---

BEAN STEW (GREEK)

3/4 quart shelled beans (fresh)	1/4 teaspoon salt
2 cups tomatoes (canned)	1/4 teaspoon pepper
1 small onion	4 tablespns. olive oil
1/4 cup water	
3/4 cup lamb (cut into small pieces)	

Put meat in hot oil and fry until nearly cooked, adding onion, chopped fine. Add tomato, beans, water, salt, and pepper. Cover well and cook over a rather slow fire.

———

Source: Bertha M. Wood, *Foods of the Foreign-Born in Relation to Health* (Boston: Whitcomb & Barrows, 1922), 81.

gefilte fish, the unleavened bannocks of the Indians, Mexican chilies, Asian rice, the pork and cornbread of blacks—all these were reminders of settling differences." The cooking school administrators and cookbook authors of this time period, such as Fannie Farmer, advocated "dainty" and bland food. They favored covering vegetables and meats with white sauce to such an alarming degree that "some critics have blamed white sauce for encouraging a conservative American food style that favored bland and creamy." Typical of these dishes were stewed celery, stewed mushrooms, and stewed mushrooms in cream, which Fannie Farmer suggested serving over "small pieces of dry toast."[9]

NATIVE AMERICAN STEWS

Most reports of 17th-, 18th-, and early-19th-century Native American stewed dishes come from the accounts of white explorers and travelers. Explorer James W. Biddle, for example, recalled a dish he encountered during his travels in early-19th-century Wisconsin. "The Indian women used to make a favorite dish of wild rice, corn and fish, boiled together, and called *Tassimanonny*. I remember it to this day as an object of early love."[10]

Native American tribes in the 17th-century Chesapeake area ate a well-balanced diet based on the staples of squash, beans, and corn, supplemented by berries and nuts, roots, shellfish, fish, and game. Often a pot of stew simmered all day, the ingredients changing daily, depending on what was foraged or shot. Usually by the afternoon, meat or fish that had been killed or collected could be added to the stewpot. One scholar notes, "[S]had, herring, and mussels were especially popular catches for the Chesapeake Native Americans." Greens that had been gathered that day were added to the stew, then the stew was thickened with cornmeal or tuckahoe, a tuber that grows in marshy areas.[11]

A remarkable study done by Gilbert Livingstone Wilson in the early-20th century focuses on Buffalo Bird Woman of the Hidatsa Indian tribe. In this work, she described to Wilson the agricultural and social practices of her tribe, and she discussed many of the foods they ate and how they were prepared. At one point, she said her family thought Four-Vegetables-Mixed, which combined beans, dried squash, and meal made from parched sunflower seeds and pounded dried corn, was "our very best dish." Her detailed description below describes exactly how they prepared the dish. Although she did not use standard American measurements, Buffalo Bird Woman did provide very precise directions on how much of each ingredient was used and how the dish was served.

FOUR-VEGETABLES-MIXED

Sunflower meal was used in making a dish that we called do'patsa-makihi'ke, or four-vegetables-mixed; from do'patsa, four things; and makihi'ke, mixed or put together. Four-vegetables-mixed we thought our very best dish.

To make this dish, enough for a family of five, I did as follows:

I put a clay pot with water on the fire.

Into the pot I threw one double-handful of beans. This was a fixed quantity; I put in just one double-handful whether the family to be served was large or small; for a larger quantity of beans in this dish was apt to make gas on one's stomach.

When we dried squash in the fall we strung the slices upon strings of twisted grass, each seven Indian fathoms long; an Indian fathom is the distance between a woman's two hands outstretched on either side. From one of these seven-fathom strings I cut a piece as long as from my elbow to the tip of my thumb; the two ends of the severed piece I tied together, making a ring; and this I dropped into the pot with the beans.

When the squash slices were well cooked I lifted them out of the pot by the grass string into a wooden bowl. With a horn spoon I chopped and mashed the cooked squash slices into a mass, which I now returned to the pot with the beans. The grass string I threw away.

To the mess I now added four or five double-handfuls of mixed meal, of pounded parched sunflower seed and pounded parched corn. The whole was boiled for a few minutes more, and was ready for serving.

I have already told how we parched sunflower seed; and that I used two or three double-handfuls of seed to a parching. I used two parchings of sunflower seed for one mess of four-vegetables-mixed. I also used two parchings of corn; but I put more corn into the pot at a parching than I did of sunflower seed.

Pounding the parched corn and sunflower seed reduced their bulk so that the four parchings, two of sunflower seed and two of corn, made but four or five double-handfuls of the mixed meal.

Four-vegetables-mixed was eaten freshly cooked; and the mixed corn-and-sunflower meal was made fresh for it each time. A little alkali salt might be added for seasoning, but even this was not usual. No other seasoning was used. Meat was not boiled with the mess, as the sunflower seed gave sufficient oil to furnish fat.

Four-vegetables-mixed was a winter food; and the squash used in its making was dried, sliced squash, never green, fresh squash.

The clay pot used for boiling this and other dishes was about the size of an iron dinner pot, or even larger. For a large family, the pot might be as much as thirteen or fourteen inches high. . . .

When a mess of four-vegetables-mixed was cooked, I did not remove the pot from the coals, but dipped out the vegetables with a mountain-sheep horn spoon, into wooden bowls.

Source: Gilbert Livingstone Wilson, ed., Buffalo Bird Woman's Garden Recounted by Maxi'diwiac (Buffalo Bird Woman) of the Hidatsa Indian Tribe (ca. 1839–1932 (1917) 21, http://digital.library.upenn.edu/women/buffalo/garden/garden.html#IV.

Nomadic tribes often dried food to make it easier to carry with them. Such foods could be eaten as the tribes moved. When there was time and opportunity, however, buffalo jerky or posole could be combined with additional ingredients to make stews. Posole is a type of hominy; the term also refers to a spicy, popular southwestern Indian stew using the ingredient posole along with pork and chilies. During Christmas and New Year's Eve, posole is served in American Indian, Hispanic, and Anglo homes throughout New Mexico and Arizona. Most who prepare the dish prefer using posole made from blue corn, but white and yellow corn are also used.[12]

Most American Indian tribes made stews of some sort from the game or fish they caught. For example, northwestern Indian game hunters prepared stews made from elk. Various tribes used different methods to hunt these large animals. Some tribes wore snowshoes, permitting them to pursue elk across the snow. Others trapped the elk, which the Shawnee called *wapiti,* or pale deer, by using dogs or by driving them through mountain passes or into rivers. Often the hunters drank the blood of the deer after the hunt. A traditional elk stew sometimes included *wapato,* a tuber that is similar to a Jerusalem artichoke and wild parsnips.[13]

SUCCOTASH

Succotash is truly an American dish. Pilgrims and Indians ate succotash in 17th-century Plymouth, Massachusetts, but it was not the vegetable mixture of sweet corn, lima beans, and bits of red and green pepper that most present-day Americans picture. The succotash eaten then, later known as Plymouth succotash or winter succotash, was a stew of corn (maize) or hominy (dried corn kernels treated with lye), beans, and fresh or dried meat and/or fish. Eastern Native American tribes commonly kept pots of succotash simmering over the fire and added to them as needed.

Daniel Gookin, a 17th-century Puritan magistrate from Cambridge, Massachusetts, made one of the earliest references to the mixture in his 1674 manuscript *Historical Collections of the Indians in New England*. Although he does not use the word, *succotash,* the mixture he described was a mixture of boiled beans, maize, and other ingredients. "Their food is generally boiled maize, or Indian corn, mixed with kidney-beans, or sometimes without. Also they frequently boil in this pottage fish and flesh of all sorts, either new taken or dried, as shads, eels, alewives or a kind of herring . . . also venison, beaver, bear's flesh, moose, otters, raccoon." Gookin most likely meant that the Indians added what was available, and not that these ingredients were necessarily added together. He also mentioned that the Indians sometimes added Jerusalem artichokes, groundnuts, and other roots and that they sometimes added dried and ground acorns or chestnuts to thicken the pottage.[14]

Historians of New England food and foodways have commented on Gookin's use of the term *pottage,* which links the Native American mixture to the ubiquitous English yeoman's dish. The typical diet of 17th-century New England colonists consisted of stews of meat and vegetables that simmered over the fire all day long. Succotash, some scholars assert, was "the most widely distributed . . . dish of the potage type" in New England, if not throughout the American colonies.[15] By the 19th century, however, recipes for succotash sometimes included meat, but frequently did not, because succotash evolved into a vegetable side dish, rather than the main dish.[16]

References to succotash range throughout American popular culture. James Fennimore Cooper mentions it in his 1826 novel *The Last of the Mohicans,* as does Harriet Beecher Stowe in her 1869 book *Old Time Folks.* The early-19th-century Rhode Island Quaker, shepherd, manufacturer, and author Thomas Robinson Hazard recalled, "[S]uccotash, the Indian for dried sweet-corn and beans, which my grandmother used to always caution me about eating too much of, as she had once known a naughty boy who burst asunder in the middle from having eaten too much heartily of the tempting dish." And, of course, Sylvester the Cat of Warner Brothers cartoon fame frequently exclaimed, "Sufferin' Succotash" as some misfortune befell him.[17]

BEEF STEW

Beef stew has gone through countless variations in American cookery. Many Americans are familiar with *boeuf bourguignon,* the elaborate beef stew made famous by Julia Child in *Mastering the Art of French Cooking* (first published in 1961), and then made popular again with the movie *Julie and Julia,* Nora Ephron's 2009 movie about blogger Julie Powell's quest to prepare every recipe in Child's cookbook. The recipe calls for braised cubes of beef and includes wine and bacon, with garnishes of braised pearl onions and sautéed mushrooms.

A recipe To Stew Beefe Steaks in Martha Washington's *Booke of Cookery* consists of layers of beef slices (with fat) flavored with vinegar, mint, savory, parsley, onions, and an anchovy. Water was added to the mixture, and the dish was then simmered in a tightly covered container over a low heat. The directions for this stew and others of this era often direct the cook to let the stew simmer between two dishes. Chafing dishes were often used for this purpose. At least a few Americans owned chafing dishes imported from England in the early-18th century, although they would have been too expensive for most colonists. Chafing dishes, which were usually made of brass and set on tripods to make them portable, were filled with hot coals. The stew was placed in one dish, covered with another dish, and then set within the chafing dish to simmer.[18]

The beef stew recipe contributed by reformer Josephine P. Holland to Hattie A. Burr's 1896 *Woman Suffrage Cook Book* was also a layered

BEEF STEW

Three pounds beef (round) cut inch pieces, four or five onions peeled and sliced. Put in a layer of onions. Dredge well with salt, pepper and flour. Repeat until all the meat and onions are used. Add two quarts boiling water, and simmer three hours. Then add one quart of potatoes peeled and sliced, and three tablespoons flour mixed with one cup of cold water. Simmer thirty minutes longer.

———

Source: Hattie A. Burr, *The Woman Suffrage Cook Book* (Boston: Hattie A. Burr, 1886), 24.

dish. It was a rather bland preparation, lacking both the spices of 17th- and early-18th-century dishes and the wine and flavorings of Child's 20th-century recipe.

SON OF A BITCH STEW

After the Civil War, cattle herders spent much time and effort driving cattle from ranches in Texas to northern markets. The popular Abilene Trail went from the Rio Grande to Abilene, Kansas. From there, cattle could be shipped east on the Union Pacific Railroad. According to one authority, a herding crew consisted of about 11 men, including the trail boss, cowboys, wrangler, and cook. She further asserts, "[T]he most important member of the crew, however, was the cook, who often became confidant and mediator for the entire crew, who depended on him for nourishment."[19] These trail cooks performed their own special magic in the mobile vehicles known as chuck wagons. Many of these cowboy cooks were black, often freed or former slaves. Because of their positions, they held some degree of respect and authority, even with white cowboys—because few wanted to anger the person who was responsible for feeding them on the trail.

One popular dish prepared by cowboy cooks was known as Son of a Bitch Stew or Son of a Gun Stew. The stew was made after a nursing calf was killed. One scholar notes, "The essential item that gave Son of a Gun Stew its distinctive taste was the young calf's 'marrow gut' (a tube connecting the two stomachs of a calf that is filled with a marrowlike substance when a calf is on a milk diet)." The stew included the heart, brains, liver, and tongue, as well as the rest of flesh of the calf. Some cooks included onions, as well.[20]

CHILI

An examination of American stews would not be complete without a discussion of chili. Chili probably originated in what is now Texas in the mid-19th century. The dish was usually made of beef, cubed or ground, that was cooked in fat, then simmered with red chilies and other spices, such as cumin and oregano, and water or some other liquid. Sometimes onions and tomatoes were added. Traditionally, Texas chili does not include beans.

Although many Texans cling to the traditional beef, no beans, version, chili has many variations, including vegetarian versions. Recipes that do use beans most often call for pinto or kidney beans, but black beans, white beans, and even lima beans are sometimes included in chili recipes. There are regional versions of chili, as well. In Cincinnati, for example, Five-Way Chili is a favorite. This dish consists of spaghetti topped with a chili sauce layer, then a layer of kidney beans, and finally layers of chopped onions and shredded cheddar cheese. In areas of the Midwest, Chili Mac, or chili with pasta, is frequently served.

Between 1902 and 1917, the *Los Angeles Times* published a series of cookbooks that collected the recipes entered in cooking contests held by the newspaper. These recipes demonstrate how Mexican dishes and flavors influenced Southern California cooks and homemakers. There are many chili recipes in the collection, as well as recipes for a variety of Spanish stews. Typically, the recipes include pieces of beef that are fried, chopped onion, about one tablespoon of chili powder, beans, and tomatoes. Some of the recipes also included potatoes, and many call for chili peppers rather than chili powder. Mrs. Shook's recipe below states that the beef should be boiled, minced, and then browned in a skillet.

Chili became very popular in the 1930s, and chili joints opened throughout the country. As the country weathered the Great Depression, the Sunday Night Supper emerged as a popular, inexpensive way

---

NO. 13. CHILI CON CARNE

Mrs. Jeff D. Shook, New York street, Garvanza, Cal,—Take a good-sized piece of soup meat (not a soup bone) boil till thoroughly tender; take out of water; mince very fine; have ready two good-sized onions, also minced fine. Put into a skillet a tablespoonful of butter, and after having coated the meat with flour, turn same with the onions into the skillet and brown. Add to it the water in which the meat was boiled and one teacup of bayou beans that have been boiled done; boil slowly for about three hours. Just before taking from the fire, add salt to taste and a heaping tablespoon of chili powder or sufficient to make it hot; must be rich and hot with pepper to be good. On a cool, damp evening, this is a most palatable dish.

Source: *Los Angeles Times Cook Book-No. 2: One Thousand Toothsome Cooking and Other Recipes Including Old-Time California, Spanish, and Mexican Dishes, Recipes of Famous Pioneer Spanish Settlers* (Times-Mirror Company, 1905?), 3.

to entertain friends. At these suppers, hosts and guests usually ate one-dish meals that were served family style. Dishes such as Welsh rarebit, creamed chipped beef, and waffles were very popular. Chili, also called chili con carne, was another favorite meal at Sunday Night suppers.[21]

Since it first became popular, chili has had legions of fans, and many are not only passionate, they are devoted. According to legend, Jesse James enjoyed the chili at one chili joint so much that he spared the town and did not rob its bank. While filming *Cleopatra* in Rome in the 1960s, Elizabeth Taylor paid for Chasen's Restaurant in Los Angeles to airlift their famous chili to her. The same restaurant also delivered chili to Clark Gable when he was in the hospital. The Chili Appreciation Society International (founded in 1951) is an organization whose "mission is to promote chili and raise money for charity." The organization sponsors chili cookoffs throughout the country, and its original motto was, "The aroma of good chili should generate rapture akin to a lover's kiss."[22]

Tabasco, a brand of pepper sauce manufactured by the McIlhenny Company, includes on its website a section about chili cookoffs. It provides history and recipes (all using Tabasco brand products, of course), and offers advice on how to host a chili competition. According to the site, after the 1968 Terlingua, Texas, chili cookoff, which was the first documented chili cookoff, the idea of chili cookoffs "spread like good gossip."[23]

If one can gauge how culturally relevant something is by its appearance on the television show, *The Simpsons,* then chili cookoffs make the list. In 1997, during the eighth season of *The Simpsons,* the show featured an episode in which Homer goes to the annual Springfield Chili Cookoff, where he eats Guatemalan insanity peppers. The peppers cause him to hallucinate, and he encounters a space coyote played by Johnny Cash. Perhaps it is best to avoid Guatemalan insanity peppers when preparing chili, and stick with the more traditional chili peppers instead.[24]

NOTES

1. Reay Tannahill, *Food in History* (New York: Three Rivers Press, 1988), 14–16; Beverly Cox and Martin Jacobs, *Spirit of the Harvest: North American Indian Cooking* (New York: Stewart, Tabori, & Chang, 1991), 124.

2. The recipe for Veal Stew with Dried Pear is included in Jane Ziegelman, *97 Orchard: An Edible History of Five Immigrant Families in One New York Tenement* (New York: Smithsonian Books, 2010), 11.

3. Keith Stavely and Kathleen Fitzgerald, *Northern Hospitality: Cooking by the Book in New England* (Amherst: University of Massachusetts Press, 2011), 136.

4. David Donald, ed., *Gone for Soldier: The Civil War Memoirs of Private Alfred Bellard* (Boston: Little, Brown, 1975), 122, quoted in William C. Davis, *A Taste for War: The Culinary History of the Blue and the Gray* (Lincoln: University of Nebraska Press, 2003), 25.

5. *Twentieth Century Club War Time Cook Book* (Pittsburgh: Pierpont, Siviter, 1918), 52.

6. Claudia Rodan, *The Book of Jewish Food: An Odyssey from Samarkand to New York* (New York: Knopf, 2003), 146–49; Joan Nathan, "To Revive Jewish Dishes, Some Cooks Look to the Shtetl," *New York Times,* November 23, 2010, http://www.nytimes.com/2010/11/24/dining/24hanukkah.html?ref=dining.

7. For a discussion of corned beef and cabbage and Irish American history, see Ziegelman, *97 Orchard,* 77–82.

8. Bertha M. Wood, *Foods of the Foreign-Born in Relation to Health,* Foreword by Michael M. Davis, Jr. (Boston: Whitcomb & Barrows, 1922), 3.

9. Laura Schenone, *A Thousand Years over a Hot Stove: A History of American Women Told through Food, Recipes, and Remembrances* (New York: Norton, 2003), 251–53; Fannie Merritt Farmer, *The Boston Cooking-School Cook Book* (Boston: Little, Brown, & Co., 1896), 260, 273–74.

10. James W. Biddle, *Recollections of Green Bay in 1816–17,* Collections of the State Historical Society of Wisconsin, 1:49–63, 1855, http://lincoln.lib.niu.edu/file.php?file=biddle.html.

11. James E. McWilliams, *A Revolution in Eating: How the Quest for Food Shaped America* (New York: Columbia University Press, 2005), 96–99.

12. Cox and Jacobs, *Spirit of the Harvest,* 177.

13. Cox and Jacobs, *Spirit of the Harvest,* 219.

14. Daniel Gookin, *Historical Collections of the Indians in New England* (1792), Special Collections Publications. Paper 13, p. 150, http://digitalcommons.uri.edu/sc_pubs/13.

15. Quoted in Keith Stavely and Kathleen Fitzgerald, *America's Founding Food: The Story of New England Cooking* (Chapel Hill: University of North Carolina Press, 2004), 40–41.

16. Stavely and Fitzgerald, *Northern Hospitality,* 118–19.

17. Thomas Robinson Hazard, *The Jonny-Cake Papers of "Shepherd Tom": Together with Reminiscences of Narragansett Schools of Former Days* (Boston: Merrymount Press, 1915), 51.

18. Karen Hess, ed., *Martha Washington's Booke of Cookery* (New York: Columbia University Press, 1981), 24, 40, 78–79.

19. Jessica B. Harris, *High on the Hog: A Culinary Journey from Africa to America* (New York: Bloomsbury, 2011), 146.

20. Harris, *High on the Hog,* 146, 147, 149.

21. Sylvia Lovegren, *Fashionable Food: Seven Decades of Food Fads* (Chicago: University of Chicago Press, 2005), 44–58.

22. Lovegren, *Fashionable Food*, 59–60; The Chili Appreciation Society International, Inc., http://www.chili.org/mission.html.

23. Sandra Day, "Chili Cookoff," http://www.tabasco.com/taste_tent/menu_planning/chili_hosting.cfm.

24. *The Simpsons*, "El Viaje Misterioso de Nuestro Jomer" (The mysterious voyage of Homer), first broadcast January 5, 1997. For information on chili peppers, see The Chile Pepper Institute at New Mexico State, http://www.chilepepperinstitute.org/.

CHAPTER 11

New Technology and Trends in Cooking

> They say you can't even understand parsnips until you've had Zero G parsnips.
> —Patron of El Chemistri Restaurant in "The Food Wife" episode, *The Simpsons* (2011)

In the 1980s, scientists who were interested in food and food science began to investigate the intersection more thoroughly. Physical chemist Hervé This recalls that he and the late Nicholas Kurti, an Oxford University physics professor, decided to "create a new scientific discipline to investigate culinary transformations" in 1988. This discipline became known as *molecular gastronomy*. According to This, it is "the chemistry and physics behind the preparation of any dish; for example, why a mayonnaise becomes firm or why a soufflé swells."[1]

Molecular gastronomy has inspired chefs to create a wide variety of new dishes, such as potato foam gnocchi, fake caviar created from sodium alginate, and ice cream made instantly with the help of liquid nitrogen. (The well-known chefs who have made this cuisine famous call it Technoemotional Cuisine or Modernist Cuisine.) The movement and cuisine began in Europe with innovative chefs, such as Catalan chef Ferran Adrià, ranked the world's number one chef in many polls. His restaurant in Spain, El Bulli, now closed, was considered to be among the top restaurants in the world. Chefs in the United States have also used the techniques of molecular gastronomy. There are many websites dedicated to molecular gastronomy. One enthusiastic

A chef demonstrates cooking with liquid nitrogen. (Focke Strangmann/DAPD)

molecular gastronomy blogger explains that molecular gastronomy recipes usually must be "followed precisely." Moreover, "steps need to be followed in a very specific sequence or the whole dish will be a disaster."[2]

The eagerly anticipated six-volume set *Modernist Cuisine* was published in 2011.[3] The publication is the work of former Microsoft chief technology officer Nathan Myhrvold and chefs Chris Young and Maxime Bilet. The work for the book was done in a test kitchen located inside a Seattle area warehouse that also houses Myhrvold's research lab, Intellectual Ventures.[4] The expensive multivolume, 2,483-page set most likely will be purchased by professionals, libraries, and only the most enthusiastic home cooks, but it provides history, methodology, techniques, and recipes for modernist cuisine. It also explains much about the science of cooking.

Those who do not want to buy the book or who want to learn more about it first can look over the recipes in the recipe library located on the *Modernist Cuisine* website. Some of them, such as the recipe for Microwaved Tilapia, do not require any unusual ingredients or equipment. Each recipe lists the ingredients (in grams), and gives precise directions and timings. There are also tips and substitutions. For example, the Pressure-Cooker Vegetable Risotto has a chart listing the amounts to be used and the cooking time needed for many different grains that can be used to make risotto. It explains how parboiling the grain and chilling it makes the final cooking go more quickly and easily, particularly if the cooking is done in a pressure cooker. The parboiling and chilling can be done up to a week before the final cooking. The rice is then mixed with sautéed shallots, carrot juice, celery juice, vermouth, and vegetable stock and cooked in the pressure cooker. After cooking, finely grated Gouda cheese and butter are added to the hot risotto.[5]

Modernist Cuisine, the techniques, as well as the book, has its proponents and opponents. Some see it as the latest in a long line of cooking innovations that have developed over centuries, and they believe it marries food science with the art and creativity of invention and presentation. Others see it as a fad that uses expensive equipment and techniques to produce spectacle rather than substance. Most likely both viewpoints have some truth. Most people are not likely to buy a centrifuge for their kitchens; they might decide to revisit the pressure cooker, however, or invest in an iSi Whip (for whipping cream) or crème brulée blowtorch.[6]

As Hervé This explains, "[M]olecular gastronomy makes it possible to place cooking on more secure foundations by recognizing it at last as the chemical art that it quite obviously is." Nevertheless, he also believes in the art of cooking. He has written:

> Does molecular gastronomy threaten to kill off classic cooking? Ask yourself whether synthesizers are likely to destroy the music of Bach and Mozart. In culinary art, as in musical art, there are technical and artistic components. Knowledge enables artists to refine their technique and helps their art to grow. Nonetheless, it is the artist who decides to work in a different way from his predecessors, not science; it is the artist who bears responsibility for his art, and not science. As for Bach and Mozart, it is up to us to decide whether we wish to keep listening to them or not.[7]

The modernist cuisine inspired by molecular gastronomy creates "a world where your intuition fails you completely," Myhrvold says. And it often requires special tools and ingredients to create new dishes and deconstruct old ones. The list of unusual products include, among others, liquid nitrogen to produce instant freezing, hydrocolloids, tapioca starches, and sodium alginate. Nitrous oxide whipped cream chargers can be used to make foams or infuse foods. Dehydrating machines are used creatively to produce such items as crispy sheets composed of fruit or vegetables, mixed with sugars and isomalt, crispy sheets of meringuelike foams, and dried herbs and other ingredients that can be made to resemble edible dirt or to be used as garnishes. Fish tank air pumps are used to create bubbles. Innovative chefs are also using hair dryers to just slightly warm dishes, blowtorches for browning them, and microwaves to create new delicacies. Chef Ferran Adrià has said, "You might see the microwave in every home kitchen yet it is definitely a vanguard technology."[8]

Microwaves are used often in modernist cuisine. One of the new dishes created by This is called Vauquelin, after Nicolas Vauquelin (1763–1829), a teacher of the famous French chemist Antoine Lavoisier. The dish consists of egg whites, which are foamed by adding more water, or fruit juice and sugar ("to increase viscosity and to stabilize the foam before cooking"). The foam is then cooked in a microwave oven.[9]

New York Times columnist Melissa Clark challenged Nathan Myhrvold to come up with a dinner party menu that she could "whip up" "without having to buy any new equipment or bizarre ingredients (like low-acyl gellan and sodium tripolyphosphate, which are sprinkled throughout the book's recipes like so much salt and pepper)." Myhrvold responded with a menu, and gave Clark a personal cooking lesson. One dish used a fake sous vide method (discussed in the following section) to prepare salmon fillets. To prepare this dish, the fillets are placed in plastic resealable bags and submerged in warm (115° F) water for 30 minutes. The fillets are then removed from the warm water bath, the skin is removed, and they are finished in pan of melted butter combined with a hazelnut-coriander spice mixture. The rest of the menu consisted of seared (with a blowtorch) frozen steaks that were then cooked in a low oven to produce steaks that were grilled on the outside but perfectly pink on the inside; squash caramelized in a pressure cooker and then pureed, and panna cotta (Italian custard) prepared with citric acid and balsamic vinegar. To start the meal, Myhrvold suggested apple-infused celery, that is, celery that tastes like apples. Clark tweaked the recipe to make gin-infused celery instead as a sort of solid cocktail. The method was the same, using a pressurized whipped-cream siphon to infuse the celery.[10]

SOUS VIDE COOKING

> God ordained things should be boiled or baked or fried. Those
> are the missionary positions of cuisine.
>   —Stephen Colbert to Nathan Myhrvold, episode #07039,
>   *The Colbert Report,* March 23, 2011

A frequently used technique in modernist cuisine is sous vide cooking.
Sous vide is French for "under vacuum." One authority describes it "as
a method of cooking in vacuumized plastic pouches at precisely controlled temperatures. Precise temperature control gives more choice
over doneness and texture than traditional cooking methods."[11] In
using the method of cooking, the raw food is sealed in plastic bags
(good quality resealable bags) and placed in a water bath. The temperature of the water and the length of cooking time must be kept
exact. When cooked, the food looks poached. Meat that has been
cooked sous vide is often finished by searing or saucing.

Myhrvold recommends sous vide cooking "to achieve the perfect
cooking rate necessary for great barbecue." There are two steps to
barbecuing this way: smoking and sous vide cooking. Smoking can be
done before or after the sous vide cooking. Myhrvold suggests people
should try it both ways to see which way they prefer. A longer smoking time is required if the smoking is done after the sous vide cooking,
however, because the flesh is not as reactive to the smoke after it has
already been cooked.[12]

PRESSURE COOKERS

Few Americans today use pressure cookers, although the trend is changing. In Betty McDonald's 1945 account of her adjustment to rural and
married life on a chicken farm, *The Egg and I,* she chronicled her ordeals
with the much-loathed gadget. She was overjoyed when it exploded—
but then her husband began looking for a newer model.[13] Many people
are scarred by vivid memories of pressure cooker explosions they wit-
nessed in the homes of relatives; others, who have never actually seen a
pressure cooker, *fear* that it will explode. New model pressure cookers,
however, have safety features that prevent such explosions.

Pressure cookers are ideal for making stocks and braised meats and
vegetables. One writer describes it this way, "As steam builds in a

sealed vessel, the boiling point of the water within increases from 212 to 250 degrees Fahrenheit. That allows the contents to repose as if in a sauna, while their aromas are squeezed out of them in a hot bear hug." The pressure cooker permits all this to happen more quickly than it would in a conventional pot, and because of the high temperatures, browning can also take place. In modernist cuisine, pressure cookers are often used to produce stock, risotto, and other dishes.[14]

NEW NORDIC

Many believe the New Nordic cuisine has replaced modernist cuisine. Instead of using chemicals and stabilizers and new techniques, this cuisine emphasizes the use of seasonal food and local ingredients, sometime foraged, and old cooking techniques such as drying and smoking. One writer describes the high-end dishes in the era of modernist cuisine as "tight, geometric, slicked-down," but "the new Nordic dishes have bed head, with artfully ruffled herbs and tufts of grass sticking out everywhere." The movement, influenced somewhat by the Slow Food movements in Spain and Italy, spread from Copenhagen throughout Scandinavia, and then throughout Europe and the United States.[15]

New Nordic cuisine often uses fish, game, produce, and other foods, such as Icelandic skyr, a type of yogurt-like product, that are unique to the Nordic countries. Some Nordic chefs have also redesigned the traditional smørrebrød, or open-faced sandwiches, believing that it is particularly ripe for exporting abroad. They note that this is "a tradition that is surprisingly similar to that of sushi: it consists of a small square-ish carbohydrate base with raw fish and other meat and highly decorative toppings including horseradish." Smørrebrød-sjomfruer, are specialized chefs, similar to sushi chefs.[16]

SOLAR COOKING

Solar cooking is almost the direct opposite of modernist cuisine. It relies on the sun, along with common supplies and ingredients. According to Solar Cookers International, the first recorded use of a solar cooker in the United States was by Samuel P. Langley, who used one during his climb of Mt. Whitney in California in 1881. Early solar cookers were expensive and difficult to manage. Growing fuel shortages and environmental concerns sparked a new interest in solar cooking in the 1970s. Solar Cookers International, a nonprofit organization, was founded in 1987 to promote solar cooking around the world.[17]

Solar cooking is an important and effective method for preparing food and pasteurizing water and milk, especially in areas where fuel is scarce. In some areas of the world, women and children must walk long distances, often in remote or war-torn areas, to obtain wood for cooking fires. Campers and people who want to have "smoke-free barbecues" can also use solar cookers. As long as there are several hours of sunlight without strong winds, most foods can be prepared in solar cookers.

The most common solar cookers cook at 180°–250°F. There are three main types of solar cookers: box cookers, curved concentrator cookers (parabolic cookers), and combination cookers. Box cookers are the most widely used and are common in India. Curved concentrator cookers reach higher temperatures, but they have to be adjusted frequently and require supervision. Many are used in western China. Combination cookers are inexpensive. Because they can be folded, they are portable and easy to store. They can be made easily from cardboard covered with aluminum foil. This encases and reflects sunlight onto a dark, shallow, covered pot that is enclosed in a plastic bag. It takes longer to cook foods using a solar cooker than it does to use an oven or a pot over a heat source; to prepare a meal, food needs to be placed in the solar cooker several hours in advance. Baked goods require 2–3 hours to cook in a solar cooker. Solar cookers cannot be used at night or on cloudy days.[18]

Fads and trends in cooking, like everything else, come and go. White bread is now out; artisan bread is in. And people are baking it at home. One scholar sees echoes of the late-19th and early-20th-century domestic science movement in the claims and practices of molecular gastronomy. As she notes, "[T]he most compelling difference between what Ellen Richards [one of the founders of the domestic science movement] called 'the chemistry of cooking' and what This and his colleagues regarded as 'how chemistry and physics can lead to new ways of cooking' is that the latter was instantly hailed by scientists, chefs, and critics as a thrilling new breakthrough."[19]

Although many people claim that Americans no longer cook, I beg to differ.[20] It is true that many Americans, overburdened with a long workday followed by chauffeuring their children to various activities, opt to microwave a quick dinner or pick up a fast-food meal. They do not cook every night, yet many of them do cook on weekends and holidays. Others have become devoted to purchasing local produce, which they have learned to cook after facing the problem of what one does with boxes filled with Swiss chard or turnips.

The number of food and cooking blogs that literally spring up overnight attest to an interest in cooking. Cooking helps to connect people. Social media sites have helped to fuel an interest in cooking. My daughters, friends, and I share recipes on a daily basis on various sites. Do we cook all of them? Of course not. Although there is a great deal of lusting over photos and ingredients (also known as the drool factor), a lack of time—and inclination—prevents every exchanged recipe from getting made. Still, many of them are made, and commented on, and enjoyed. Cooking is a way of sharing traditions, a way of transferring culture. In my house and, I suspect, in many American households, cooking, that is, to prepare food by heating it, remains not only an essential nutritional practice, it is an essential social one, as well.

NOTES

1. Hervé This, "Food for Tomorrow?" *EMBO Reports* 7, no. 11 (2006), 1063, 1062.

2. See http://www.molecularrecipes.com/molecular-gastronomy/.

3. Nathan Myhrvold, Chris Young, and Maxime Bilet, *Modernist Cuisine: The Art and Science of Cooking* (Bellevue, WA: The Cooking Lab, 2011). There is also a website with a blog, http://modernistcuisine.com/.

4. Paul Adams, "A Tour of the Modernist Cuisine Kitchen Laboratory," Popsci, posted February 1, 2011, http://www.popsci.com/technology/article/2011–02/tour-modernist-cuisine-kitchen-laboratory.

5. "Pressure-Cooked Vegetable Risotto," Recipe adapted from chapter 12, "Plant Foods," in Myhrvold, Young, and Bilet, *Modernist Cuisine,* http://modernistcuisine.com/cook/recipe-library/pressure-cooked-vegetable-risotto/.

6. For a defense of *Modernist Cuisine,* see Rob Mifsud, "Pro: Modernist Cuisine Skeptics Just Don't Get It, " *Globe and Mail,* March 29, 2011, http://www.theglobeandmail.com/life/food-and-wine/trends/trends-features/pro-modernist-cuisine-skeptics-just-dont-get-it/article1961698/. For a criticism of *Modernist Cuisine,* see Mark Schatzker, "Con: Modernist Cuisine Mistakes the Chef for the Great Creator," *Globe and Mail,* March 29, 2011, http://www.theglobeandmail.com/life/food-and-wine/trends/trends-features/modernist-cuisine-mistakes-the-chef-for-the-great-creator/article1961552/.

7. Hervé This, *Building a Meal: From Molecular Gastronomy to Culinary Constructivism,* trans. M.B. DeBevoise (New York: Columbia University Press, 2009), 88.

8. Jerry Adler, "Food Like You've Never Seen Before," *Smithsonian Magazine,* June 2011, http://www.smithsonianmag.com/arts-culture/Food-Like-

Youve-Never-Seen-Before.html; Matt Preston, "The New Frontier," *The Age,* April 29, 2008, http://www.theage.com.au/news/epicure/the-new-frontier/2008/04/28/1209234716017.html.

9. This, "Food for Tomorrow?" 1064. For directions and pictures, see Martin Lersch, "Egg White Foam + Microwave = Vauquelin," February 4, 2007, http://blog.khymos.org/2007/02/04/egg-white-foam-microwave-vauquelin/.

10. Melissa Clark, "Sorcerer's Apprentice Hosts a Dinner Party," *New York Times,* January 17, 2012, http://www.nytimes.com/2012/01/18/dining/modernist-cuisine-adapted-to-home-entertaining.html?pagewanted=all.

11. Douglas E. Baldwin, "Sous Vide Cooking: A Review," *International Journal of Gastronomy and Food Science* 1, no. 1 (2012), 15.

12. Nathan Myhrvold, "The Chemistry of the Barbecue Stall," Modernistecuisine.com, August 30, 2012, http://modernistcuisine.com/2012/08/barbecue-stall/.

13. Betty McDonald, "That Infernal Machine, the Pressure Cooker," in *The Egg and I* (Philadelphia: J. B. Lippincott, 1945), 182–85.

14. Rob Mifsud, "A Pot with Benefits," *Slate Magazine,* February 29, 2012, http://www.slate.com/articles/life/food/2012/02/the_pressure_cooker_makes_a_comeback_.single.html.

15. Julia Moskin, "New Nordic Cuisine Draws Disciples," *New York Times,* August 23, 2011, http://www.nytimes.com/2011/08/24/dining/new-nordic-cuisine-draws-disciples.html?pagewanted=all.

16. Jens Martin Skibsted and Bo Lindegaard, "Smørrebrød: Designing and Deconstructing the Vernacular," Core77, February 20, 2012, http://www.core77.com/blog/food/smrrebrd_designing_and_deconstructing_the_vernacular_21785.asp.

17. *Solar Cookers: How to Make, Use and Enjoy,* 10th ed., (Sacramento, CA: Solar Cookers International, 2004), 52.

18. For instructions on how to build a solar cooker and some recipes, see *Solar Cookers: How to Make, Use and Enjoy.*

19. Laura Shapiro, *Perfection Salad: Women and Cooking at the Turn of the Century,* with a new afterword (Berkeley and Los Angeles: University of California Press, 2009), 230–31.

20. See for example, Michael Pollan, "Out of the Kitchen, Onto the Couch," *New York Times,* July 29, 2009, http://www.nytimes.com/2009/08/02/magazine/02cooking-t.html?pagewanted=all.

Selected Bibliography and Resources

Allen, Ann. *The Housekeeper's Assistant, Composed Upon Temperance Principles, With Instructions in the Art of Making Plain and Fancy Cakes, Puddings, Pastry, Confectionery, Ice Creams, Jellies, Blanc Mange, Also for Cooking of all the Various Kinds of Meats and Vegetables; With Variety of Useful Information And Receipts Never Before Published.* Boston: James Munroe & Co., 1845.

Anderson, Virginia DeJohn. *Creatures of Empire: How Domestic Animals Transformed Early America.* New York: Oxford University Press, 2004.

An Old Housekeeper [Ann Allen]. *The Housekeeper's Assistant, Composed Upon Temperance Principles, With Instructions in the Art of Making Plain and Fancy Cakes, Puddings, Pastry, Confectionery, Ice Creams, Jellies, Blanc Mange, Also for Cooking of all the Various Kinds of Meats and Vegetables; With Variety of Useful Information And Receipts Never Before Published.* Boston: James Munroe & Co., 1845.

Bailey, Floral L. "Navaho Foods and Cooking Methods." *American Anthropologist* 42, no. 2 (April–June 1940): 270–90.

Baldwin, Douglas E. "Sous Vide Cooking: A Review." *International Journal of Gastronomy and Food Science* 1, no. 1 (2012): 15–30.

Beard, James, *James Beard's American Cookery.* With a new foreword by Tom Colicchio. New York: Little, Brown, 2010.

Beecher, Catharine. *Miss Beecher's Domestic Receipt Book: Designed as a supplement to her Treatise on Domestic Economy.* 3rd ed. New York: Harper and Brothers, 1850.

Beecher, Catharine, and Harriet Beecher Stowe. *The American Woman's Home: or Principles of Domestic Science.* New York: J. B. Ford & Co.; Boston: H. A. Brown & Co., 1869.

Berkin, Carol. *Revolutionary Mothers: Women in the Struggle for America's Independence.* New York: Knopf, 2005.

Berzok, Linda Murray. *American Indian Food.* Santa Barbara, CA: Greenwood, 2005.

Bittman, Mark. *How to Cook Everything Vegetarian: Simple Meatless Recipes for Great Food.* New York: John Wiley & Sons, 2007.

Bobrow-Strain, Aaron. *White Bread: A Social History of the Store-Bought Loaf.* Boston: Beacon Press, 2012.

Brown, Rick, and Jack Bettridge, *Barbecue America: A Pilgrimage in Search of America's Best Barbecue.* Alexandria, VA: Time-Life Books, 1999.

Burr, Hattie A. *The Woman Suffrage Cook Book.* Boston: Hattie A. Burr, 1890.

Child, Lydia Maria. *The American Frugal Housewife.* New introduction by Jan Longone. Mineola, NY: Dover, 1999.

Civitello, Linda. *Cuisine and Culture: A History of Food and People.* 3rd ed. Hoboken, NJ: John Wiley & Sons, 2011.

Coe, Sophie D. *America's First Cuisines.* Austin: University of Texas Press, 1994.

Collins, A.M. *The Great Western Cook Book, or Table Receipts, adapted to Western Housewifery by Mrs. A.M. Collins.* New York: A.S. Barnes & Co., 1857.

Collins, Suzanne. *The Hunger Games.* New York: Scholastic Press, 2008.

Cornelius, Mary Hooker. *The Young Housekeeper's Friend.* Rev. ed. Boston: Thompson, Brown, & Co., 1873.

Covey, Herbert C., and Dwight Eisnach, *What the Slaves Ate: Recollections of African American Foods and Foodways from the Slave Narratives.* Santa Barbara, CA: ABC-CLIO, 2009.

Cox, Beverly, and Martin Jacobs. *Spirit of the Harvest: North American Indian Cooking.* New York: Stewart, Tabori, & Chang, 1991.

Crane, Elaine Forman, ed. *The Diary of Elizabeth Drinker.* Boston: Northeastern University Press, 1991.

Crosby, Alfred W., Jr. *The Columbian Exchange: Biological and Cultural Consequences of 1492.* Westport, CT: Praeger, 2003.

Crump, Nancy Carter. *Hearthside Cooking: Early American Southern Cuisine Updated for Today's Hearth and Cookstove.* 2nd ed. Chapel Hill: University of North Carolina Press, 2008.

Davis, William C. *A Taste for War: The Culinary History of the Blue and the Gray.* Lincoln: University of Nebraska Press, 2011.

Deetz, James. *In Small Things Forgotten: The Archaeology of Early American Life.* New York: Doubleday, Anchor Books ed., 1977.

Edge, John T. *Fried Chicken: An American Story.* New York: G.P. Putnam's Sons, 2004.

Estes, Rufus. *Good Things to Eat as Suggested by Rufus.* Chicago: Published by the Author, 1911.

Farmer, Fannie Merritt. *The Boston Cooking-School Cook Book*. Boston: Little, Brown, & Co., 1896.

Ferris, Marcie Cohen. *Matzoh Ball Gumbo: Culinary Tales of the Jewish South*. Chapel Hill: University of North Carolina Press, 2005.

Fitch, Noël Riley. *Appetite for Life: The Biography of Julia Child*. New York: Doubleday, 1997.

Fox, Minnie C. *The Blue Grass Cook Book*. New York: Fox, Duffield, 1904.

Fussell, Betty. *The Story of Corn*. Albuquerque: University of New Mexico Press, 2004.

Gentile, Maria. *The Italian Cook Book: The Art of Eating Well*. New York: Italian Book Co., 1919.

Haber, Barbara. *From Hardtack to Home Fries: An Uncommon History of Cooks and Meals*. New York: Free Press, 2002.

Harland, Marion. *Common Sense in the Household: A Manual of Practical Housewifery*. New York: Scribner, Armstrong, and Co., 1873.

Harris, Jessica B. *High on the Hog: A Culinary Journey from Africa to America*. New York: Bloomsbury, 2011.

Hazard, Thomas Robinson. *The Jonny-Cake Papers of "Shepherd Tom."* Introduction by Rowland Gibson Hazard. Boston: Merrymount Press, 1915.

Hedges, Ken. *Fibers and Forms: Native American Basketry of the West*. San Diego: San Diego Museum of Man, 1997.

Henderson, Mary Newton Foote. *Practical Cooking and Dinner Giving*. New York: Harper & Brothers, 1877.

Henry, Fern L. *My Checkered Life: Luzena Stanley Wilson in Early California*. Nevada City, CA: Carl Mautz Publishing, 2003.

Hess, Karen. *The Carolina Rice Kitchen: The African Connection*. Columbia: University of South Carolina Press, 1992.

Hess, Karen, ed. *Martha Washington's Booke of Cookery*. New York: Columbia University Press, 1981.

Horne, Field, ed. *The Diary of Mary Cooper: Life on a Long Island Farm, 1768–1773*. Oyster Bay, NY: Oyster Bay Historical Society, 1981.

Howland, Esther Allen. *The American Economical Housekeeper and Family Receipt Book*. Cincinnati, OH: H.W. Derby, 1845.

Jones, Jacqueline. *Labor of Love, Labor of Sorrow: Black Women, Work, and the Family, from Slavery to the Present*. New York: Vintage Books, 1986.

Keoleian, Ardashes H. *The Oriental Cook Book*. New York: Sully & Kleinteich, 1913.

Kephart, Horace. *Camp Cookery*. New York: Outing Publishing Co., 1910

King, Caroline Howard. *When I Lived in Salem, 1822–1866*. Preface by Louisa L Dressel. Brattleboro, VT: Stephen Daye Press, 1937.

Lahiri, Jhumpa. *The Namesake*. New York: Houghton Mifflin, Mariner Books ed., 2004.

Larcon, Lucy. *A New England Girlhood: Outlined from Memory.* Boston: Houghton, Mifflin, 1889.

Lee, Jennifer 8. *The Fortune Cookie Chronicles: Adventures in the World of Chinese Food.* New York: Twelve, 2008.

Lee, N.K.M. *The Cook's Own Book. Being a Complete Culinary Encyclopedia Comprehending all Valuable Receipts for cooking Meat, Fish, and Fowl, and Composing every kind of Soup, Gravy, Pastry, Preserves, Essences, &c. that have been Published OR Invented During The Last Twenty Years particularly the very best of those in the Cook's Oracle, Cook's Dictionary, and other systems of Domestic Economy with Numerous Original Receipts, and a complete system of Confectionary.* Boston: Munroe & Francis, 1832.

Leslie, Eliza. *Directions for Cookery, In Its Various Branches.* 10th ed. Philadelphia: E. L. Carey & A. Hart, 1840.

Lovegren, Sylvia. *Fashionable Food: Seven Decades of Food Fads.* Chicago: University of Chicago Press, 2005.

Mann, Charles C. *Uncovering the New World Columbus Created.* New York: Knopf, 2011.

McCulloch-Williams, Martha. *Dishes & Beverages of the Old South.* New York: McBride, Nast & Co., 1913.

McGee, Harold. *On Food and Cooking: The Science and Lore of the Kitchen.* Rev. ed. New York: Scribner, 2004.

McWilliams, James E. *A Revolution in Eating: How the Quest for Food Shaped America.* New York: Columbia University Press, 2005.

Miller, Tim. "The Birth of the Patio Daddy-O: Outdoor Grilling in Postwar America." *Journal of American Culture* 33, no. 1 (2010): 5–11, http://www3.interscience.wiley.com/cgi-bin/fulltext/123326799/HTMLSTART.

Nylander, Jane C. *Our Own Snug Fireside: Images of the New England Home, 1760–1860.* New Haven, CT: Yale University Press, 1994.

Oliver, Sandra L. *Food in Colonial and Federal America.* Santa Barbara, CA: Greenwood Press, 2005.

Oliver, Sandra L. *Saltwater Foodways: New Englanders and Their Food, at Sea and Ashore, in the 19th Century.* Mystic, CT: Mystic Seaport Museum, 1995.

Olmert, Michael. "Smokehouses." *Colonial Williamsburg Journal* (Winter 2004–5), http://www.history.org/foundation/journal/winter04-05/smoke.cfm.

O'Neill, Molly, ed. *American Food Writing: An Anthology with Classic Recipes.* New York: Library of America, 2009.

Parloa, Maria. *Miss Parloa's New Cook Book: A Guide to Marketing and Cooking.* New York: Charles T. Dillingham, 1882.

Raffald, Elizabeth. *The Experienced English Housekeeper, for the Use and Ease of Ladies, Housekeepers, Cooks, &co.* 10th ed. London: R. Baldwin, 1786.

Randolph, Mary. *The Virginia Housewife: Or, Methodical Cook*. Stereotype ed. Baltimore: Plaskitt & Cugle, 1838.

Rosengarten, David. *It's All American Food: The Best Recipes for More Than 400 New American Classics*. Boston: Little, Brown, 2003.

Rundell, Maria Eliza. *A New System of Domestic Cookery, Formed Upon Principles of Economy, and Adapted to the Use of Private Families*. Boston: W. Andrews, 1807.

Schlissel, Lillian. *Women's Diaries of the Westward Journey*. New York: Schocken Books, 1982.

Shapiro, Laura. *Perfection Salad: Women and Cooking at the Turn of the Century*. With a new afterword. Berkeley and Los Angeles: University of California Press, 2009.

Shapiro, Laura. *Something from the Oven: Reinventing Dinner in 1950s America*. New York: Penguin, 2004.

Sharp, Patricia. "New Zion Barbecue." *Saveur*, May 26, 2009, http://www.saveur.com/article/Travels/New-Zion-Barbecue.

Simmons, Amelia. *American Cookery, or the art of dressing viands, fish, poultry, and vegetables, and the best modes of making pastes, puffs, pies, tarts, puddings, custards, and preserves, and all kinds of cakes, from the imperial plum to plain cake: Adapted to this country and all grades of life*. Hartford, CT: Printed for Simeon Butler, Northampton, 1798.

Sklar, Kathryn Kish. *Catharine Beecher: A Study in American Domesticity*. New York: W.W. Norton, 1976.

Smith, Andrew F. *The Tomato in America: Early History, Culture, and Cookery*. Champaign: University of Illinois Press, 2001.

Smith, Andrew F. *The Turkey: An American Story*. Urbana: University of Illinois Press, 2006.

Smith, Andrew F., ed. *The Oxford Companion to American Food and Drink*. New York: Oxford University Press, 2007.

Smith, Billy G. *The "Lower Sort": Philadelphia's Laboring People, 1750–1800*. Ithaca, NY: Cornell University Press, 1990.

Staib, Walter, with Beth D'Addono, *City Tavern Cookbook: 200 Years of Classic Recipes from America's First Gourmet Restaurant*. Philadelphia: Running Press, 1999.

Stavely, Keith, and Kathleen Fitzgerald, *America's Founding Food: The Story of New England Cooking*. Chapel Hill: University of North Carolina Press, 2004.

Stevens, Molly. *All About Braising: The Art of Uncomplicated Cooking*. New York: Norton, 2004.

This, Hervé. *Building a Meal: From Molecular Gastronomy to Culinary Constructivism*. Translated by M.B. DeBevoise. New York: Columbia University Press, 2009.

Twentieth Century Club War Time Cook Book. Pittsburgh: Pierpont, Siviter, 1918.

Tyree, Marion Fontaine Cabell. *Housekeeping in Old Virginia, Containing Contributions from Two Hundred and Fifty Ladies in Virginia and Sister States, Distinguished for Their Skill in the Culinary Art and Other Branches of Domestic Economy.* Richmond, VA: J.W. Randolph & English, 1878.

Ulrich, Laurel Thatcher. *Good Wives: Image and Reality in the Lives of Women in Northern New England, 1650–1750.* New York: Oxford University Press, 1982.

Ulrich, Laurel Thatcher. *A Midwife's Tale: The Life of Martha Ballard, Based on Her Diary, 1785–1812.* New York: Knopf, 1990.

Van Rensselaer, Martha, Flora Rose, and Helen Canon, comps. *A Manual of Home-Making.* New York: Macmillan, 1920.

Walsh, Lorena S. "Feeding the 18th-Century Town Folk, or, Whence the Beef?" Colonial Williamsburg Interpreter 21, no. 2 (2000), http://research.history.org/Historical_Research/Research_Themes/Theme Respect/Feeding.cfm.

Weaver, William Woys. *A Quaker Woman's Cookbook: The Domestic Cookery of Elizabeth Ellicott Lea.* Rev. ed. Mechanicsburg, PA: Stackpole Books, 2004.

Weaver, William Woys. *Thirty-Five Recipes from "The Larder Invaded."* Philadelphia: The Library Company of Philadelphia and The Historical Society of Pennsylvania, 1986.

Williams, Jacqueline. *Wagon Wheel Kitchens: Food on the Oregon Trail.* Lawrence: University Press of Kansas, 1993.

Williams, Susan. *Food in the United States, 1820s–1890.* Santa Barbara, CA: Greenwood, 2006.

Wragham, Richard. *Catching Fire: How Cooking Made Us Human.* New York: Basic Books, 2009.

Ziegelman, Jane. *97 Orchard: An Edible History of Five Immigrant Families in One New York Tenement.* New York: Smithsonian Books, 2010.

WEBSITES

Food sites, food organizations, and food blogs have grown exponentially over the past few years. Here are a few that I have found helpful.

The Association for the Study of Food and Culture, professional organization of food scholars, http://legacy.www.nypl.org/research/chss/grd/res guides/culinary/culinary.cfm

The Food Timeline, http://www.foodtimeline.org/

The New York Public Library Culinary History Guide, http://legacy.www.nypl.org/research/chss/grd/resguides/culinary/culinary.cfm

The Old Foodie, Janet Clarkson's blog on food and history, http://www.
     theoldfoodie.com/
The Online Culinary History Network, http://culinaryhistory.org/
The 3 Men Website, http://www.3men.com/allabout1.htm#TheHistory
     ofBarbecue

SOME MOVIES WITH MEMORABLE FOOD SCENES

This is not a definitive list. It is simply a list of some movies with great food
scenes. Because this book is about cooking in America, I have not included
movies such as *Tampopo, Tom Jones,* and *Babette's Feast.*

Annie Hall (d. Woody Allen, 1977). Woody Allen and Diane Keaton at-
     tempt to boil lobsters.
The Apartment (d. Billy Wilder, 1960). Jack Lemmon memorably cooks spa-
     ghetti and meatballs for Shirley MacLaine, using a tennis racquet as
     a strainer.
Big Night (d. Campbell Scott and Stanley Tucci, 1996). Two brothers
     (Stanley Tucci and Tony Shaloub) try to save their Italian restaurant
     by preparing one special dinner.
Cool Hand Luke (d. Stuart Rosenberg, 1967). A convict played by Paul
     Newman famously attempts to eat 50 hard-boiled eggs.
Fried Green Tomatoes (d. Jon Avnet, 1991). Recipes for fried green tomatoes
     and other southern fare.
Goodfellas (d. Martin Scorsese, 1990). Cooking in prison. Paul Sorvino's
     ability to thinly slice garlic with a razor blade has spawned a term,
     "Goodfella's thin."
The Help (d. Tate Taylor, 2011). Many scenes of southern foods and cook-
     ing done by the black household help, including fried chicken and the
     infamous chocolate pie.
It Happened One Night (d. Frank Capra, 1934). Clark Gable teaches
     Claudette Colbert how to dunk donuts, among other things.
Julie and Julia (d. Nora Ephron, 2009). Blogger Julie Powell (Amy Adams)
     attempts to cook all of the recipes in Julia Child's *Mastering the Art of
     French Cooking.* Julia Child is played by Meryl Streep.
Lady and the Tramp (d. Clyde Geronomi, Wilfred Jackson, Hamilton Luske,
     1955). This animated classic includes the wonderful and romantic
     scene where Lady and the Tramp share a plate of spaghetti.
Tortilla Soup (d. Maria Ripoli, 2001). A remake of the Chinese movie *Eat,
     Drink, Man, Woman,* it features many scenes of the father cooking
     Mexican American meals, including tortilla soup.
Waitress (d. Adrienne Shelly, 2007). A pregnant waitress (Keri Russell) in an
     unhappy marriage bakes incredible pies with names, such as "I Don't
     Want Earl's Baby Pie."

Index

About the Author

Merril D. Smith is an independent scholar, author, and editor of several books, including *Encyclopedia of Rape* (2004), *Women's Roles in Seventeenth-Century America* (2008), and *Women's Roles in Eighteenth-Century America* (2010).